Frommer's®

Italian
PhraseFinder &
Dictionary

1st Edition

WILEY
Wiley Publishing, Inc.

Published by:

Wiley Publishing, Inc.

111 River St.
Hoboken, NJ 07030-5774

ISBN-13: 978-0-471-77331-3
ISBN-10: 0-471-77331-X

Italian Editor: Amanda Castleman
Series Editor: Maureen Clarke
Photo Editor: Richard H. Fox
Cover design by Fritz Metsch

Interior Design, Content Development, Translation, Copyediting, Proofreading,
Production, and Layout by:
Publication Services, Inc., 1802 South Duncan Road, Champaign, IL 61822
Linguists: Paola Bartolotti-van Loon & Rosaria Tenace

For information on our other products and services or to obtain technical support,
please contact our Customer Care Department within the U.S. at 800/762-2974, outside the U.S. at 317/572-3993 or fax 317/572-4002.
Wiley also publishes its books in a variety of electronic formats. Some content that
appears in print may not be available in electronic formats.

Manufactured in the United States of America

5 4 3 2 1

Contents

An Invitation to the Reader

In researching this book, we discovered many wonderful sayings and terms useful to travelers in Italy. We're sure you'll find others. Please tell us about them, so we can share the information with your fellow travelers in upcoming editions. If you were disappointed with an aspect of this book, we'd like to know that, too. Please write to:

Frommer's Italian PhraseFinder & Dictionary, 1st Edition
Wiley Publishing, Inc.
111 River St. • Hoboken, NJ 07030-5774

An Additional Note

The packager, editors, and publisher cannot be held responsible for the experiences of readers while traveling. Your safety is important to us, however, so we encourage you to stay alert and be aware of your surroundings. Keep a close eye on cameras, purses, and wallets, all favorite targets of thieves and pickpockets.

Frommers.com

Now that you have the language for a great trip, visit our website at **www.frommers.com** for travel information on more than 3,000 destinations. With features updated regularly, we give you instant access to the most current trip-planning information available. At Frommers.com, you'll also find the best prices on airfares, accommodations, and car rentals—and you can even book travel online through our travel booking partners. At Frommers.com, you'll also find:

- Online updates to our most popular guidebooks
- Vacation sweepstakes and contest giveaways
- Newsletter highlighting the hottest travel trends
- Online travel message boards with featured travel discussions

INTRODUCTION: HOW TO USE THIS BOOK

More than 70 million people speak Italian, a language so melodious it can make a chore list resemble an opera aria. This rich tongue is already somewhat familiar to most chefs, artists, musicians, and others who savor Italy's rich cultural heritage.

As a Romance language, Italian is closely related to Latin, French, Italian, Portuguese, and Romanian. The modern nation of Italy is a patchwork of former city-states—and its dialects still reflect these strong regional loyalties. Thus you may hear variations on the phrases found here. But rest assured: Native speakers have carefully reviewed all the material.

Our intention is not to teach you Italian: A class or audio program is best for that. Rather, we offer an easy-to-use travel tool. You don't need to memorize the contents or flip frantically to locate a topic, as with other books. Rather, Frommer's has fingertip referencing and an extensive PhraseFinder dictionary at the back.

Say a taxi driver accidentally hands you €5 instead of €10. Look up "change" in the dictionary and discover how to say: "Sorry, but this isn't the right change." Then follow the cross-reference to numbers, so you can explain exactly how much is missing.

This book may even be useful to advanced students, because it supplies speedy access to exact idioms. Elegance and *bella figura*—cutting a fine figure—are important to Italians. So is the right phrase at the right time.

As Tim Parks observed in *An Englishman in Verona*: "While Italians usually seem to like foreigners, the foreigners they like most are the ones who know the score, the ones who have caved in and agreed that the Italian way of doing things is best. . . . There is an order to follow in all things; follow it, even when it borders on the superstitious and ritualistic."

Thus, from the novice to the conversationally adept, travelers can benefit from the detailed conversation and etiquette tips here. At each turn, we've researched the traditions and travails, striving to make this phrasebook accessible, practical, and indispensable.

We've also tried to make this volume useful to all English speakers, though Frommer's is based in the United States. As with all our publications, we hope this enriches your travel experience greatly. And with that, we offer this wish: *Fate il miglior viaggio possibile!*

CHAPTER ONE

SURVIVAL ITALIAN

If you tire of toting around this phrasebook, tear out or photocopy
this chapter. You should be able to get around using only the terms
found in the next 35 pages.

BASIC GREETINGS

For a full list of greetings, see p111.

Hello.	**Salve.**
	SAHL-veh
How are you?	**Come sta?**
	KOH-meh stah
I'm fine, thanks.	**Bene, grazie.**
	BEH-neh GRAH-tsyeh
And you?	**E lei?**
	eh lay
My name is ____.	**Mi chiamo ____.**
	mee KYAH-moh
And yours?	**E lei?**
	eh lay
It's a pleasure to meet you.	**Piacere di conoscerla.**
	pyah-CHEH-reh dee KOH-noh-shehr-lah
Please.	**Per favore.**
	pehr fah-VOH-reh
Thank you.	**Grazie.**
	GRAH-tsyeh
Yes.	**Sì.**
	SEE
No.	**No.**
	noh

1

OK.

OK. / Va bene.
OK / vah BEH-neh

No problem.

Nessun problema.
nehs-SOON proh-BLEH-mah

I'm sorry, I don't
understand.

Mi dispiace, non capisco.
*mee dee-SPYAH-cheh nohn kah-
PEE-skoh*

Would you speak slower,
please?

**Può parlare più lentamente, per
favore?**
*PWOH pahr-LAH-reh PYOO lehn-
tah-MEHN-teh pehr fah-VOH-reh*

Would you speak louder,
please?

**Può parlare più ad alta voce, per
favore?**
*PWOH pahr-LAH-reh PYOO ahd
AHL-tah VOH-cheh pehr fah-
VOH-reh*

Do you speak English?

Parla inglese?
PAHR-lah een-GLEH-seh

Do you speak any other
languages?

Parla altre lingue?
PAHR-lah AHL-treh LEEN-gweh

I speak ____ better than
Italian.

Parlo ____ meglio che italiano.
*PAHR-loh ____ MEH-lyoh keh ee-
tah-LYAH-noh*

Would you spell that?

Può dirmi come si scrive?
*PWOH DEER-mee KOH-meh see
SKREE-veh*

Would you please repeat
that?

Può ripetere, per favore?
*PWOH ree-PEH-teh-reh pehr fah-
VOH-reh*

Would you point that out
in this dictionary?

**Può indicarlo su questo
dizionario?**
*PWOH een-dee-KAHR-loh soo
KWEHS-toh dee-tsyoh-NAH-ryoh*

THE KEY QUESTIONS

With the right hand gestures, you can get a lot of mileage from the following list of single-word questions and answers.

Who?	**Chi?**
	kee
What?	**Cosa?**
	KOH-sah
When?	**Quando?**
	KWAHN-doh
Where?	**Dove?**
	DOH-veh
Why?	**Perché?**
	pehr-KEH
How?	**Come?**
	KOH-meh
Which?	**Quale?**
	KWAH-leh
How many / much?	**Quanto -a? / Quanti -e?**
	KWAHN-toh -tah / KWAHN-tee -teh

THE ANSWERS: WHO

For full coverage of pronouns, see p19.

I	**Io**
	EE-oh
you	**Lei / tu**
	lay / too
him	**lui**
	LOO-ee
her	**lei**
	lay
us	**noi**
	NOH-ee
them	**loro**
	LOH-roh

THE ANSWERS: WHEN

For full coverage of time, see p12.

now	**ora**
	OH-rah
later	**più tardi**
	PYOO TAHR-dee
in a minute	**fra un minuto**
	frah oon mee-NOO-toh
today	**oggi**
	OHD-jee
tomorrow	**domani**
	doh-MAH-nee
yesterday	**ieri**
	YEH-ree
in a week	**fra una settimana**
	frah oonah seht-tee-MAH-nah
next week	**la settimana prossima**
	lah set-tee-MAH-nah prohs-SEE-mah
last week	**la settimana scorsa**
	lah set-tee-MAH-nah SKOHR-sah
next month	**il mese prossimo**
	eel MEH-zeh prohs-SEE-moh
At ____	**Alle ____**
	AHL-leh
ten o'clock this morning.	**dieci di stamattina.**
	DYEH-chee dee stah-maht-TEE-nah
two o'clock this afternoon.	**due di oggi pomeriggio.**
	DOO-eh dee OHD-jee poh-meh-REED-joh
seven o'clock this evening.	**sette di stasera.**
	SEHT-teh dee stah-SEH-rah

For full coverage of numbers, see p7.

THE ANSWERS: WHERE

here	**qui / qua**
	kwee / kwah
there	**lì / là**
	LEE / LAH
near	**vicino**
	vee-CHEE-noh
closer	**più vicino**
	PYOO vee-CHEE-noh
closest	**il più vicino**
	eel PYOO vee-CHEE-noh
far	**lontano**
	lohn-TAH-noh
farther	**più lontano**
	PYOO lohn-TAH-noh
farthest	**il più lontano**
	eel PYOO lohn-TAH-noh
across from	**di fronte a**
	dee FROHN-teh ah
next to	**di fianco a**
	dee FYAHN-koh ah
behind	**dietro a**
	DYEH-troh ah
straight ahead	**diritto**
	dee-REET-toh
left	**a sinistra**
	ah see-NEES-trah
right	**a destra**
	ah DEHS-trah
up	**su**
	soo
down	**giù**
	JOO
lower	**più giù**
	PYOO JOO

higher	**più su**
	PYOO soo
forward	**avanti**
	ah-VAHN-tee
back	**indietro**
	een-DYEH-troh
around	**attorno**
	aht-TOHR-noh
across the street	**dall'altra parte della strada**
	dahl-LAHL-trah PAHR-teh DEHL-la STRAH-dah
down the street	**più avanti**
	PYOO ah-VAHN-tee
on the corner	**all'angolo**
	ahl-LAHN-goh-loh
kittycorner	**all'angolo opposto**
	ahl-LAHN-goh-loh ohp-POHS-toh
____ blocks from here	**____ traverse più in là**
	____ trah-VEHR-seh PYOO een LAH

For a full list of numbers, see the next page.

THE ANSWERS: WHICH

this one	**questo -a**
	KWEHS-toh -tah
that	**quello -la**
	KWEHL-loh -lah
these	**questi -e**
	KWEHS-tee -teh
those	**quelli -le**
	KWEHL-lee -leh

NUMBERS & COUNTING

one	**uno** *OO-noh*	seventeen	**diciassette** *dee-chahs-SEHT-teh*
two	**due** *DOO-eh*	eighteen	**diciotto** *dee-CHOT-toh*
three	**tre** *treh*	nineteen	**diciannove** *dee-chahn-NOH-veh*
four	**quattro** *KWAHT-troh*	twenty	**venti** *VEHN-tee*
five	**cinque** *CHEEN-kweh*	twenty-one	**ventuno** *vehn-TOO-noh*
six	**sei** *SEH-ee*	thirty	**trenta** *TREHN-tah*
seven	**sette** *SEHT-teh*	forty	**quaranta** *kwah-RAHN-tah*
eight	**otto** *OHT-toh*	fifty	**cinquanta** *cheen-KWAN-tah*
nine	**nove** *NOH-veh*	sixty	**sessanta** *sehs-SAHN-tah*
ten	**dieci** *dee-EH-chee*	seventy	**settanta** *seht-TAHN-tah*
eleven	**undici** *OON-dee-chee*	eighty	**ottanta** *oht-TAHN-tah*
twelve	**dodici** *DOH-dee-chee*	ninety	**novanta** *noh-VAHN-tah*
thirteen	**tredici** *TREH-dee-chee*	one hundred	**cento** *CHEHN-to*
fourteen	**quattordici** *KWAHT-tohr-dee-chee*	two hundred	**duecentos** *DOO-eh-CHEHN-toh*
fifteen	**quindici** *KWEEN-dee-chee*	one thousand	**mille** *MEEL-leh*
sixteen	**sedici** *SEH-dee-chee*		

FRACTIONS & DECIMALS

one eighth	**un ottavo** *oon oht-TAH-voh*
one quarter	**un quarto** *oon KWAHR-toh*
three eighths	**tre ottavi** *treh oht-TAH-vee*
one third	**un terzo** *oon TEHR-tsoh*
one half	**mezzo** *MEHD-dzoh*
two thirds	**due terzi** *DOO-eh TEHR-tsee*
three quarters	**tre quarti** *treh KWAHR-tee*
double	**doppio** *DOHP-pyoh*
triple	**triplo** *TREE-ploh*
one-tenth	**un decimo** *oon DEH-chee-moh*
one-hundredth	**un centesimo** *oon chehn-TEH-zee-moh*
one-thousandth	**un millesimo** *oon meel-LEH-zee-moh*

MATH

addition	**addizione** *ahd-deet-TSYOH-neh*
2 + 1	**due più uno** *DOO-eh PYOO OO-noh*
subtraction	**sottrazione** *soht-traht-TSYOH-neh*
2 − 1	**due meno uno** *DOO-eh MEH-noh OO-noh*

multiplication	**moltiplicazione** *mohl-tee-plee-kaht-TSYOH-neh*
2 × 3	**due per tre** *DOO-eh pehr treh*
division	**divisione** *dee-vee-ZYOH-neh*
6 ÷ 3	**sei diviso tre** *SEH-ee dee-VEE-zoh treh*

ORDINAL NUMBERS

first	**primo -a** *PREE-moh -mah*
second	**secondo -a** *seh-KOHN-doh -dah*
third	**terzo -a** *TEHR-tsoh -tsah*
fourth	**quarto -a** *KWAHR-toh -tah*
fifth	**quinto -a** *KWEEN-toh -tah*
sixth	**sesto -a** *SEHS-toh -tah*
seventh	**settimo -a** *SEHT-tee-moh -mah*
eighth	**ottavo -a** *oht-TAH-voh -vah*
ninth	**nono -a** *NOH-noh -nah*
tenth	**decimo -a** *DEH-chee-moh -mah*
last	**ultimo -a** *OOL-tee-moh -mah*

MEASUREMENTS

Measurements are usually metric, though you may need a few Imperial measurement terms.

centimeter	**centimetro** *chehn-TEE-meh-troh*
meter	**metro** *MEH-troh*
kilometer	**chilometro** *kee-LOH-meh-troh*
millimeter	**millimetro** *meel-LEE-meh-troh*
hectares	**ettari** *EHT-tah-ree*
a distance squared is	**quadrato** *kwah-DRAH-toh*
short	**corto -a** *KOHR-toh -tah*
long	**lungo -a** *LOON-goh -gah*

VOLUME

milliliters	**millilitro** *meel-LEE-lee-troh*
liter	**litro** *LEE-troh*
cup	**tazza** *TAHT-sah*

QUANTITY

some (always singular)	**qualche** *KWAHL-keh*
none	**niente** *NYEHN-teh* **nessuno** *nehs-SOO-noh*

Dos and Don'ts

Italians measure foodstuffs by the kilogram or smaller 100g unit (**ettogrammo** abbreviated to *etto*: equivalent to just under 4oz). **Pizzerie al taglio** (pizza slice shops) generally run on this system, but hand gestures can suffice. A good server poises the knife, then asks for approval before cutting. **Più** (PYOO) is "more," **meno** (MEH-noh) "less." **Basta** (BAHS-tah) means "enough." To express "half" of something, do say **mezzo** (MEHD-zoh).

all	**tutto -a / tutti -e**
	TOOT-toh -tah / TOOT-tee -teh
much / many	**molto -a / molti -e**
	MOHL-toh -tah / MOHL-tee -teh
A little bit (can be used for quantity or for time)	**poco -a**
	POH-koh -kah
dozen	**dozzina**
	dot-SEE-nah

SIZE

small	**piccolo -a**
	PEEK-koh-loh-lah
the smallest (literally "the most small")	**il / la più piccolo -a**
	eel / lah PYOO PEEK-koh-loh -lah
medium	**medio -a**
	MEH-dyoh -dyah
big	**grande**
	GRAHN-deh
fat	**grasso -a**
	GRAHS-soh -sah
really fat	**molto grasso -a**
	MOHL-toh GRAHS-soh -sah

the biggest	**il / la più grande**
	eel / lah PYOO GRAHN-deh
wide	**largo -a**
	LAHR-goh -gah
narrow	**stretto -a**
	STREHT-toh -tah

TIME

Time in Italian is referred to, literally, by the hour. **Che ora è?** translates as "What's the hour?"
For full coverage of number terms, see p7.

HOURS OF THE DAY

What time is it?	**Che ora è?**
	keh OH-rah EH
At what time?	**A che ora?**
	ah keh OH-rah
For how long?	**Per quanto tempo?**
	pehr KWAHN-toh TEHM-poh

A little tip

By adding a diminutive suffix, **-ino -a**, **-etto -a**, or a combination of the two, you can make anything smaller or shorter. These endings replace the original *-o* and *-a*, respectively:

| a really little bit | **pochino -a** (*poh-KEE-noh -nah*) |
| a really teeny tiny bit | **pochettino -a** (*poh-keht-TEE-noh -nah*) |

It's one o'clock.	**È l'una.** *EH LOO-nah*
It's two o'clock.	**Sono le due.** *SOH-noh leh DOO-eh*
It's two thirty.	**Sono le due e mezzo.** *SOH-noh leh DOO-eh eh MEHD-dzoh*
It's two fifteen.	**Sono le due e un quarto.** *SOH-noh leh DOO-eh eh oon KWAHR-toh*
It's a quarter to three.	**Sono le tre meno un quarto. / Manca un quarto alle tre.** *SOH-noh leh treh MEH-noh oon KWAHR-toh / MAHN-kah oon KWAHR-toh AHL-leh treh*
It's noon.	**È mezzogiorno.** *EH mehd-dzoh -JOHR-noh*
It's midnight.	**È mezzanotte.** *EH mehd-dzah-NOHT-teh*
It's early.	**È presto.** *EH PREHS-toh*
It's late.	**È tardi.** *EH TAHR-dee*
in the morning	**al mattino** *ahl maht-TEE-noh*
in the afternoon	**al pomeriggio** *ahl poh-meh-REED-joh*
at night	**di notte** *dee NOHT-teh*
dawn	**l'alba** *LAHL-bah*

DAYS OF THE WEEK

Sunday	**domenica**
	doh-MEH-nee-kah
Monday	**lunedì**
	loo-neh-DEE
Tuesday	**martedì**
	mahr-teh-DEE
Wednesday	**mercoledì**
	mehr-koh-leh-DEE
Thursday	**giovedì**
	joh-veh-DEE
Friday	**venerdì**
	veh-nehr-DEE
Saturday	**sabato**
	SAH-bah-toh
today	**oggi**
	OHD-jee
tomorrow	**domani**
	doh-MAH-nee
yesterday	**ieri**
	YEH-ree
the day before yesterday	**avantieri**
	ah-vahn-TYEH-ree
these last few days	**questi ultimi giorni**
	KWEHS-tee OOL-tee-mee
	JOHR-nee
one week	**una settimana**
	OO-nah seht-tee-MAH-nah
next week	**la prossima settimana**
	lah PROHS-see-mah seht-tee-
	MAH-nah
last week	**la settimana scorsa**
	lah seht-tee-MAH-nah SKOHR-sah

MONTHS OF THE YEAR

January	**gennaio**
	jehn-NAH-yoh

February	**febbraio**
	fehb-BRAH-yoh
March	**marzo**
	MAHR-tso
April	**aprile**
	ah-PREE-leh
May	**maggio**
	MAHD-joh
June	**giugno**
	JEWN-nyo
July	**luglio**
	LOOL-lyo
August	**agosto**
	ah-GOHS-toh
September	**settembre**
	seht-TEHM-breh
October	**ottobre**
	oht-TOH-breh
November	**novembre**
	noh-VEHM-breh
December	**dicembre**
	dee-CHEHM-breh
one month	**un mese**
	oon MEH-zeh
next month	**il prossimo mese**
	eel PROHS-see-moh MEH-zeh
last month	**il mese scorso**
	eel MEH-zeh SKOHR-soh

SEASONS OF THE YEAR

spring	**la primavera**
	lah pree-mah-VEH-rah
summer	**l'estate**
	lehs-TAH-teh
autumn	**l'autunno**
	low-TOON-noh
winter	**l'inverno**
	leen-VEHR-noh

ITALIAN GRAMMAR BASICS

Classified as a Romance language, Italian is closely related to Latin, French, Spanish, Portuguese, and Romanian. It arose from the Vulgar Latin of the late Roman Empire.

THE ALPHABET

The Italian alphabet has 21 letters. The letters **h**, **j**, **k**, **w**, **x**, and **y** are used only in words taken from other languages (such as jazz). Certain combinations of letters have special sounds in Italian, just as **ch**, **sh**, **th**, and **ng** have special sounds in English.

Letter	Name	Pronunciation
a	a	**ah** as in *father* - **La Scala** *lah SKAH-lah*
b	bi	**b** as in *bud* - **bacio** *BAH-choh* (kiss)
c	ci	**ca, co, cu, che, chi:** hard **k** sound as in *car* - **cane** *KAH-neh* (dog)
		ce, ci: ch as in *cheap* - **ciao** *CHAH-oh*
d	di	**d** as in *day* - **dente** *DEHN-teh* (tooth)
e	e	**eh** as in *bell* - **bene** *BEH-neh* (good, well)
f	effe	**f** as in *fan* - **forte** *FOHR-teh* (strong, loud)
g	gi	**ga, go, gu, ghe, ghi:** hard **g** as in *good* - **gatto** *GAHT-toh* (cat)
		ge, gi: soft **j** as in *jelly* - **gelato** *jeh-LAH-toh* (ice cream)
		gli: lly close to *million* - **figlio** *FEEL-lyoh* (son)
		gn: ny as in *poignant* - **bagno** *BAHN-nyoh* (bathroom, restroom)
h	acca	silent before vowels, stresses **a** and **o**: **ho** *OH* (I have), **hai** *AH-ee* (you have)
i	i	**ee** as in *eel* - **ieri** *ee-EH-ree* (yesterday)
l	elle	**l** as in *lunch* - **letto** *LET-toh* (bed)
m	emme	**m** as in *Mary* - **mano** *MAH-noh* (hand)
n	enne	**n** as in *nail* - **nero** *NEH-roh* (black)
o	o	**oh** as in *pot* - **oggi** *OHD-jee* (today)
p	pi	**p** as in *pet* - **pasta** *PAHS-tah*
q	cu	**q** as in *quick* - **questo** *KWEHS-toh* (this)
r	erre	trilled, as in the Scottish **r** - **Roma**

Letter	Name	Pronunciation
s	esse	**s** as in *soon* - **sasso** *SAHS-soh* (rock)
		z as in *rose* between vowels - **casa** *KAH-zah* (house, home)
		sce, sci: sh as in *shop* - **pesce** *PEH-sheh* (fish)
		sche, schi: sk as in *skip* - **schifo** *SKEE-foh* (disgust)
t	ti	**t** as in *tea* - **Torino** *toh-REE-noh* (Turin)
u	u	**oo** as in *boom* - **uno** *OO-noh* (one)
v	vu	**v** as in *very* - **Verona** *veh-ROH-nah*
z	zeta	**dz** or **ts** as in *mezzo* and *matzo* **zucchero** *DZOOK-keh-roh* (sugar) **pizza** *PEET-sah*

Foreign letters

j	i lunga	**j** as *jazz*
k	kappa	**k** sound
w	doppia vu	**w** sound

PRONUNCIATION

Italian has few pitfalls like silent letters; a word's sound closely resembles its written form. Such straightforward pronunciation makes this melodious language accessible and appealing to even the most casual student.

Often **c** and **g** are stumbling blocks for beginners. Both have a soft sound before **e** or **i**, a hard sound before **a**, **o**, and **u**. Think **cubo** *KOO-boh* (cube) versus **arrivederci** *ahr-ree-veh-DEHR-chee* (bye) and **gala** *GAH-lah* versus **Luigi** *loo-EE-jee*.

Double consonants should be pronounced twice—or lengthened and intensified. English speakers are already familiar with this from phrases such as gra**b b**ag, bla**ck c**at, goo**d d**ay, hal**f f**ull, goo**d j**ob, ho**t t**ea and ki**ds z**one.

Enjoy the language's drama and richness, but don't slip into an operatic parody. Italians often accuse foreigners of doubling all consonants. Yet no native, when listening to an aria, would ever confuse **m'ama** (she loves me) with **mamma** (mom)!

GENDER, ADJECTIVES, MODIFIERS

The ending of an Italian noun reveals its gender (masculine or feminine) and number (singular and plural). Those ending in *o* are generally masculine and become *i* (plural); those ending in *a* are typically feminine and become *e* (plural). Ones that conclude in *e* can be masculine or feminine, and shift to *i* (plural). Adjectives agree in gender and number, and usually follow the nouns.

	Singular	Plural
Masculine	**il piatto bianco** (the white plate)	**i piatti bianchi** (the white plates)
	il cane grande (the large dog)	**i cani grandi** (the large dogs)
Feminine	**la pizza calda** (hot pizza)	**le pizze calde** (hot pizzas)
	la carne tenera (tender meat)	**le carni tenere** (tender meats)

Nouns often are accompanied by a masculine or feminine definite article (the): **il**, **lo**, **la** (singular); **i**, **gli**, **le** (plural). Indefinite articles (a, an, some)—**un**, **una** (singular) and **dei**, **delle** (plural)—must also correspond to the nouns they modify.

The Definite Article ("The")

	Masculine	Feminine
Singular	**il** cane (the dog) **lo** stivale (the boot)	**la** tavola (the table) **la** rete (the net)
Plural	**i** cani (the dogs) **gli** stivali (the boots)	**le** tavole (the tables) **le** reti (the nets)

The Indefinite Article ("A" or "An")

	Masculine	Feminine
Singular	**un** cane (a dog)	**una** tavola (a table)
Plural	**dei** cani (some dogs)	**delle** tavole (some tables)

PERSONAL PRONOUNS

English	Italian	Pronunciation
I	io	EE-oh
You (singular, familiar)	tu	TOO
He / She / You (singular, formal)	lui / lei / Lei	LOO-ee / lay / lay
We	noi	NOH-ee
You (plural, familiar)	voi	VOH-ee
They / You (plural, formal)	loro / Loro	LOH-roh

PRONOUNS

English	Italian	Pronunciation
This	questo -a	KWEHS-toh -tah
That	quello -a	KWEHL-loh -lah
These	questi -e	KWEHS-tee -teh
Those	quelli -e	KWEHL-lee -leh

Hey, You!

Italian has two words for "you"—**tu**, spoken among friends and familiars, and to address children; and **Lei / Loro**, used among strangers or as a sign of respect toward elders and authority figures. When speaking with a stranger, expect to use **Lei / Loro** unless you are invited to do otherwise. The trend is toward using the second person familiar form (**voi**) to replace the formal **Loro**.

REGULAR VERB CONJUGATIONS

Italian verb infinitives end in ARE (e.g. **parlare**, to speak), ERE (e.g. **vendere**, to sell), and IRE (e.g. **partire**, to leave). Drop the last three letters to determine the word's stem. Then add endings that reveal who did the action—and when. Following are the present-tense conjugations for regular verbs.

Present Tense

ARE Verbs	PARLARE "To Talk, To Speak"	
I talk.	Io parl*o*.	PAHR-loh
You (singular, familiar) **talk.**	Tu parl*i*.	PAHR-lee
He / She talks. You (singular, formal) **talk.**	Lui / Lei / Lei parl*a*.	PAHR-lah
We talk.	Noi parl*iamo*.	pahr-LYAH-moh
You (plural, familiar) **talk.**	Voi parl*ate*.	pahr-LAH-teh
They / You (plural, formal) **talk.**	Loro / Loro parl*ano*.	PAHR-lah-noh

ERE Verbs	VENDERE "To Sell"	
I sell.	Io vend*o*.	VEHN-doh
You (singular, familiar) **sell.**	Tu vend*i*.	VEHN-dee
He / She sells. You (singular, formal) **sell.**	Lui / Lei / Lei vend*e*.	VEHN-deh
We sell.	Noi vend*iamo*.	vehn-DYAH-moh
You (plural, familiar) **sell.**	Voi vend*ete*.	vehn-DEH-teh
They / You (plural, formal) **sell.**	Loro / Loro vend*ono*.	VEHN-doh-noh

IRE Verbs	PARTIRE "To Leave"	
I leave.	Io part*o.*	PAHR-toh
You (singular, familiar) **leave.**	Tu part*i.*	PAHR-tee
He / She leaves. You (singular, formal) **leave.**	Lui / Lei / Lei parte.	PAHR-teh
We leave.	Noi part*iamo.*	pahr-TYAH-moh
You (plural, familiar) **leave.**	Voi part*ite.*	pahr-TEE-teh
They / You (plural, formal) **leave.**	Loro / Loro part*ono.*	PAHR-toh-noh

Past Tense

Italian has five past tenses. The present perfect most often expresses the simple past (equivalent to the English "I have eaten" or "I ate"). The imperfect tense conveys an unfinished or continuing action ("I was eating"). So for verbs like **essere** (to be) we've supplied that form instead. Below are examples for regular verbs.

ARE Verbs	PARLARE "To Talk, To Speak"	
I talked.	Io *ho* parl*ato.*	oh pahr-LAH-toh
You (singular, familiar) **talked.**	Tu *hai* parl*ato.*	eye pahr-LAH-toh
He / She / You (singular, formal) **talked.**	Lui / Lei / Lei *ha* parl*ato.*	AH pahr-LAH-toh
We talked.	Noi *abbiamo* parl*ato.*	ahb-BYAH-moh pahr-LAH-toh
You (plural, familiar) **talked.**	Voi *avete* parl*ato.*	ah-VEH-teh pahr-LAH-toh
They / You (plural, formal) **talked.**	Loro / Loro *hanno* parl*ato.*	AHN-noh pahr-LAH-toh

ERE Verbs

VENDERE "To Sell"

I sold.	Io *ho* vend*uto*.	oh vehn-DOO-toh
You (singular, familiar) **sold.**	Tu *hai* vend*uto*.	eye vehn-DOO-toh
He / She / You (singular, formal) **sold.**	Lui / Lei / Lei *ha* vend*uto*.	AH vehn-DOO-toh
We sold.	Noi *abbiamo* vend*uto*.	ahb-BYAH-moh vehn-DOO-toh
You (plural, familiar) **sold.**	Voi *avete* vend*uto*.	ah-VEH-teh vehn-DOO-toh
They / You (plural, formal) **sold.**	Loro / Loro *hanno* vend*uto*.	AHN-noh vehn-DOO-toh

IRE Verbs

PARTIRE "To Leave"

I left.	Io *sono* part*ito*.	SOH-noh pahr-TEE-toh
You (singular, familiar) **left.**	Tu *sei* part*ito*.	SEH-ee pahr-TEE-toh
He / She / You (singular, formal) **left.**	Lui / Lei / Lei *è* part*ito*.	EH pahr-TEE-toh
We left.	Noi *siamo* part*iti*.	SYAH-moh pahr-TEE-tee
You (plural, familiar) **left.**	Voi *siete* part*iti*.	SYEH-teh pahr-TEE-tee
They / You (plural, formal) **left.**	Loro / Loro *sono* part*iti*.	SOH-noh pahr-TEE-tee

The Future Tense

ARE Verbs	PARLARE "To Talk, To Speak"	
I will talk.	Io parlerò.	pahr-leh-ROH
You (singular, familiar) will talk.	Tu parlerai.	pahr-leh-REYE
He / she / you (singular, formal) will talk.	Lui / Lei / Lei parlerà.	pahr-leh-RAH
We will talk.	Noi parleremo.	pahr-leh-REH-moh
You (plural, familiar) will talk.	Voi parlerete.	pahr-leh-REH-teh
They / You (plural, formal) will talk.	Loro / Loro parleranno.	pahr-leh-RAHN-noh

ERE Verbs	VENDERE "To Sell"	
I will sell.	Io venderò.	vehn-deh-ROH
You (singular, familiar) will sell.	Tu venderai.	vehn-deh-REYE
He / She / You (singular, formal) will sell.	Lui / Lei / Lei venderà.	vehn-deh-RAH
We will sell.	Noi venderemo.	vehn-deh-REH-moh
You (plural, familiar) will sell.	Voi venderete.	vehn-deh-REH-teh
They / You (plural, formal) will sell.	Loro / Loro venderanno.	vehn-deh-RAHN-noh

IRE Verbs	PARTIRE "To Leave"	
I will leave.	Io partir*ò*.	pahr-tee-ROH
You (singular, familiar) **will leave.**	Tu partir*ai*.	pahr-tee-REYE
He / She / You (singular, formal) **will leave.**	Lui / Lei / Lei partir*à*.	pahr-tee-RAH
We will leave.	Noi partir*emo*.	pahr-tee-REH-moh
You (plural, familiar) **will leave.**	Voi partir*ete*.	pahr-tee-REH-teh
They / You (plural, formal) **will leave.**	Loro / Loro partir*anno*.	pahr-tee-RAHN-noh

TO BE OR NOT TO BE

Italian has two verbs that mean "to be" (am, are, is, was, were). One is for physical location or temporary conditions (**stare**), and the other is for fixed qualities or conditions (**essere**). **Stare** is used in courtesy expressions with **bene** or **male** (well, unwell), e.g. **Come sta? Sto bene / male** (How are you? I'm fine / not well) and to express a progressive -ing action, e.g. **Sto mangiando** (I am eating). **Essere** is used most of the time to express fixed qualities or conditions (as in English) and health states other than **bene** or **male**, e.g. **Sono stanco** (I'm tired).

I am here. (temporary, stare)	Io sto qua.
What are you doing? (temporary, stare)	Cosa sta facendo?
The train is slow. (quality, essere)	Il treno è lento.

Stare "To Be, To Stay" (conditional)

Present Tense

I am.	Io sto.	stoh
You (singular, familiar) are.	Tu stai.	steye
He / She is. You (singular, formal) are.	Lui / Lei / Lei sta.	stah
We are.	Noi stiamo.	STYAH-moh
You (plural, familiar) are.	Voi state.	STAH-teh
They / You (plural, formal) are.	Loro / Loro stanno.	STAHN-noh

Past (imperfect) Tense

I was.	Io stavo.	STAH-voh
You (singular, familiar were.	Tu stavi.	STAH-vee
He / She was. You (singular, formal) were.	Lui / Lei / Lei stava.	STAH-vah
We were.	Noi stavamo.	stah-VAH-moh
You (plural, familiar) were.	Voi stavate.	stah-VAH-teh
They / You (plural, formal) were.	Loro / Loro stavano.	STAH-vah-noh

Essere "To Be" (permanent)

Present Tense

I am.	Io *sono*.	SOH-noh
You (singular, familiar) **are.**	Tu *sei*.	SEH-ee
He /She is. You (singular, formal) **are.**	Lui / Lei / Lei *è*.	EH
We are.	Noi *siamo*.	SYAH-moh
You (plural, familiar) **are.**	Voi *siete*.	SYEH-teh
They / You (plural, formal) **are.**	Loro / Loro *sono*.	SOH-noh

Past (imperfect) Tense

I was.	Io *ero*.	EH-roh
You (singular, familiar) **were.**	Tu *eri*.	EH-ree
He / She was. You (singular, formal) **were.**	Lui / Lei / Lei *era*.	EH-rah
We were.	Noi *eravamo*.	eh-rah-VAH-moh
You (plural, familiar) **were.**	Voi *eravate*.	eh-rah-VAH-teh
They / You (plural, formal) **were.**	Loro / Loro *erano*.	EH-rah-noh

IRREGULAR VERBS

Italian has numerous irregular verbs that stray from the standard **-ARE**, **-ERE**, and **-IRE** conjugations. Rather than bog you down with too much grammar, we're providing the present tense conjugations for the most common irregular verbs.

AVERE "To Have"

I have.	Io *ho.*	OH
You (singular, familiar) **have.**	Tu *hai.*	EYE
He / She has. You (singular, formal) **have.**	Lui / Lei / Lei *ha.*	AH
We have.	Noi *abbiamo.*	ahb-BYAH-moh
You (plural, familiar) **have.**	Voi *avete.*	ah-VEH-teh
They / You (plural, formal) **have.**	Loro / Loro *hanno.*	AHN-noh

ANDARE "To Go"

I go.	Io *vado.*	VAH-doh
You (singular, familiar) **go.**	Tu *vai.*	VAH-ee
He / She goes. You (singular, formal) **go.**	Lui / Lei / Lei *va.*	vah
We go.	Noi *andiamo.*	ahn-DYAH-moh
You (plural, familiar) **go.**	Voi *andate.*	ahn-DAH-teh
They / You (plural, formal) **go.**	Loro / Loro *vanno.*	VAHN-noh

DARE "To Give"

I give.	Io do.	DOH
You (singular, familiar) give.	Tu dai.	DAH-ee
He / She gives. You (singular, formal) give.	Lui / Lei / Lei dà.	DAH
We give.	Noi diamo.	DYAH-moh
You (plural, familiar) give.	Voi date.	DAH-teh
They / You (plural, formal) give.	Loro / Loro danno.	DAHN-noh

FARE "To Do, To Make"

I do / make.	Io faccio.	FAHT-choh
You (singular, familiar) do / make.	Tu fai.	FAH-ee
He / She does / makes. You (singular, formal) do / make.	Lui / Lei / Lei fa.	FAH
We do / make.	Noi facciamo.	faht-CHAH-moh
You (plural, familiar) do / make.	Voi fate.	FAH-teh
They / You (plural, formal) do / make.	Loro / Loro fanno.	FAHN-noh

Fare

The verb *fare* means to make or do. It's also used to describe the weather. For example:

Fa caldo. It's hot.
  (Literally: It makes hot.)
Fa freddo. It's cold.
  (Literally: It makes cold.)

Be careful not to say **Sono freddo**, as this translates "I'm a cold person" or "I'm sexually frigid". Instead, say **Ho freddo / caldo.** (Literally: I have cold / hot.) Likewise, **Sono caldo** can mean "hot to trot."

BERE "To Drink"		
I drink.	Io bevo.	BEH-voh
You (singular, familiar) drink.	Tu bevi.	BEH-vee
He / She drinks. You (singular, formal) drink.	Lui / Lei / Lei beve.	BEH-veh
We drink.	Noi beviamo.	beh-VYAH-moh
You (plural, familiar) drink.	Voi bevete.	beh-VEH-teh
They / You (plural, formal) drink.	Loro / Loro bevono.	BEH-voh-noh

DOVERE "Must, To Have To"

I must / have to.	Io devo.	DEH-voh
You (singular, familiar) must / have to.	Tu devi.	DEH-vee
He / She must / has to. You (singular, formal) must / have to.	Lui / Lei / Lei deve.	DEH-veh
We must / have to.	Noi dobbiamo.	dohb-BYAH-moh
You (plural, familiar) must / have to.	Voi dovete.	doh-VEH-teh
They / You (plural, formal) must / have to.	Loro / Loro devono.	DEH-voh-noh

POTERE "Can, To Be Able"

I can / am able.	Io posso.	POHS-soh
You (singular, familiar) can / are able.	Tu puoi.	poo-OH-ee
He / She can/ is able. You (singular, formal) can / are able.	Lui /Lei / Lei può.	poo-OH
We can / are able.	Noi possiamo.	pohs-SYAH-moh
You (plural, familiar) can / are able.	Voi potete.	poh-TEH-teh
They / You (plural, formal) can / are able.	Loro / Loro possono.	POHS-soh-noh

SAPERE "To Know"

I know.	Io so.	soh
You (singular, familiar) **know.**	Tu sai.	SAH-ee
He / She knows. You (singular, formal) **know.**	Lui / Lei / Lei sa.	SAH
We know.	Noi sappiamo.	sahp-PYAH-moh
You (plural, familiar) **know.**	Voi sapete.	sah-PEH-teh
They / You (plural, formal) **know.**	Loro / Loro sanno.	SAHN-noh

VOLERE "To Want"

I want.	Io voglio.	VOHL-lyoh
You (singular, familiar) **want.**	Tu vuoi.	VWOH-ee
He / She wants. You (singular, formal) **want.**	Lui / Lei / Lei vuole.	VWOH-leh
We want.	Noi vogliamo.	vohl-LYAH-moh
You (plural, familiar) **want.**	Voi volete.	voh-LEH-teh
They / You (plural, formal) **want.**	Loro / Loro vogliono.	VOHL-lyoh-noh

USCIRE "To Get Out"

I get out.	Io *esco*.	EHS-koh
You (singular, familiar) **get out.**	Tu *esci*.	EH-shee
He / She gets out. You (singular, formal) **get out.**	Lui / Lei / Lei *esce*.	EH-sheh
We get out.	Noi usc*iamo*.	oo-SHAH-moh
You (plural, familiar) **get out.**	Voi usc*ite*.	oo-SHEE-teh
They / You (plural, formal) **get out.**	Loro / Loro *escono*.	EHS-koh-noh

VENIRE "To Come"

I come.	Io ven*go*.	VEHN-goh
You (singular, familiar) **come.**	Tu v*ieni*.	VYEH-nee
He / She comes. You (singular, formal) **come.**	Lui / Lei / Lei v*iene*.	VYEH-neh
We come.	Noi ven*iamo*.	veh-NYAH-moh
You (plural, familiar) **come.**	Voi ven*ite*.	veh-NEE-teh
They / You (plural, formal) **come.**	Loro / Loro ven*gono*.	VEHN-goh-noh

Piacere

The Italian for "to like" is *piacere*, which literally means to please. So, rather than "I like chocolate," Italians say, "Chocolate is pleasing to me."

Mi piace il cioccolato. I like chocolate.
(Literally: Chocolate is pleasing to me.)

Mi piacciono i dolci. I like sweets / desserts.
(Literally: Sweets are pleasing to me.)

Piacere "To Like"

Present Tense	Singular	Plural
I like.	*Mi* piace. PYAH-cheh	*Mi* piacciono. PYAHT-choh-noh
You (informal, singular) **like.**	*Ti* piace.	*Ti* piacciono.
He / She likes. You (formal, singular) **like.**	*Gli / Le / Le* piace.	*Gli / Le / Le* piacciono.
We like.	*Ci* piace.	*Ci* piacciono.
You (informal, plural) **like.**	*Vi* piace.	*Vi* piacciono.
They / You (formal, plural) **like.**	*Gli / Loro* piace.	*Gli / Loro* piacciono.

Past Tense	Singular	Plural
I liked.	*Mi* piaceva. pyah-CHEH-vah	*Mi* piacevano. pyah-CHEH-vah-noh
You (informal, singular) **liked.**	*Ti* piaceva.	*Ti* piacevano.
He / She/ You (formal, singular) **liked.**	*Gli / Le / Le* piaceva.	*Gli / le / Le* piacevano.
We liked.	*Ci* piaceva.	*Ci* piacevano.
You (informal, plural) **liked.**	*Vi* piaceva.	*Vi* piacevano.
They / You (formal, plural) **liked.**	*Gli / Loro* piaceva.	*Gli / Loro* piacevano.

REFLEXIVE VERBS

Italian has many more reflexive verbs than English. A verb is reflexive when both its subject and object refer to the same person or thing. For example: "Maria looks at herself in the mirror," **Maria si guarda allo specchio**. The following common verbs are used reflexively: **vestirsi** (to get dressed, literally to dress oneself), **bagnarsi** (to get oneself wet), and **svegliarsi** (to wake up, literally to wake oneself up).

VESTIRSI "To Get Dressed"

I get dressed.	Io *mi* vesto.	mee VEHS-toh
You (singular, familiar) get dressed.	Tu *ti* vesti.	tee VEHS-tee
He / She gets dressed. **You** (singular, formal) get dressed.	Lui / Lei / Lei *si* veste.	see VEHS-teh
We get dressed.	Noi *ci* vestiamo.	chee vehs-TYAH-moh
You (plural, familiar) get dressed.	Voi *vi* vestite.	vee vehs-TEE-teh
They / You (plural, formal) **get dressed.**	Loro / Loro *si* vestono.	see VEHS-toh-noh

CHAPTER TWO

GETTING THERE & GETTING AROUND

This section deals with every form of transportation. Whether you've just reached your destination by plane or you're renting a car to tour the countryside, you'll find the necessary phrases in the next 30 pages.

AT THE AIRPORT

I am looking for ____	**Cerco ____**
	CHEHR-koh
a porter.	**un facchino.**
	oon fahk-KEE-noh
the check-in counter.	**il check-in.**
	eel check-in
the ticket counter.	**la biglietteria.**
	lah beel-lyeht-teh-REE-ah
arrivals.	**l'area arrivi.**
	LAH-reh-ah ahr-REE-vee
departures.	**l'area partenze.**
	LAH-reh-ah pahr-TEHN-tseh
gate number ____.	**l'uscita numero ____.**
	loo-SHEE-tah NOO-meh-roh

For full coverage of numbers, see p7.

the waiting area.	**l'area d'attesa.**
	LAH-reh-ah daht-TEH-zah
the men's restroom.	**la toilette uomini.**
	lah twa-LEHT WOH-mee-nee
the women's restroom.	**la toilette donne.**
	lah twa-LEHT DOHN-neh
the police station.	**la stazione di polizia.**
	lah stah-TSYOH-neh dee
	poh-lee-TSEE-ah

a security guard.	**una guardia di sicurezza.** *OOH-nah GWAHR-dyah dee see-koo-RET-sah*
the smoking area.	**l'area fumatori.** *LAH-reh-ah foo-mah-TOH-ree*
the information booth.	**l'ufficio informazioni.** *loof-FEE-choh een-FOHR-mah- TSYOH-nee*
a public telephone.	**un telefono pubblico.** *oon teh-LEH-foh-noh POOB-blee-koh*
an ATM / cashpoint.	**un bancomat.** *oon BAHN-koh-maht*
baggage claim.	**il ritiro bagagli.** *eel ree-TEE-roh bah-GAHL-lyee*
a luggage cart.	**un carrello portabagagli.** *oon kahr-REHL-loh POHR-tah- bah-GAHL-lyee*
a currency exchange.	**un cambiavalute.** *oon KAHM-byah-vah-LOO-teh*
a café.	**un caffè.** *oon kahf-FEH*
a restaurant.	**un ristorante.** *oon ree-stoh-RAHN-teh*
a bar.	**un bar.** *oon bar*
a bookstore or newsstand.	**una libreria o un'edicola.** *OO-nah lee-breh-REE-ah oh oon eh-DEE-koh-lah*
a duty-free shop.	**un duty-free.** *oon duty-free*

GETTING THERE

Is there Internet access here?	**C'è un accesso a Internet qui?** *ch-EH oon atch-CHESS-oh ah Internet kwee*
I'd like to page someone.	**Vorrei far chiamare qualcuno.** *vohr-RAY fahr kyah-MAH-reh kwahl-KOO-noh*
Do you accept credit cards?	**Prendete la carta di credito?** *prehn-DEH-teh lah KAHR-tah dee KREH-dee-toh*

CHECKING IN

I would like a one-way ticket to ___.	**Vorrei un biglietto di andata per ___.** *vohr-RAY oon beel-LYEHT-toh dee ahn-DAH-tah pehr*
I would like a round trip ticket to ___.	**Vorrei un biglietto di andata e ritorno per ___.** *vohr-RAY oon beel-LYEHT-toh dee ahn-DAH-tah eh ree-TOHR-noh pehr*
How much are the tickets?	**Quanto costano i biglietti?** *KWAHN-toh KOHS-tah-noh ee beel-LYEHT-tee*
Do you have anything less expensive?	**C'è qualcosa di meno caro?** *ch-EH kwahl-KOH-zah dee MEH-noh KAH-roh*
What time does flight ___ leave?	**A che ora parte il volo ___?** *ah keh OH-rah PAHR-teh eel VOH-loh*
What time does flight ___ arrive?	**A che ora arriva il volo ___?** *ah keh OH-rah ahr-REE-vah eel VOH-loh*

For full coverage of numbers, see p7.
For full coverage of time, see p12.

Common Airport Signs

Arrivi	Arrivals
Partenze	Departures
Terminal	Terminal
Uscita	Gate
Emissione biglietti	Ticketing
Dogana	Customs
Ritiro bagagli	Baggage Claim
Spingere	Push
Tirare	Pull
Vietato fumare	No Smoking
Entrata	Entrance
Uscita	Exit
Uomini	Men's
Donne	Women's
Bus navetta	Shuttle Buses
Taxi	Taxis

GETTING THERE

How long is the flight?

Quanto dura il volo?
KWAHN-toh DOO-rah eel VOH-loh

Do I have a connecting flight?

C'è una coincidenza?
ch-EH OO-nah koh-een-chee-DEHN-tsa

Do I need to change planes?

Devo cambiare aereo?
DEH-voh kahm-BYAH-reh ah-EH-reh-oh

My flight leaves at __:__.

Il mio aereo parte alle __:__.
eel MEE-oh ah-EH-reh-oh PAHR-teh ahl-leh

What time will the flight arrive?

A che ora arriva l'aereo?
ah keh OH-rah ahr-REE-vah lah-EH-reh-oh

Is the flight on time?	**Il volo è in orario?** *eel VOH-loh EH een oh-RAH-ryoh*
Is the flight delayed?	**Il volo è in ritardo?** *eel VOH-loh EH een ree-TAHR-doh*
From which terminal is flight ____ leaving?	**Da che terminal parte il volo ____?** *dah keh TEHR-mee-nahl PAHR-teh eel VOH-loh*
From which gate is flight ____ leaving?	**Da che uscita parte il volo ____?** *dah keh oo-SHEE-tah PAHR-teh eel VOH-loh*

For full coverage of numbers, see p7.

How much time do I need for check-in?	**Quanto tempo ci vuole per fare il check-in?** *KWAHN-toh TEHM-poh chee VWOH-leh pehr FAH-reh eel check-in*
Is there an express check-in line?	**C'è una fila rapida per il check-in?** *ch-EH OO-nah FEE-lah RAH-pee-dah pehr eel check-in*
Is there electronic check-in?	**C'è un check-in elettronico?** *ch-EH oon check-in eh-leht-TROH-nee-koh*

Seat Preferences

I would like ____ ticket(s) in ____	**Vorrei ____ biglietto -i in ____** *vohr-RAY ____ beel-LYEHT-toh -ee een*
first / business class.	**prima classe.** *PREE-mah KLAHS-seh*
economy class.	**classe turistica.** *KLAHS-seh too-REES-tee-kah*
I would like ____	**Vorrei ____** *vohr-RAY*
Please don't give me ____	**Per favore non mi dia ____** *pehr fah-VOH-reh nohn mee DEE-ah*
a window seat.	**un posto vicino al finestrino.** *oon POHS-toh vee-CHEE-noh ahl fee-nehs-TREE-noh*
an aisle seat.	**un posto sul corridoio.** *oon POHS-toh sool kohr-ree-DOH-yoh*
an emergency exit row seat.	**un posto vicino all'uscita di sicurezza.** *oon POHS-toh vee-CHEE-noh ahl-loo-SHEE-tah dee see-koo-RET-sah*
a bulkhead seat.	**un posto in prima fila.** *oon POHS-toh een PREE-mah FEE-lah*
a seat by the restroom.	**un posto vicino alle toilette.** *oon POHS-toh vee-CHEE-noh AHL-leh twa-LEHT*
a seat near the front.	**un posto nella parte anteriore.** *oon POHS-toh NEHL-lah PAHR-teh ahn-teh-RYOH-reh*

a seat near the middle.	**un posto nella zona centrale.** *oon POHS-toh NEHL-lah DZOH-nah chehn-TRAH-leh*
a seat near the back.	**un posto verso il retro.** *oon POHS-toh VEHR-soh eel REH-troh*
Is there a meal on the flight?	**Viene servito un pasto durante il volo?** *VYEH-neh sehr-VEE-toh oon PAHS- toh doo-RAHN-teh eel VOH-loh*
I'd like to order ____	**Vorrei ordinare ____** *vohr-RAY ohr-dee-NAH-reh*
a vegetarian meal.	**un pasto vegetariano.** *oon PAHS-toh veh-jeh-tah-RYAH-noh*
a kosher meal.	**un pasto kasher.** *oon PAHS-toh KAH-shehr*
a diabetic meal.	**un pasto per diabetici.** *oon PAHS-toh pehr dyah-BEH- tee-chee*
I am traveling to ____.	**Sto andando a ____.** *stoh ahn-DAHN-doh ah*
I am coming from ____.	**Vengo da ____.** *VEHN-goh dah*
I arrived from ____.	**Arrivo da ____.** *ahr-REE-voh dah*

For full coverage of country terms, see English / Italian dictionary.

I'd like to change / cancel / confirm my reservation.	**Vorrei cambiare / annullare / confermare la mia prenotazione.** *vohr-RAY kahm-BYAH-reh / ahn- nool-LAH-reh / kohn-fehr-MAH- reh lah MEE-ah preh-noh-tah- TSYOH-neh*

I have ____ bags to check.	**Ho ____ bagagli da registrare.** *OH ____ bah-GAHL-lyee dah reh-jees-TRAH-reh*

For full coverage of numbers, see p7.

Passengers with Special Needs

Is that handicap accessible?	**C'è accesso ai disabili?** *ch-EH atch-CHESS-oh eye dee-ZAH-bee-lee*
May I have a wheelchair / a walker please?	**Posso avere una sedia a rotelle / un deambulatore, per favore?** *POHS-soh ah-VEH-reh OO-nah SEH-dyah ah roh-TEHL-leh / oon deh-ahm-boo-lah-TOH-reh pehr fah-VOH-reh*
I need some assistance boarding.	**Ho bisogno di assistenza all'imbarco.** *OH bee-ZOHN-nyoh dee ahs-sees-TEHN-tsa ahl-leem-BAHR-koh*
I need to bring my service dog.	**Devo portare il mio cane d'assistenza.** *DEH-voh pohr-TAH-reh eel MEE-oh KAH-neh dahs-sees-TEHN-tsa*
Do you have services for the hearing impaired?	**Ci sono servizi per ipoudenti?** *chee SOH-noh sehr-VEE-tsee pehr EE-poh-oo-DEHN-tee*
Do you have services for the visually impaired?	**Ci sono servizi per ipovedenti?** *chee SOH-noh sehr-VEE-tsee pehr EE-poh-oo-veh-DEHN-tee*

Trouble at Check-In

How long is the delay?	**Di quanto è il ritardo?**
	dee KWAHN-toh EH eel ree-TAHR-doh
My flight was late.	**Il mio volo era in ritardo.**
	eel MEE-oh VOH-loh EH-rah een ree-TAHR-doh
I missed my flight.	**Ho perso il volo.**
	OH PEHR-soh eel VOH-loh
When is the next flight?	**Quand'è il prossimo volo?**
	kwahn-DEH eel PROHS-see-moh VOH-loh
May I have a meal voucher?	**Posso avere un buono pasto?**
	POHS-soh ah-VEH-reh oon BWOH-noh PAHS-toh
May I have a room voucher?	**Posso avere un buono stanza?**
	POHS-soh ah-VEH-reh oon BWOH-noh STAHN-tsah

AT CUSTOMS / SECURITY CHECKPOINTS

I'm traveling with a group.	**Viaggio con un gruppo.**
	VYAHD-joh kohn oon GROOP-poh
I'm on my own.	**Viaggio da solo -a.**
	VYAHD-joh dah SOH-loh -ah
I'm traveling on business.	**Sono in viaggio d'affari.**
	SOH-noh een VYAHD-joh dahf-FAH-ree
I'm on vacation.	**Sono in vacanza.**
	SOH-noh een vah-KAHN-tsah
I have nothing to declare.	**Non ho nulla da dichiarare.**
	nohn OH NOOL-lah dah dee-kyah-RAH-reh
I would like to declare ____.	**Vorrei dichiarare ____.**
	vohr-RAY dee-kyah-RAH-reh
I have some liquor.	**Ho un po' di liquore.**
	OH oon POH dee lee-KWOH-reh

I have some cigars.	**Ho dei sigari.**
	OH day SEE-gah-ree
They are gifts.	**Sono regali.**
	SOH-noh reh-GAH-lee
They are for personal use.	**Sono per uso personale.**
	SOH-noh pehr OO-zoh pehr-soh-NAH-leh
That is my medicine.	**È la mia medicina.**
	EH lah MEE-ah meh-dee-CHEE-nah
I have my prescription.	**Ho la mia ricetta.**
	OH lah MEE-ah ree-CHET-tah
My children are traveling on the same passport.	**I miei bambini viaggiano con lo stesso passaporto.**
	ee mee-EH-ee bahm-BEE-nee VYAHD-jah-noh kohn loh STEHS-soh pahs-sah-POHR-toh
I'd like a female / male officer to conduct the search.	**Vorrei un agente donna / uomo per la perquisizione.**
	vohr-RAY oon ah-JEN-teh DOHN-nah / WOH-moh pehr lah pehr-kwee-zee-TSYOH-neh

GETTING THERE

Listen Up: Security Lingo

Per favore, ____	Please ____
si tolga le scarpe.	remove your shoes.
si tolga la giacca / la maglia.	remove your jacket / sweater.
si tolga i gioielli.	remove your jewelry.
metta le borse sul trasportatore.	place your bags on the conveyor belt.
Si sposti di qua.	Step to the side.
Dobbiamo fare un'ispezione manuale.	We have to do a hand search.

Trouble at Security

Help me. I've lost ___	**Mi aiuti. Ho perso ___** *mee ah-YOO-tee OH PEHR-soh*
my passport.	**il passaporto.** *eel pahs-sah-POHR-toh*
my boarding pass.	**la carta d'imbarco.** *lah KAHR-tah deem-BAHR-koh*
my identification.	**il documento d'identità.** *eel doh-koo-MEHN-toh dee-dehn-tee-TAH*
my wallet.	**il portafoglio.** *eel pohr-tah-FOHL-lyoh*
my purse.	**la borsa.** *lah BOHR-sah*
Someone stole my purse / wallet!	**Mi hanno rubato la borsa / il portafoglio!** *mee AHN-noh roo-BAH-toh lah BOHR-sah / eel pohr-tah-FOHL-lyoh*

IN-FLIGHT

It's unlikely you'll need much Italian on the plane, but these phrases will help if a bilingual flight attendant is unavailable or if you need to talk to an Italian-speaking neighbor.

I think that's my seat.	**Credo che quello sia il mio posto.** *KREH-doh keh KWEHL-loh SEE-ah eel MEE-oh POHS-toh*
May I have ___	**Posso avere ___** *POHS-soh ah-VEH-reh*
water?	**dell'acqua?** *dehl-LAHK-wah*
sparkling water?	**gassata?** *gas-SAH-tah*
orange juice?	**del succo d'arancia?** *dehl SOOK-koh dah-RAHN-chah*

soda?	**una bibita?**
	OO-nah BEE-bee-tah
diet soda?	**una bibita light?**
	OO-nah BEE-bee-tah light
a beer?	**una birra?**
	OO-nah BEER-rah
wine?	**del vino?**
	dehl VEE-noh

For a complete list of drinks, see p88.

a pillow?	**un cuscino?**
	oon koo-SHEE-noh
a blanket?	**una coperta?**
	OO-nah koh-PEHR-tah
headphones?	**le cuffie?**
	leh KOOF-fyeh
a magazine or	**una rivista o un giornale?**
newspaper?	*OO-nah ree-VEES-tah oh oon*
	johr-NAH-leh
When will the meal be	**Quando sarà servito il pasto?**
served?	*KWAHN-doh sah-RAH*
	sehr-VEE-toh eel PAHS-toh
How long until we land?	**Quanto manca all'atterraggio?**
	KWAHN-toh MAHN-kah
	ahl-laht-tehr-RAHD-joh
May I move to another	**Posso cambiare posto?**
seat?	*POHS-soh kahm-BYAH-reh*
	POHS-toh
How do I turn the light	**Come si accende / spegne la luce?**
on / off?	*KOH-meh see atch-CHEN-deh /*
	SPEHN-nyeh lah LOO-cheh

Trouble In-Flight

These headphones are	**Queste cuffie sono guaste.**
broken.	*KWEHS-teh KOOF-fyeh SOH-noh*
	GWAHS-teh

I spilled.	**Mi si è rovesciato.**
	mee see EH roh-veh-SHAH-toh
My child spilled.	**Si è rovesciato al bambino.**
	see EH roh-veh-SHAH-toh ahl bahm-BEE-noh
My child is sick.	**Il mio bambino / la mia bambina sta male.**
	eel MEE-oh bahm-BEE-noh / lah MEE-ah bahm-BEE-nah stah MAH-leh
I need an airsickness bag.	**Mi serve un sacchetto per il mal d'aria.**
	mee SEHR-veh oon sahk-KEHT-toh perh eel mahl DAHR-yah
I smell something strange.	**Sento uno strano odore.**
	SEHN-toh OO-noh STRAH-noh oh-DOH-reh
That passenger is behaving suspiciously.	**Quel passeggero si comporta in modo sospetto.**
	kwehl pahs-sed-JEH-roh see kohm-POHR-tah een MOH-doh sohs-PEHT-to

BAGGAGE CLAIM

Where is baggage claim for flight ____?	**Dov'è il ritiro bagagli per il volo ____?**
	doh-VEH eel ree-TEE-roh bah-GAHL-lyee pehr eel VOH-loh
Would you please help with my bags?	**Può aiutarmi con i bagagli?**
	PWOH ah-yoo-TAHR-mee kohn ee bah-GAHL-lyee
I am missing ____ bags.	**Mi mancano ____ borse.**
	mee MAHN-kah-noh ____ BOHR-seh

For full coverage of numbers, see p7.

My bag is ____	**La mia borsa è ____** *lah MEE-ah BOHR-sah EH*
lost.	**smarrita.** *zmahr-REE-tah*
damaged.	**danneggiata.** *dahn-ned-JAH-tah*
stolen.	**stata rubata.** *STAH-tah roo-BAH-tah*
a suitcase.	**una valigia.** *OO-nah vah-LEE-jah*
a briefcase.	**una valigetta.** *OO-nah vah-lee-JEHT-tah*
a carry-on.	**un bagaglio a mano.** *oon bah-GAHL-lyoh ah MAH-noh*
a suit bag.	**una borsa portabiti.** *OO-nah BOHR-sah pohr-TAH-bee-tee*
a trunk.	**un baule.** *oon bah-OO-leh*
golf clubs.	**mazze da golf.** *MAHT-seh dah golf*

For colors terms, see English / Italian Dictionary.

hard.	**rigido -a.** *REE-jee-doh -ah*
made out of ____	**fatto -a di ____** *FAHT-toh -ah dee*
canvas.	**tela.** *TEH-lah*
vinyl.	**vinile.** *vee-NEE-leh*
leather.	**pelle.** *PEHL-leh*

hard plastic.	**plastica dura.** *PLAHS-tee-kah DOO-rah*
aluminum.	**alluminio.** *ahl-loo-MEE-nyoh*

RENTING A VEHICLE

Is there a car rental agency in the airport?	**C'è un'agenzia di autonoleggio in aeroporto?** *ch-EH oon-ah-jehn-TSEE-ah dee ow-toh-noh-LEHD-joh een ah-EH-roh-POHR-toh*
I have a reservation.	**Ho una prenotazione.** *OH OO-nah preh-noh-tah-TSYOH-neh*

Vehicle Preferences

I would like to rent ____	**Vorrei noleggiare ____** *vohr-RAY noh-lehd-JAH-reh*
an economy car.	**un'auto economica.** *oon-OW-toh eh-koh-NOH-mee-kah*
a midsize car.	**un'auto di media dimensione.** *oon-OW-toh dee MEH-dyah dee-mehn-SYOH-neh*
a sedan.	**una berlina.** *OO-nah berh-LEE-nah*
a convertible.	**un'auto convertibile.** *oon-OW-toh kohn-vehr-TEE-bee-leh*
a van.	**un furgoncino.** *oon foor-gohn-CHEE-noh*
a sports car.	**un'auto sportiva.** *oon-OW-toh spohr-TEE-vah*
a 4-wheel-drive vehicle.	**una quattro per quattro.** *OO-nah KWAHT-troh pehr KWAHT-troh*

a motorcycle.	**una moto.** *OO-nah MOH-toh*
a scooter.	**uno scooter.** *OO-noh scooter*
Do you have one with ____	**C'è un'auto con ____** *ch-EH oon-OW-toh kohn*
air conditioning?	**climatizzatore?** *klee-mah-teed-zsah-TOH-reh*
a sunroof?	**tettuccio apribile?** *teht-TOOT-choh ah-PREE-bee-leh*
a CD player?	**lettore di CD?** *leht-TOH-reh dee chee-DEE*
satellite radio?	**radio satellitare?** *RAH-dyoh sah-tehl-lee-TAH-reh*
satellite tracking?	**navigazione satellitare?** *nah-vee-gah-TZYOH-neh* *sah-tehl-lee-TAH-reh*
an onboard map?	**sistema di navigazione?** *see-STEH-mah dee* *nah-vee-gah-TSYOH-neh*
a DVD player?	**lettore di DVD?** *leht-TOH-reh dee dee-voo-DEE*
child seats?	**sedili per bambini?** *seh-DEE-lee pehr bahm-BEE-nee*
Do you have a ____	**C'è ____** *ch-EH*
smaller car?	**un'auto più piccola?** *oon-OW-toh PYOO PEEK-koh-lah*
bigger car?	**un'auto più grande?** *oon-OW-toh PYOO GRAHN-deh*
cheaper car?	**un'auto più economica?** *oon-OW-toh PYOO* *eh-koh-NOH-mee-kah*

Do you have a non-smoking car?	**C'è un'auto per non fumatori?**
	ch-EH oon-OW-toh pehr nohn foo-mah-TOH-ree
I need an automatic transmission.	**Mi serve un'auto con cambio automatico.**
	mee SEHR-veh oon-OW-toh kohn KAHM-byoh ow-toh-MAH-tee-koh
A standard transmission is okay.	**Con cambio manuale va bene.**
	kohn KAHM-byoh mah-NWAH-leh vah BEH-neh
May I have an upgrade?	**Posso avere una categoria superiore?**
	POHS-soh ah-VEH-reh OO-nah kah-teh-goh-REE-ah soo-peh-RYOH-reh

Money Matters

What's the daily / weekly / monthly rate?	**Qual è la tariffa giornaliera / settimanale / mensile?**
	kwah-LEH lah tah-REEF-fah johr-nah-LYEH-rah / seht-tee-mah-NAH-leh / mehn-SEE-leh
What is the mileage rate?	**Qual è la tariffa chilometrica?**
	kwah-LEH lah tah-REEF-fah kee-loh-MEH-tree-kah
How much is insurance?	**Quanto costa l'assicurazione?**
	KWAHN-toh KOHS-tah lahs-see-koo-raht-SYOH-neh
Are there other fees?	**Ci sono altri costi?**
	chee SOH-noh AHL-tree KOHS-tee
Is there a weekend rate?	**C'è una tariffa per il weekend?**
	ch-EH OO-nah tah-REEF-fah pehr eel weekend

Technical Questions

What kind of gas does it take?

Che tipo di benzina prende?
keh TEE-poh dee behn-DZEE-nah PREHN-deh

Do you have the manual in English?

Ha il manuale in inglese?
AH eel mah-NWA-leh een een-GLEH-zeh

Do you have an English booklet with the local traffic laws?

Ha un codice della strada in inglese?
AH oon KOH-dee-cheh DEHL-lah STRAH-dah een een-GLEH-zeh

Car Troubles

The _____ doesn't work.

_____ non funziona.
nohn foon-TSYOH-nah

See diagram on p54 for car parts.

It is already dented.

È già ammaccata.
EH JAH ahm-mahk-KAH-tah

It is scratched.

È graffiata.
EH grahf-FYAH-tah

The windshield is cracked.

Il parabrezza è crepato.
eel pah-rah-BREHT-sah EH kreh-PAH-toh

The tires look low.

Le gomme sembrano sgonfie.
leh GOHM-meh SEHM-brah-noh SGOHN-fyeh

It has a flat tire.

Ha una gomma a terra.
AH OO-nah GOHM-mah ah TEHR-rah

Whom do I call for service?

Chi chiamo per l'assistenza?
kee KYAH-moh pehr lahs-sees-TEHN-tsa

It won't start.

Non parte.
nohn PAHR-teh

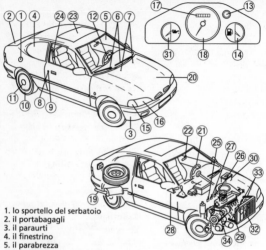

1. lo sportello del serbatoio
2. il portabagagli
3. il paraurti
4. il finestrino
5. il parabrezza
6. I tergicristalli
7. Il liquido tergicristalli
8. la serratura
9. la serratura automatica
10. I pneumatici
11. le ruote
12. l'accensione
13. la spia
14. l'indicatore di livello di carburante
15. gli indicatori di direzione
16. I fanali
17. il contachilometri
18. il tachimetro
19. la marmitta
20. il cofano
21. il volante
22. lo specchietto retrovisore
23. il tettuccio apribile
24. la cintura di sicurezza

25. l'acceleratore
26. la frizione
27. il freno
28. il freno d'emergenza
29. il motore
30. la batteria
31. l'indicatore di livello dell'olio
32. il radiatore
33. il tubo del radiatore
34. la cinghia del ventilatore

It's out of gas.	**È a secco.**
	EH ah SEHK-koh
The Check Engine light is on.	**La spia del motore è accesa.**
	lah SPEE-ah dehl moh-TOH-reh
	EH aht-CHEH-zah
The oil light is on.	**La spia dell'olio è accesa.**
	lah SPEE-ah dehl-LOH-lyoh EH
	aht-CHEH-zah
The brake light is on.	**La spia dei freni è accesa.**
	lah SPEE-ah day FREH-nee EH
	aht-CHEH-zah
It runs rough.	**Non va bene, fa rumore.**
	nohn vah BEH-neh fah roo-MOH-reh
The car is over-heating.	**L'auto si surriscalda.**
	LOW-toh see soor-ree-SKAHL-dah

Asking for Directions

Excuse me.	**Mi scusi.**
	mee SKOO-zee
How do I get to ____?	**Come si arriva a ____?**
	KOH-meh see ahr-REE-vah ah
Go straight.	**Vada dritto.**
	VAH-dah DREET-toh
Turn left.	**Giri a sinistra.**
	JEE-ree ah see-NEES-trah
Continue right.	**Continui a destra.**
	kohn-TEE-nwee ah DEHS-trah
It's on the right.	**E' sulla destra.**
	EH SOOL-lah DEHS-trah
Can you show me on the map?	**Può mostrarmi sulla cartina?**
	PWOH mohs-TRAHR-mee SOOL-lah
	kahr-TEE-nah
How far is it from here?	**Quanto dista da qui?**
	KWAHN-toh DEES-tah dah kwee
Is this the right road for ____?	**Questa è la strada giusta per ____?**
	KWEHS-tah EH lah STRAH-dah
	JOOS-tah pehr

I've lost my way.	**Mi sono perso -a.**
	mee SOH-noh PEHR-soh -sah
Would you repeat that, please?	**Può ripetere, per favore?**
	PWOH ree-PEH-teh-reh pehr fah-VOH-reh
Thanks for your help.	**Grazie per l'aiuto.**
	GRAH-tsyeh pehr lah-YOO-toh

For full coverage of direction-related terms, see p5.

Sorry, Officer

What is the speed limit?	**Qual è il limite di velocità?**
	kwah-LEH eel LEE-mee-teh dee veh-loh-chee–TAH
I wasn't going that fast.	**Non andavo così veloce.**
	nohn ahn-DAH-voh koh-ZEE veh-LOH-cheh
How much is the fine?	**Quant'è la multa?**
	kwahn-TEH lah MOOL-tah
Where do I pay the fine?	**Dove si paga la multa?**
	DOH-veh see PAH-gah lah MOOL-tah

Road Signs

Limite di velocità	Speed Limit
Stop	Stop
Dare la precedenza	Yield
Pericolo	Danger
Strada senza sbocco	No Exit
Senso unico	One Way
Vietato l'accesso	Do Not Enter
Strada chiusa	Road Closed
Pagamento pedaggio	Toll
Solo contanti	Cash Only
Parcheggio vietato	No Parking
Tariffa di parcheggio	Parking fee
Parcheggio	Parking garage

Do I have to go to court?	**Devo andare in tribunale?** *DEH-voh ahn-DAH-reh een tree-boo-NAH-leh*
I had an accident.	**Ho avuto un incidente.** *OH ah-VOO-toh oon een-chee-DEHN-teh*
The other driver hit me.	**L'altro autista mi ha investito -a.** *LAHL-troh ow-TEES-tah mee AH een-vehs-TEE-toh -tah*
I'm at fault.	**È colpa mia.** *EH KOHL-pah MEE-ah*

BY TAXI

Where is the taxi stand?	**Dov'è la fermata dei taxi?** *doh-VEH lah fehr-MAH-tah day taxi*
Is there a limo / bus / van for my hotel?	**C'è un servizio di limousine / bus / navetta per il mio hotel?** *ch-EH oon sehr-VEE-tsyoh dee limousine / boos / nah-VEHT-tah pehr eel MEE-oh hotel*
I need to get to ____.	**Devo andare a ____.** *DEH-voh ahn-DAH-reh ah*
How much will that cost?	**Quanto mi costa?** *KWAHN-toh mee KOHS-tah*
How long will it take?	**Quanto tempo ci vuole?** *KWAHN-toh TEHM-poh chee VWOH-leh*

Listen Up: Taxi Lingo

Salga!	Get in!
Lasci i bagagli, faccio io.	Leave your luggage, I got it.
Sono cinque euro al pezzo.	It's 5 Euros for each bag.
Quanti passeggeri?	How many passengers?
Ha fretta?	Are you in a hurry?

Can you take me / us to the train / bus station?	**Può portarmi / portarci alla stazione dei treni / degli autobus?**
	PWOH pohr-TAHR-mee / chee AHL-lah stah-TSYOH-neh day TREH-nee / DEHL-lye OW-toh-boos
I am in a hurry.	**Ho fretta.**
	OH FREHT-tah
Slow down.	**Rallenti.**
	rahl-LEHN-tee
Am I close enough to walk?	**Sono abbastanza vicino da andarci a piedi?**
	SOH-noh ahb-bahs-TAHN-tsah vee-CHEE-noh dah ahn-DAHR-chee ah PYEH-dee
Let me out here.	**Mi lasci qui.**
	mee LAH-shee kwee
That's not the correct change.	**Il resto non è giusto.**
	eel REH-stoh nohn EH JOOS-toh

BY TRAIN

How do I get to the train station?	**Come si arriva alla stazione ferroviaria?**
	KOH-meh see ahr-REE-vah AHL-lah stah-TSYOH-neh fehr-roh-VYAH-ryah
Would you take me to the train station?	**Può portarmi alla stazione ferroviaria?**
	PWOH pohr-TAHR-mee AHL-lah stah-TSYOH-neh fehr-roh-VYAH-ryah
How long is the trip to ____?	**Quanto ci vuole fino a ____?**
	KWAHN-toh chee VWOH-leh FEE-noh ah
When is the next train?	**Quand'è il prossimo treno?**
	kwahn-DEH eel PROHS-see-moh TREH-noh

Do you have a schedule / timetable?	**Ha un orario?** *AH oon oh-RAH-ryoh*
Do I have to change trains?	**Devo cambiare treni?** *DEH-voh kahm-BYAH-reh TREH-nee*
a one-way ticket	**un biglietto di sola andata** *oon beel-LYEHT-toh dee SOH-lah ahn-DAH-tah*
a round-trip ticket	**un biglietto di andata e ritorno** *oon beel-LYEHT-toh dee ahn-DAH-tah eh ree-TOHR-noh*
Which platform does it leave from?	**Da che binario parte?** *dah keh bee-NAH-ryoh PAHR-teh*
Is there a bar car?	**C'è una carrozza bar?** *ch-EH OO-nah kahr-ROHT-sah bar*
Is there a dining car?	**C'è una carrozza ristorante?** *ch-EH OO-nah kahr-ROHT-sah ree-stoh-RAHN-teh*
Which car is my seat in?	**In quale carrozza è il mio posto?** *een KWAH-leh kahr-ROHT-sah EH eel MEE-oh POHS-toh*
Is this seat taken?	**È occupato questo posto?** *EH ohk-koo-PAH-toh KWEHS-toh POHS-toh*
Where is the next stop?	**Dov'è la prossima fermata?** *doh-VEH lah PROHS-see-mah fehr-MAH-tah*
How many stops to ___?	**Quante fermate fino a ___?** *KWAHN-teh fehr-MAH-teh FEE-noh ah*
What's the train number and destination?	**Qual è il numero del treno e la destinazione?** *kwah-LEH eel NOO-meh-roh dehl TREH-noh eh lah dehs-tee-nah-TSYOH-neh*

BY BUS

How do I get to the bus
station?

**Come si arriva alla stazione degli
autobus?**
*KOH-meh see ahr-REE-vah ahl-LAH
stah-TSYOH-neh DEHL-lye
OW-toh-boos*

Would you take me to the
bus station?

**Può portarmi alla stazione degli
autobus?**
*PWOH pohr-TAHR-mee ahl-LAH
stah-TSYOH-neh DEHL-lye
OW-toh-boos*

May I have a bus schedule?

**Posso avere un orario degli
autobus?**
*POHS-soh ah-VEH-reh oon oh-RAH-
ryoh DEHL-lye OW-toh-boos*

Which bus goes to ____?

Quale autobus va a ____?
KWAH-leh OW-toh-boos vah ah

Where does it leave from?

Da dove parte?
dah DOH-veh PAHR-teh

How long does the bus
take?

**Quanto tempo ci impiega
l'autobus?**
*KWAHN-toh TEHM-poh chee
eem-PYEH-gah LOW-toh-boos*

How much is it?

Quanto costa?
KWAHN-toh KOHS-tah

Is there an express bus?

C'è un autobus espresso?
*ch-EH oon OW-toh-boos ehs-
PREHS-soh*

Does it make local stops?	**Fa fermate locali?** *fah fehr-MAH-teh loh-KAH-lee*
Does it run at night?	**Fa servizio notturno?** *fah sehr-VEE-tsyoh noht-TOOR-noh*
When is the next bus?	**Quand'è il prossimo autobus?** *kwahn-DEH eel PROHS-see-moh* *OW-toh-boos*
a one-way ticket	**un biglietto di sola andata** *oon beel-LYEHT-toh dee SOH-lah* *ahn-DAH-tah*
a round-trip ticket	**un biglietto di andata e ritorno** *oon beel-LYEHT-toh dee ahn-DAH-* *tah eh ree-TOHR-noh*
How long will the bus be stopped?	**Quanto tempo sta fermo l'autobus?** *KWAHN-toh TEHM-poh stah* *FEHR-moh LOW-toh-boos*
Is there an air conditioned bus?	**C'è un autobus con aria condizionata?** *ch-EH oon OW-toh-boos kohn* *AH-ryah kohn-dee-tsyoh-NAH-tah*
Is this seat taken?	**È occupato questo posto?** *EH ohk-koo-PAH-toh KWEHS-toh* *POHS-toh*

Ticket etiquette

Travelers in Italy often need to validate their tickets before embarking. In a train station, search for a yellow **macchina obliteratrice** (stamping machine), which prints the time and date in the space marked **convalida** (validation). These usually stand at the end of each **binario** (platform). Many subways have a similar system, but buses validate onboard. If you forget—or can't reach the machine in a crowd—write the details in pen.

Where is the next stop?	**Dov'è la prossima fermata?** *doh-VEH lah PROHS-see-mah* *fehr-MAH-tah*
Please tell me when we reach ____.	**Mi dice quando arriviamo a ____,** **per favore.** *mee DEE-cheh KWAHN-doh ahr-ree-* *VYAH-moh ah pehr fah-VOH-reh*
Let me off here.	**Mi lasci qui.** *mee LAH-shee kwee*

BY BOAT OR SHIP

Would you take me to the port?	**Può portarmi al porto?** *PWOH pohr-TAHR-mee ahl* *POHR-toh*
When does the ship sail?	**Quando salpa la nave?** *KWAHN-doh SAHL-pah lah NAH-veh*
How long is the trip?	**Quanto dura il viaggio?** *KWAHN-toh DOO-rah eel* *VYAHD-joh*
Where are the life preservers?	**Dove sono i salvagenti?** *DOH-veh SOH-noh ee sahl-vah-* *JEHN-tee*
I would like a private cabin.	**Vorrei una cabina privata.** *vohr-RAY OO-nah kah-BEE-nah* *pree-VAH-tah*
Is the trip rough?	**È una traversata agitata?** *EH OO-nah trah-vehr-SAH-tah* *ah-jee-TAH-tah*
I feel seasick.	**Ho mal di mare.** *OH eel mahl dee MAH-reh*
I need some seasick pills.	**Ho bisogno di pastiglie** **antinausea.** *OH bee-ZOHN-nyoh dee pahs-* *TEEL-lyeh ahn-tee-NOW-seh-ah*
Where is the bathroom?	**Dov'è la toilette?** *doh-VEH lah twah-LEHT*

Does the ship have a casino?	**C'è un casinò sulla nave?** *ch-EH oon kah-zee-NOH SOOL-lah NAH-veh*
Will the ship stop at ports along the way?	**La nave si ferma nei porti lungo il tragitto?** *lah NAH-veh seeFEHR-mah NAY POHR-tee LOON-goh eel trah-JEET-oh*

BY SUBWAY

Where's the subway station?	**Dov'è la stazione del metrò?** *doh-VEH lah stah-TSYOH-neh dehl meh-TROH*
Where can I buy a ticket?	**Dove si comprano i biglietti?** *DOH-veh see KOHM-prah-noh ee beel-LYEHT-tee*

GETTING THERE

SUBWAY TICKETS

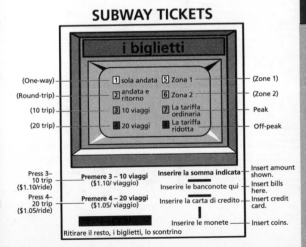

(One-way)	1 sola andata
(Round-trip)	2 andata e ritorno
(10 trip)	3 10 viaggi
(20 trip)	20 viaggi

5 Zona 1	(Zone 1)
6 Zona 2	(Zone 2)
7 La tariffa ordinaria	Peak
La tariffa ridotta	Off-peak

i biglietti

| Press 3– 10 trip ($1.10/ride) | **Premere 3 – 10 viaggi** ($1.10/ viaggio) |
| Press 4– 20 trip ($1.05/ride) | **Premere 4 – 20 viaggi** ($1.05/ viaggio) |

Inserire la somma indicata	Insert amount shown.
Inserire le banconote qui	Insert bills here.
Inserire la carta di credito	Insert credit card.
Inserire le monete	Insert coins.

Ritirare il resto, i biglietti, lo scontrino

Could I have a map of the subway?	**Mi da' una cartina del metrò?** *mee DAH OO-nah kahr-TEE-nah dehl meh-TROH*
Which line should I take for ____?	**Che linea devo prendere per ____?** *keh LEE-neh-ah DEH-voh PREHN-deh-reh pehr*
Is this the right line for ____?	**Questa è la linea giusta per ____?** *KWEHS-tah EH lah LEE-neh-ah JOOS-tah pehr*
Which stop is it for ____?	**Qual è la fermata per ____?** *kwah-LEH lah fehr-MAH-tah pehr*
How many stops is it to ____?	**Quante fermate per ____?** *KWAHN-teh fehr-MAH-teh pehr*
Is the next stop ____?	**La prossima fermata è ____?** *lah PROHS-see-mah fehr-MAH-tah EH*
Where are we?	**Dove siamo?** *DOH-veh see-AH-moh*
Where do I change to ____?	**Dove devo cambiare per ____?** *DOH-veh DEH-voh kahm-BYAH-reh pehr*
What time is the last train to ____?	**A che ora parte l'ultimo treno per ____?** *ah keh OH-rah PAHR-teh LOOL-tee-moh TREH-noh pehr*

CONSIDERATIONS FOR TRAVELERS WITH SPECIAL NEEDS

Do you have wheelchair access?	**C'è accesso alle sedie a rotelle?** *ch-EH atch-CHESS-oh ALH-leh SEH-dyeh ah roh-TEHL-leh*
Do you have elevators? Where?	**Ci sono ascensori? Dove?** *chee SOH-noh ah-shehn-SOH-ree DOH-veh*

Do you have ramps? Where?	**Ci sono rampe? Dove?**
	chee SOH-noh RAHM-peh DOH-veh
Are the restrooms wheelchair accessible?	**Le toilettes hanno accesso alle sedie a rotelle?**
	leh twa-LEHT AHN-noh atch-CHESS-oh ALH-leh SEH-dyeh ah roh-TEHL-leh
Do you have audio assistance for the hearing impaired?	**C'è assistenza audio per ipoudenti?**
	ch-EH ahs-sees-TEHN-tsa OW-dyoh pehr EE-poh-oo-DEHN-tee
I am deaf.	**Sono ipoudente.**
	SOH-noh ee-poh-oo-DEHN-teh
May I bring my service dog?	**Posso portare il mio cane di assistenza?**
	POHS-soh pohr-TAH-reh eel MEE-oh KAH-neh dee ahs-sees-TEHN-tsa
I am blind.	**Sono ipovedente.**
	SOH-noh ee-poh-veh-DEHN-teh
I need to charge my power chair.	**Devo caricare la mia sedia a rotelle.**
	DEH-voh kah-ree-KAH-reh lah MEE-ah SEH-dyah ah roh-TEHL-leh

CHAPTER THREE

LODGING

This chapter will help you find the right accommodations, at the right price—and the amenities you might need during your stay.

ROOM PREFERENCES

Please recommend ____	**Per favore, mi consigli ____** *pehr fah-VOH-reh mee* *kohn-SEEL-lyee*
a clean hostel.	**una locanda pulita.** *OO-nah loh-KAHN-dah* *poo-LEE-tah*
a moderately priced hotel.	**un albergo non caro.** *oon ahl-BEHR-goh nohn KAH-roh*
a moderately priced B&B.	**una pensione non cara.** *OO-nah pehn-SYOH-neh nohn* *KAH-rah*
a good hotel / motel.	**un buon hotel / motel.** *oon BWON hotel / motel*
Does the hotel have ____	**L'hotel ha ____** *loh-TEL AH*
a pool?	**una piscina?** *OO-nah pee-SHEE-nah*
a casino?	**un casinò?** *oon kah-zee-NOH*
suites?	**delle suite?** *DEHL-leh suite*
a balcony?	**un balcone?** *oon bahl-KOH-neh*
a fitness center?	**una palestra?** *OO-nah pah-LEHS-trah*
a spa ?	**un centro fitness?** *oon CHEN-troh fitness*

a private beach?	**una spiaggia privata?** *OO-nah SPYAD-jah pree-VAH-tah*
a tennis court?	**un campo da tennis?** *oon KAHM-poh dah tennis*
I would like a room for ____	**Vorrei una stanza per ____** *vohr-RAY OO-nah STAHN-tsah pehr*

For full coverage of numbers, see p7.

I would like ____	**Vorrei ____** *vohr-RAY*
a king-sized bed.	**un letto matrimoniale king size.** *oon LET-toh mah-tree-moh-NYAH-leh (king size)*
a double bed.	**un letto matrimoniale.** *oon LET-toh mah-tree-moh-NYAH-leh*
twin beds.	**due letti singoli.** *DOO-eh LET-tee SEEN-goh-lee*
adjoining rooms.	**stanze adiacenti.** *STAHN-tseh ah-dyah-CHEN-tee*
a smoking room.	**una stanza per fumatori.** *OO-nah STAHN-tsah pehr foo-mah-TOH-ree*

Listen Up: Reservations Lingo

Non abbiamo stanze libere.	We have no vacancies.
Quanto si ferma?	How long will you be staying?
Per fumatori o non fumatori?	Smoking or non smoking?
Abbiamo solo mezza pensione / pensione completa.	We only have full / half board.
Devo tenere il passaporto fino a domani.	I need to keep your passport overnight.

a nonsmoking room.	**una stanza per non fumatori.**
	OO-nah STAHN-tsah pehr nohn
	foo-mah-TOH-ree
a private bathroom.	**un bagno privato.**
	oon BAHN-nyoh pree-VAH-toh
a shower.	**la doccia.**
	lah DOT-chah
a bathtub.	**la vasca da bagno.**
	lah VAHS-kah dah BAHN-nyoh
air conditioning.	**l'aria condizionata.**
	LAH-ryah kohn-dee-tsyoh-
	NAH-tah
television.	**la televisione.**
	lah teh-leh-vee-ZYOH-neh
cable.	**la televisione via cavo.**
	lah teh-leh-vee-ZYOH-neh
	VEE-ah KAH-voh
satellite TV.	**la TV satellitare.**
	lah tee-VOO
	sah-tehl-lee-TAH-reh
a telephone.	**un telefono.**
	oon teh-LEH-foh-noh
Internet access.	**accesso a Internet.**
	atch-CHESS-oh ah internet
high-speed Internet access.	**accesso ad Internet ad alta velocità.**
	atch-CHESS-oh ah internet ahd
	AHL-tah veh-loh-chee-TAH
a refrigerator.	**un frigorifero.**
	oon free-goh-REE-feh-roh
a beach view.	**una vista sulla spiaggia.**
	OO-nah VEES-tah SOOL-lah
	SPYAD-jah
a city view.	**una vista sulla città.**
	OO-nah VEES-tah SOOL-lah
	cheet-TAH

a kitchenette.	**un angolo cottura.** *oon AHN-goh-loh koht-TOO-rah*
a balcony.	**un balcone.** *oon bahl-KOH-neh*
a suite.	**una suite.** *OO-nah suite*
a penthouse.	**un attico.** *oon AHT-tee-koh*
I would like a room ____	**Vorrei una stanza ____** *vohr-RAY OO-nah STAHN-tsah*
on the ground floor.	**sul pianterreno.** *SOOL pyahn-tehr-REH-noh*
near the elevator.	**vicino all'ascensore.** *vee-CHEE-noh ahl-ash-ehn-SOH-reh*
near the stairs.	**vicino alle scale.** *vee-CHEE-noh AHL-leh SKAH-leh*
near the pool.	**vicino alla piscina.** *vee-CHEE-noh AHL-lah pee-SHEE-nah*
away from the street.	**lontano dalla strada.** *lohn-TAH-noh DAHL-lah STRAH-dah*
I would like a corner room.	**Vorrei una stanza d'angolo.** *vohr-RAY OO-nah STAHN-tsah DAHN-goh-loh*
Do you have ____	**C'è ____** *ch-EH*
a crib?	**una culla?** *OO-nah KOOL-lah*
a foldout bed?	**un lettino pieghevole?** *oon leht-TEE-noh pyeh-GHE-voh-leh*

LODGING

FOR GUESTS WITH SPECIAL NEEDS

I need a room with ___	**Mi serve una stanza con ___** *mee SEHR-veh OO-nah STAHN-tsah kohn*
wheelchair access.	**accesso a sedia a rotelle.** *atch-CHESS-oh ah SEH-dyah ah roh-TEHL-leh*
services for the visually impaired.	**servizi per ipovedenti.** *sehr-VEET-see pehr ee-poh-veh-DEHN-tee*
services for the hearing impaired.	**servizi per ipoudenti.** *sehr-VEET-see pehr ee-poh-oo-DEHN-tee*
I am traveling with a service dog.	**Viaggio con un cane di assistenza.** *VYAHD-joh kohn oon KAH-neh dee ahs-sees-TEHN-tsa*

MONEY MATTERS

I would like to make a reservation.	**Vorrei fare una prenotazione.** *vohr-RAY FAH-reh OO-nah preh-noh-tah-TSYOH-neh*
How much per night?	**Quanto costa per notte?** *KWAHN-toh KOHS-tah pehr NOHT-teh*
Is breakfast included?	**È compresa la colazione?** *EH kohm-PREH-zah lah koh-lah-TSYOH-neh*
Do you have a ___	**C'è una tariffa ___** *ch-EH OO-nah tah-REEF-fah*
weekly / monthly rate?	**settimanale / mensile?** *seht-tee-mah-NAH-leh / mehn-SEE-leh*
a weekend rate?	**per il weekend?** *pehr eel weekend*

We will be staying for ____ days / weeks.

Staremo per ____ giorni / settimane.
stah-REH-moh pehr ___ JOHR-nee / seht-tee-MAH-neh

For full coverage of number terms, see p7.

When is checkout time?

A che ora è il check-out?
ah keh OH-rah EH eel check-out

For full coverage of time-related terms, see p12.

Do you accept credit cards / travelers checks?

Prendete la carta di credito / i traveller's cheques?
PREHN-deh-teh lah KAHR-tah dee KREH-dee-toh / ee traveller's cheques

May I see a room?

Posso vedere la stanza?
POHS-soh veh-DEH-reh lah STAHN-tsah

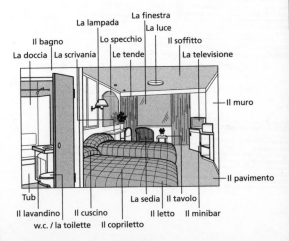

La finestra
La lampada
La luce
Lo specchio
Il soffitto
Le tende
La televisione
Il bagno
La doccia
La scrivania
Il muro
Il pavimento
Tub
Il lavandino
Il cuscino
La sedia
Il tavolo
w.c. / la toilette
Il copriletto
Il letto
Il minibar

LODGING

Is there a service charge?

C'è una tariffa per il servizio?
*ch-EH OO-nah tah-REEF-fah pehr
eel sehr-VEE-tsyoh*

I'd like to speak with the manager.

Vorrei parlare con il direttore.
*vohr-RAY pahr-LAH-reh kohn eel
dee-reht-TOH-reh*

IN-ROOM AMENITIES

I'd like _____

to place an international call.

to place a long-distance call.

directory assistance in English.

Vorrei _____
vohr-RAY
fare una chiamata internazionale.
*FAH-reh OO-nah KYAH-mah-tah
een-tehr-nah-tsyoh-NAH-leh*
fare una chiamata interurbana.
*FAH-reh OO-nah KYAH-mah-tah
een-tehr-oor-BAH-nah*
l'assistenza abbonati in inglese.
*lahs-sees-TEHN-tsa ahb-boh-
NAH-tee een een-GLEH-zeh*

Instructions for dialing the hotel phone

Per chiamare un'altra stanza, comporre il numero di stanza.	To call another room, dial the room number.
Per chiamate locali, comporre prima il 9.	To make a local call, dial 9 first.
Per chiamare il centralinista, comporre lo 0.	To call the operator, dial 0.

room service.	**il servizio in camera.** *eel sehr-VEE-tsyoh een KAH-meh-rah*
maid service.	**il servizio di pulizia.** *eel sehr-VEE-tsyoh dee poo-lee-TSEE-ah*
the front desk operator	**il centralinista alla reception** *eel chen-trah-lee-NEES-tah AHL-lah reception*
Do you have room service?	**Offrite il servizio in camera?** *ohf-FREE-teh eel sehr-VEE-tsyoh een KAH-meh-rah*
When is the kitchen open?	**Quando apre la cucina?** *KWAHN-doh AH-preh lah koo-CHEE-nah*
When is breakfast served?	**A che ora servite la colazione?** *ah keh OH-rah sehr-VEE-teh lah koh-lah-TSYOH-neh*

For time-related terms, see p12.

Do you offer massages?	**Offrite il servizio massaggi?** *ohf-FREE-teh eel sehr-VEE-tsyoh mahs-SAHD-jee*
Do you have a lounge?	**Avete un salotto?** *ah-VEH-teh oon sah-LOHT-toh*
Do you have a business center?	**Avete un centro d'affari?** *ah-VEH-teh oon CHEN-troh dahf-FAH-ree*
Do you serve breakfast?	**Servite la colazione?** *sehr-VEE-teh lah koh-lah-TSYOH-neh*
Do you have Wi-Fi?	**Avete il wi-fi?** *ah-VEH-teh eel wi-fi*

LODGING

May I have a newspaper in the morning?	**Posso avere il giornale al mattino?** *POHS-soh ah-VEH-reh eel johr-NAH-leh ahl maht-TEE-noh*
Do you offer a laundry service?	**Offrite il servizio di lavanderia?** *ohf-FREE-teh eel sehr-VEE-tsyoh dee lah-vahn-deh-REE-ah*
Do you offer dry cleaning?	**Offrite il sevizio di lavasecco?** *ohf-FREE-the-eel-sehr-VEE-tsyoh dee lah-vah-SEHK-koh*
May we have ____	**Possiamo avere ___** *pohs-SYAH-moh ah-VEH-reh*
clean sheets today?	**lenzuola pulite oggi?** *lehn-TSWO-lah poo-LEE-tee OHD-jee*
more towels?	**altri asciugamani?** *AHL-tree ah-shoo-gah-MAH-nee*
more toilet paper?	**altra carta igienica?** *AHL-trah KAHR-tah ee-JEH-nee-kah*
extra pillows?	**altri cuscini?** *AHL-tree koo-SHEE-nee*
Do you have an ice machine?	**C'è un distributore di ghiaccio?** *ch-EH oon dees-tree-boo-TOH-reh dee GYAT-choh*

Did I receive any ____	**Ho ricevuto ____**
	OH ree-cheh-VOO-toh
messages?	**messaggi?**
	mehs-SAHD-jee
mail?	**posta?**
	POHS-ta
faxes?	**fax?**
	fax
A spare key, please.	**Una chiave di scorta, per favore.**
	OO-nah KYAH-veh dee SKOHR-tah
	pehr fah-VOH-reh
I'd like a wake up call.	**Vorrei un servizio di sveglia.**
	vohr-RAY oon sehr-VEE-tsyoh dee
	ZVEHL-lyah

For time-related terms, see p12.

Do you have alarm clocks?	**C'è un orologio sveglia?**
	ch-EH oon oh-roh-LOD-joh
	ZVEHL-lyah
Is there a safe in the room?	**C'è una cassaforte in camera?**
	ch-EH OO-nah kahs-sah-FOHR-teh
	een KAH-meh-rah
Does the room have a hair dryer?	**C'è un asciugacapelli in camera?**
	ch-EH oon ah-SHOO-gah-kah-
	PEHL-lee een KAH-meh-rah

HOTEL ROOM TROUBLE

May I speak with the manager?	**Posso parlare con il direttore?** *POHS-soh pahr-LAH-reh kohn eel dee-REHT-toh-reh*
The ___ does not work.	**___ non funziona.** *nohn foon-TSYOH-nah*
television	**Il televisore** *eel teh-leh-vee-ZOH-reh*
telephone	**Il telefono** *eel teh-LEH-foh-noh*
air conditioning	**Il condizionatore d'aria** *eel kohn-dee-tsyoh-nah-TOH-reh DAH-ryah*
Internet access	**L'accesso a Internet** *laht-CHESS-oh ah internet*
cable TV	**La TV via cavo** *lah TV VEE-ah KAH-voh*
There is no hot water.	**Non c'è acqua calda.** *nohn ch-EH AHK-wah KAHL-dah*
The toilet is overflowing!	**Il water è l'acqua trabocca!** *eel VAH-tehr EH LAHK-wah trah-BOHK-kah*

This room is ____

    too noisy.

    too cold.

    too warm.

This room has ____

    bugs.

    mice.

I'd like a different room.

Do you have a bigger room?

I locked myself out of my room.

Do you have any fans?

The sheets are not clean.

The towels are not clean.

The room is not clean.

Questa stanza è ____
KWEHS-tah STAHN-tsah EH
    troppo rumorosa.
    TROHP-poh roo-moh-ROH-zah
    troppo fredda.
    TROHP-poh FREHD-dah
    troppo calda.
    TROHP-poh KAHL-dah

In questa stanza ci sono ____
een KWEHS-tah STAHN-tsah chee SOH-noh
    degli insetti.
    DEHL-lyee een-SEHT-tee
    dei topi.
    day TOH-pee

Vorrei un'altra stanza.
vohr-RAY oo-NAHL-trah STAHN-tsah

C'è una stanza più grande?
ch-EH OO-nah STAHN-tsah PYOO GRAHN-deh

Ho lasciato le chiavi nella stanza.
OH lah-SHAH-toh leh KYAH-vee NEHL-lah STAHN-tsah

Ci sono dei ventilatori?
chee SOH-noh day vehn-tee-lah-TOH-ree

Le lenzuola non sono pulite.
leh lehn-TSWOH-lah nohn SOH-noh poo-LEE-teh

Gli asciugamani non sono puliti.
lyee ah-shoo-gah-MAH-nee nohn SOH-noh poo-LEE-tee

La stanza non è pulita.
lah STAHN-tsah nohn EH poo-LEE-tah

The guests next door / above / below are being very loud.	**Gli ospiti a fianco / di sopra / di sotto fanno molto rumore.** *lyee OHS-pee-tee ah FYAHN-koh / dee SOH-prah / dee SOHT-toh FAHN-noh MOHL-toh roo-MOH-reh*

CHECKING OUT

I think this charge is a mistake.	**Credo questo addebito sia errato.** *KREH-doh KWEHS-toh ahd-DEH-bee-toh SEE-ah ehr-RAH-to*
Please explain this charge to me.	**Mi spieghi questo addebito, per favore.** *mee SPYEH-ghee KWEHS-toh ahd-DEH-bee-toh pehr fah-VOH-reh*
Thank you, we enjoyed our stay.	**Grazie, siamo stati contenti del soggiorno.** *GRAH-tsyeh see-AH-moh STAH-tee kohn-TEHN-tee dehl sohd-JOHR-noh*
The service was excellent.	**Il servizio è stato ottimo.** *eel sehr-VEE-tsyoh EH STAH-toh OHT-tee-moh*
The staff is very professional and courteous.	**Il personale è molto professionale e cortese.** *eel pehr-soh-NAH-leh EH MOHL-toh proh-fehs-syo-NAH-leh eh kohr-TEH-zeh*
Please call a cab for me.	**Mi chiama un taxi, per favore?** *mee KYAH-mah oon taxi pehr fah-VOH-reh*
Would someone please get my bags?	**Qualcuno può prendere le mie borse?** *kwahl-KOO-noh PWOH PREHN-deh-reh leh MEE-eh BOHR-seh*

HAPPY CAMPING

I'd like a site for _____

Vorrei un posto per_____
vohr-RAY oon POHS-toh pehr

a tent.

una tenda.
OO-nah TEHN-dah

a camper.

un camper.
oon KAHM-pehr

Are there _____

Ci sono_____
chee SOH-noh

bathrooms?

i bagni?
ee BAHN-nyee

showers?

le docce?
leh DOHT-cheh

Is there running water?

C'è acqua corrente?
ch-EH AHK-wah kohr-REHN-teh

Is the water drinkable?

L'acqua è potabile?
LAHK-wah EH poh-TAH-bee-leh

Where is the electrical
hookup?

Dove sono gli attacchi elettrici?
*DOH-veh SOH-noh lyee
aht-TAH-kee eh-LEHT-tree-keh*

CHAPTER FOUR
DINING

This chapter includes a menu reader and the language you need to communicate in a range of dining establishments and food markets.

FINDING A RESTAURANT

Would you recommend a good ____ restaurant?	**Può consigliarmi un buon ristorante** ____ *PWOH kohn-seel-LYAHR-mee oon bwon ree-stoh-RAHN-teh*
local	**locale?** *loh-KAH-leh*
French	**francese?** *frahn-CHEH-zeh*
German	**tedesco?** *teh-DEHS-koh*
Chinese	**cinese?** *chee-NEH-zeh*
Japanese	**giapponese?** *jahp-poh-NEH-zeh*
Asian	**asiatico?** *ah-ZYAH-tee-koh*
Greek	**greco?** *GREH-koh*
steakhouse	**con specialità di carne?** *kohn speh-chah-lee-TAH dee KAHR-neh*

seafood	**con specialità di pesce?** *kohn speh-chah-lee-TAH dee* *PEH-sheh*
vegetarian	**vegetariano?** *veh-jeh-tah-RYAH-noh*
buffet-style	**stile buffet?** *STEE-leh boof-FEH*
budget	**economico?** *eh-koh-NOH-mee-koh*
Would you recommend a good pizza restaurant?	**Può consigliarmi una buona pizzeria?** *PWOH kohn-seel-LYAHR-mee* *OO-nah bwon-nah peet-tseh* *REE-ah*
Which is the best restaurant in town?	**Qual è il miglior ristorante in città?** *kwah-LEH eel meel-LYOHR ree-* *stoh-RAHN-teh een cheet-TAH*
Is there a late-night restaurant nearby?	**C'è un ristorante qui vicino aperto fino a tardi?** *ch-EH oon ree-stoh-RAHN-teh* *kwee vee-CHEE-noh*
Is there a restaurant that serves breakfast nearby?	**C'è un ristorante qui vicino che serve la colazione?** *ch-EH oon ree-stoh-RAHN-teh* *kwee vee-CHEE- noh keh SEHR-veh* *lah koh-lah-TSYOH-neh*
Is it very expensive?	**È molto caro?** *EH MOHL-toh KAH-roh*
Do I need a reservation?	**Bisogna prenotare?** *bee-ZOHN-nyah preh-noh-TAH-reh*
Do I have to dress up?	**Bisogna vestirsi bene?** *bee-ZOHN-nyah vehs-TEER-see* *BEH-neh*

Do they serve lunch?	**Servono il pranzo?** *SEHR-voh-noh eel PRAHN-tsoh*
What time do they open for dinner?	**A che ora aprono per la cena?** *ah keh OH-rah AH-proh-noh pehr lah CHEH-nah*
For lunch?	**Per il pranzo?** *pehr eel PRAHN-tsoh*
What time do they close?	**A che ora chiudono?** *ah keh OH-rah KYOO-doh-noh*
Do you have a take out menu?	**C'è un menu da asporto?** *ch-EH oon meh-NOO dah ahs-POHR-toh*
Do you have a bar?	**C'è un bar?** *ch-EH oon bar*
Is there a café nearby?	**C'è un caffè qui vicino?** *ch-EH oon kahf-FEH kwee vee-CHEE-noh*

GETTING SEATED

Are you still serving?	**Siete ancora aperti?** *SYEH-teh ahn-KOH-rah ah-PEHR-tee*
How long is the wait?	**Quanto c'è da aspettare?** *KWAHN-toh ch-EH dah ahs-peht-TAH-reh*
Do you have a nonsmoking section?	**C'è una sezione per non fumatori?** *ch-EH OO-nah seh-TSYOH-neh pehr nohn foo-mah-TOH-ree*
A table for ____, please.	**Un tavolo per ____, per favore.** *oon TAH-voh-loh pehr ____ pehr fah-VOH-reh*

For a full list of numbers, see p7.

Do you have a quiet table?	**C'è un tavolo tranquillo?** *ch-EH oon TAH-voh-loh trahn-KWIL-loh*

Listen Up: Restaurant Lingo

Sezione fumatori o non fumatori? *seh-TSYOH-neh foo-mah-TOH-ree oh nohn foo-mah-TOH-ree*	Smoking or nonsmoking?
È necessaria la giacca. *EH neh-chehs-SAH-ryah lah JAHK-kah*	You'll need a jacket.
Mi dispiace, non sono permessi i pantaloni corti. *mee dee-SPYAH-cheh nohn SOH-noh pehr-MEHS-see ee pahn-tah-loh-nee KOHR-tee*	I'm sorry, no shorts are allowed.
Posso portarle qualcosa da bere? *POHS-soh pohr-TAHR-leh kwahl-KOH-zah dah BEH-reh*	May I bring you something to drink?
Gradisce la carta dei vini? *grah-DEESH-eh lah KAHR-tah day VEE-nee*	Would you like to see a wine list?
Vuol sentire le nostre specialità? *vwol sehn-TEE-reh leh NOHS-treh speh-chah-lee-TAH*	Would you like to hear our specials?
È pronto -a per ordinare? *EH PROHN-toh -ah pehr ohr-dee-NAH-reh*	Are you ready to order?
Mi dispiace signore / signora, ma la suacarta di credito è stata rifiutata. *mee dee-SPYAH-cheh seen-NYOH-reh / seen-NYOH-rah mah lah SOO-ah KAHR-tah dee KREH-dee-toh EH STAH-tah ree-few-TAH-tah*	I'm sorry sir / madame, your credit card was declined.

May we sit outside / inside please?	**Possiamo sederci fuori / dentro, per favore?** *pohs-SYAH-moh seh-DEHR-chee FWO-ree / DEHN-troh pehr fah-VOH-reh*
May we sit at the counter?	**Possiamo sederci al banco?** *pohs-SYAH-moh seh-DEHR-chee ahl BAHN-koh*
A menu please?	**Un menu per favore?** *oon meh-NOO pehr fah-VOH-reh*

ORDERING

Do you have a special tonight?	**Qual è la specialità di questa sera?** *kwah-LEH lah speh-chah-lee-TAH dee KWEHS-tah SEH-rah*
What do you recommend?	**Cosa consiglia?** *KOH-sah kohn-SEEL-lyah*
May I see a wine list?	**Posso vedere la carta dei vini?** *POHS-soh veh-DEH-reh lah KAHR-tah day VEE-nee*
Do you serve wine by the glass?	**Servite il vino a bicchiere?** *sehr-VEE-teh eel VEE-noh ah beek-KYEH-reh*
May I see a drink list?	**Posso vedere la lista delle bevande?** *POHS-soh veh-DEH-reh lah LEES-tah DEHL-leh beh-VAHN-de*
I would like it cooked ___	**Lo / La vorrei ___** *loh / lah vohr-RAY*
rare.	**cotto -a al sangue.** *KOHT-toh -ah ahl SAHN-gweh*
medium rare.	**cotto -a quasi al sangue.** *KOHT-toh -ah KWAH-zee ahl SAHN-gweh*
medium.	**cotto -a mediamente.** *KOHT-toh -ah meh-dyah-MEHN-teh*

medium well.	**cotto -a abbastanza bene.**
	KOHT-toh -ah ahb-bah-STAHN-tsah BEH-ne
well.	**ben cotto -a.**
	behn KOHT-toh -ah
charred.	**rosolato -a.**
	roh-zoh-LAH-toh -ah
Do you have a ____ menu?	**Avete un menu____**
	ah-VEH-teh oon meh-NOO
children's	**per i bambini?**
	pehr ee bahm-BEE-nee
diabetic	**per diabetici?**
	pehr dyah-BEH-tee-chee
kosher	**kasher?**
	KAH-sher
vegetarian	**vegetariano?**
	veh-jeh-tah-RYAH-noh
What is in this dish?	**Cosa c'è in questo piatto?**
	KOH-sah ch-EH een KWEHS-toh PYAHT-toh
How is it prepared?	**Come viene preparato?**
	KOH-meh VYEH-neh preh-pah-RAH-toh
What kind of oil is that cooked in?	**In che tipo di olio viene cotto?**
	een keh TEE-poh dee OH-lyoh VYEH-ne KOHT-toh
Do you have any low-salt dishes?	**Avete dei piatti poco salati?**
	ah-VEH-teh day PYAHT-tee POH-koh sah-LAH-tee
On the side, please.	**A parte, per favore.**
	ah PAHR-teh pehr fah-VOH-reh
May I make a substitution?	**Posso sostituire una cosa?**
	POHS-soh soh-stee-too-EE-reh OO-nah KOH-sah

DINING

I'd like to try that.	**Vorrei provare quello.** *vohr-RAY proh-VAH-reh* *KWEHL-loh*
Is that fresh?	**È fresco -a?** *EH FREHS-koh -ah*
Waiter!	**Cameriere -a!** *kah-meh-RYEH-reh -ah*
Extra butter, please.	**Mi porta altro burro, per favore.** *mee POHR-tah AHL-troh BOOR-* *roh pehr fah-VOH-reh*
No butter, thanks.	**Niente burro, grazie.** *NYEHN-teh BOOR-roh GRAH-tsyeh*
No cream, thanks.	**Niente panna, grazie.** *NYEHN-teh PAHN-nah GRAH-tsyeh*
No salt, please.	**Niente sale, per favore.** *NYEHN-teh SAH-leh pehr-fah-* *VOH-reh*
May I have some oil, please?	**Mi porta un po' di olio, per favore?** *mee POHR-tah oon POH dee oh-* *LYOH pehr fah-VOH-reh*
More bread, please.	**Altro pane, per favore.** *AHL-troh PAH-neh pehr fah-* *VOH-reh*
I am lactose intolerant.	**Ho intolleranza al lattosio.** *OH een-tohl-leh-RAHN-tsah ahl* *laht-TOH-zyoh*
Would you recommend something without milk?	**Mi consiglia qualcosa senza latte?** *mee kohn-SEEL-lyah kwahl-KOH-* *zah SEHN-tsah LAHT-teh*
I am allergic to_____	**Sono allergico -a ____** *SOH-noh ahl-LEHR-jee-koh -kah*
nuts.	**a noci e nocciole.** *ah NOH-chee eh noht-CHOH-leh*
peanuts.	**alle arachidi.** *AHL-leh ah-RAH-kee-dee*

seafood.	**ai frutti di mare.**
	eye FROOT-tee dee MAH-reh
shellfish.	**a molluschi e crostacei.**
	ah mohl-LOOS-kee eh krohs-TAH-cheh-ee
Water, please?	**Acqua, per favore?**
	AHK-wah pehr fah-VOH-reh
with ice	**con ghiaccio**
	kohn GYAT-choh
without ice	**senza ghiaccio**
	SEHN-tsah GYAT-choh
I'm sorry, I don't think this is what I ordered.	**Scusi, ma non credo di aver ordinato questo.**
	SKOO-zee mah nohn KREH-doh dee ah-VEHR ohr-dee-NAH-toh KWEHS-toh
My meat is a little over / under cooked.	**La carne è un po' troppo cotta / troppo poco cotta.**
	lah KAHR-neh EH oon POH TROHP-poh KOHT-tah /TROHP-poh POH-koh KOHT-tah
My vegetables are a little over / under cooked.	**Le verdure sono un po' troppo cotte / troppo poco cotte.**
	leh vehr-DOO-reh SOH-noh oon POH TROHP-poh KOHT-teh / TROHP-poh POH-koh KOHT-teh
There's a bug in my food!	**C'è un insetto nel mio cibo!**
	ch-EH oon een-SEHT-toh nehl MEE-oh CHEE-boh
May I have a refill?	**Me ne porta un altro?**
	meh neh POHR-tah oon AHL-troh
A dessert menu, please.	**Il menu dei dolci, per favore.**
	eel MEH-noo day DOHL-chee pehr fah-VOH-reh

DRINKS

Carafes of **vino della casa** (house wine) are usually three sizes:
litro *LEE-troh* (liter), **mezzo litro** (half liter) and **un quarto**
(quarter), akin to two generous glasses. Remember that standard
wine bottles hold 750ml; it's easy to underestimate the 25% extra
wallop of a liter (and Italians frown on public drunkenness, even
while encouraging **un po' di vino**—a little wine—with midday
and evening meals).

alcoholic	**alcooliche**
	ahl-KOH-lee-keh
neat / straight	**liscio -a**
	LEE-shoh -ah
on the rocks	**con ghiaccio**
	kohn GYAT-choh
with (seltzer or soda)	**con selz / acqua frizzante**
water	*kohn seltz / AHK-wah freet-*
	TSAHN-teh
beer	**birra**
	BEER-rah
wine	**vino**
	VEE-noh
house wine	**vino della casa**
	VEE-noh DEHL-lah KAH-zah
sweet wine	**vino dolce**
	VEE-noh DOHL-cheh
dry white wine	**vino bianco secco**
	VEE-noh BYAHN-koh SEHK-koh
rosé	**rosato**
	roh-ZAH-toh
light-bodied wine	**vino leggero**
	VEE-noh lehd-JEH-roh
red wine	**vino rosso**
	VEE-noh ROHS-soh

How Do You Take It?

Prendere generally means to take. But if a bartender asks, **Prende qualcosa?**, he's not inviting you to steal his fancy corkscrew. He's asking what you'd like to drink.

full-bodied wine	**vino corposo**
	VEE-noh kohr-POH-zoh
sparkling sweet wine	**spumante**
	spoo-MAHN-teh
liqueur	**liquore**
	lee-KWOH-reh
brandy	**brandy**
	brandy
cognac	**cognac**
	cognac
gin	**gin**
	gin
vodka	**vodka**
	vodka
rum	**rum**
	room
non-alcoholic	**analcolici**
	ah-nahl-KOH-lee-chee
hot chocolate	**cioccolata calda**
	chohk-koh-LAH-tah KAHL-dah
lemonade	**limonata**
	lee-moh-NAH-tah
milk shake	**frappè**
	frahp-PEH
milk	**latte**
	LAHT-teh

tea	**tè**
	teh
coffee	**caffè**
	kahf-FEH
cappuccino	**cappuccino**
	kahp-pooch-CHEE-noh
espresso	**caffè**
	kahf-FEH
iced coffee	**caffè freddo**
	kahf-FEH FREHD-doh
concentrated	**ristretto**
	rees-TREHT-toh
with a drop of alcohol	**corretto**
	kohr-REHT-toh
with a drop of milk	**macchiato**
	mahk-KYAH-toh
fruit juice	**succo di frutta**
	SOOK-koh dee FROOT-tah

For a full list of fruits, see p104.

SETTLING UP

Check please.	**Il conto per favore.**
	eel KOHN-toh pehr fah-VOH-reh
I'm full!	**Sono sazio -a!**
	SOH-noh SAH-tsyoh -tsyah
The meal was excellent.	**Il cibo era squisito.**
	eel CHEE-boh EH-rah skwee-ZEE-toh
There's a problem with my bill.	**C'è un problema con il conto.**
	ch-EH oon proh-BLEH-mah kohn eel KOHN-toh
Is the tip included?	**La mancia è inclusa?**
	lah MAHN-chah EH een-KLOO-zah
My compliments to the chef!	**I miei complimenti al cuoco!**
	ee MEE-eh-ee kohm-plee-MEHN-tee ahl KWO-koh

MENU READER

Italian cuisine varies broadly from region to region, but we've tried to make our list of classic dishes as encompassing as possible.

APPETIZERS (ANTIPASTI)

affettati misti: mixed cold cuts and vegetables (often buffet)
ahf-feht-TAH-tee MEES-tee

prosciutto: ham
proh-SHOOT-toh

  prosciutto cotto: cooked ham
  proh-SHOOT-toh KOHT-toh

  prosciutto crudo: air cured ham
  proh-SHOOT-toh KROO-doh

bruschetta: toasted bread slices with various toppings
broos-KEHT-tah

crocchette: croquettes
krohk-KEHT-teh

crostini: little toasts topped with a variety of ingredients
krohs-TEE-nee

insalata di frutti di mare: seafood salad
een-sah-LAH-tah dee FROOT-tee dee MAH-reh

mozzarella con pomodori: mozzarella and tomatoes
moht-tsah-REHL-lah kohn poh-moh-DOH-ree

insalata di nervetti: calf's foot and veal shank salad
een-sah-LAH-tah dee nehr-VEHT-tee

olive: olives
oh-LEE-veh

peperonata: mixed sweet peppers stewed with tomatoes
peh-peh-roh-NAH-tah

SALADS (INSALATI)

insalata caprese: tomato and mozzarella salad
een-sah-LAH-tah kah-PREH-zeh

insalata mista: mixed salad
een-sah-LAH-tah MEES-tah

insalata verde: green salad
een-sah-LAH-tah VEHR-deh

insalata di crescione: watercress salad
een-sah-LAH-tah dee kreh-SHOH-neh

insalata di lattuga romana: romaine salad
een-sah-LAH-tah dee laht-TOO-gah roh-MAH-nah

insalata di pomodori: tomato salad
een-sah-LAH-tah dee poh-moh-DOH-ree

insalata di rucola: arugula / rocket salad
een-sah-LAH-tah dee ROO-koh-lah

insalata di spinaci: spinach salad
een-sah-LAH-tah dee spee-NAH-chee

PIZZA TYPES

bianca: white, without tomato sauce
BYAHN-kah

capricciosa: with a mixture of toppings (artichoke hearts, ham, olives, pickled mushrooms, capers, sometimes egg)
kah-preet-CHOH-zah

con funghi: with mushrooms
kohn FOON-gy

marinara: with tomato sauce, garlic, capers, oregano, and some-times anchovies
mah-ree-NAH-rah

margherita: with tomato sauce, basil, and mozzarella
mahr-ghe-REE-tah

napoletana: with fresh tomatoes, garlic, oregano, anchovies, and mozzarella; toppings may vary
nah-poh-leh-TAH-nah

quattro stagioni: (four seasons) same toppings as capricciosa
KWAHT-troh stah-JOH-nee

siciliana: usually with capers, onions, and anchovies
see-chee-LYAH-nah

SAUCES (SALSA)

bagna cauda: hot anchovy, garlic, and oil dip
BAHN-nyah KOW-dah

pizzaiola: tomato sauce with onion and garlic
PEET-sah-YOH-lah

salsa verde: green sauce with parsley, anchovies, capers, and garlic
SAHL-sah VERH-deh

pesto: basil, pine nuts, and garlic sauce
PEHS-toh

SOUPS (ZUPPA)

acquacotta: Tuscan vegetable soup with poached egg
AHK-wah KOHT-tah

minestrone: mixed vegetable soup
mee-nehs-TROH-neh

ribollita: Tuscan bean and bread vegetable soup
ree-bohl-LEE-tah

zuppa: soup
DZOOP-pah

di pane: bread (recipes vary greatly)
dee PAH-neh

fagioli e farro: beans and spelt
fah-JOH-lee eh FAHR-roh

porri e patate: leek and potato
POHR-ree eh pah-TAH-teh

pavese: bread and egg, Pavia style
pah-VEH-zeh

PASTA DISHES

agnolotti: meat-stuffed pasta
ahn-nyoh-LOHT-tee

bucatini: hollow thick spaghetti, usually all'amatriciana (with a bacon and tomato sauce)
boo-kah-TEE-nee

cannelloni: stuffed pasta tubes, topped with a sauce and baked
kahn-nehl-LOH-nee

cappellacci alla ferrarese: pumpkin-stuffed pasta, Ferrara style
kahp-pehl-LAHT-chee AHL-lah fehr-rah-REH-zeh

cappelletti: meat-stuffed pasta usually served in broth
kahp-pehl-LEHT-tee

fusilli: spiral-shaped pasta
foo-ZEEL-lee

gnocchi: potato dumplings
NYOHK-kee

pansotti: swiss chard- and herbs-stuffed pasta, usually served
with walnut sauce, a Ligurian specialty
pahn-SOHT-tee

pappardelle alla lepre: wide pasta ribbons with hare sauce
pahp-pahr-DEHL-leh AHL-lah LEH-preh

penne strascicate: pasta quills sauteed with meat sauce
PEHN-neh strah-shee-KAH-teh

PASTA SAUCES (SUGI)

alfredo: butter and parmesan cheese
ahl-FREH-doh

amatriciana: bacon and tomato
ah-mah-tree-CHAH-nah

arrabbiata: tomato and hot pepper
ahr-rahb-BYAH-tah

bolognese: ground meat and tomato
boh-lohn-NYEH-zeh

carbonara: bacon and egg
kahr-boh-NAH-rah

panna: cream
PAHN-nah

pesto alla genovese: basil, pine nuts, and garlic
PEHS-toh AHL-lah jeh-noh-VEH-zeh

pomodoro: tomato
poh-moh-DOH-roh

puttanesca: tomato, anchovy, garlic, and capers
poot-tah-NEHS-kah

quattro formaggi: four cheeses
KWAHT-troh fohr-MAHD-jee

ragù: ground meat and tomato
rah-GOO

vongole: clams and tomato
VOHN-goh-leh

RISOTTO (RISOTTO)

risotto ai funghi: with parmesan and porcine mushrooms
ree-ZOHT-toh eye FOON-gy

risotto alla milanese: with saffron and parmesan cheese,
Milanese style
ree-ZOHT-toh AHL-lah mee-lah-NEH-zeh

risotto ai frutti di mare: with seafood
ree-ZOHT-toh eye FROOT-tee dee MAH-reh

MEAT (CARNE)

abbacchio alla romana: roasted spring lamb, Roman style
ahb-BAHK-kyoh AHL-lah roh-MAH-nah

bollito misto: boiled cuts of beef and veal served with a sauce
bohl-LEE-toh MEES-toh

carpaccio: thin slices of raw meat—beef, horse, or swordfish—
dressed with olive oil and lemon juice
kahr-PAHT-choh

cinghiale: wild boar, usually braised or roasted
cheen-GYAH-leh

involtini: thin slices of meat filled and rolled
een-vohl-TEE-nee

spezzatino: meat stew
speht-sah-TEE-noh

spiedini: skewered chunks of meat (also available with seafood)
spyeh-DEE-nee

BEEF (MANZO)

bistecca alla fiorentina: grilled T-bone steak, Florentine style
bees-TEHK-kah AHL-lah fyoh-rehn-TEE-nah

bresaola: air-dried beef, served in thin slices
breh-ZAH-oh-lah

osso buco: braised veal shank
OHS-soh BOO-koh

peposo: peppery stew
peh-POH-zoh

stracotto: beef stew with vegetables
strah-KOHT-toh

stufato: stew
stoo-FAH-toh

ORGAN MEATS (ORGANI)

busecca alla milanese: milanese tripe (beef stomach) soup
boo-SEHK-kah AHL-lah mee-lah-NEH-zeh

cervello al burro nero: brains in black-butter sauce
chehr-VEHL-loh ahl BOOR-roh NEH-roh

fegato alla veneziana: calf's liver fried with onions, Venetian style
FEH-gah-toh AHL-lah veh-neh-TSYAH-nah

VEAL (VITELLO)

bocconcini: stewed or braised chunks
bohk-kohn-CHEE-nee

cima alla genovese: flank steak Genoese style, filled with egg,
and vegetables
CHEE-mah AHL-lah jeh-noh-VEH-zeh

costoletta alla milanese: breaded cutlet, Milanese style
kohs-toh-LEHT-tah AHL-lah mee-lah-NEH-zeh

lombata di vitello: loin (recipes vary)
lohm-BAH-tah dee vee-TEHL-loh

piccata al Marsala: thin cutlets cooked in Marsala (sweet wine)
sauce
peek-KAH-tah ahl mahr-SAH-lah

saltimbocca: veal and ham rolls
sahl-teem-BOHK-kah

scaloppina alla: cutlet filled with cheese and Valdostana: ham,
   Valdostana (alpine) style, typically with gruyère or fontina
   cheese
skah-lohp-PEE-nah AHL-lah vahl-dohs-TAH-nah

vitello tonnato: cold slices of boiled veal served with tuna-
   mayonnaise sauce
vee-TEHL-loh tohn-NAH-toh

PORK (MAIALE)

arista di maiale: roast loin
ah-REES-tah dee mah-YA-leh

braciola: grilled chop
brah-CHOH-lah

zampone: sausage stuffed pig's trotter
dzahm-POH-neh

POULTRY (POLLAME)

pollo alla cacciatora: chicken braised with mushrooms in tomato
   sauce, hunter's style
POHL-loh AHL-lah kaht-chah-TOH-rah

pollo alla diavola: chicken chargrilled with lemon and pepper
POHL-loh AHL-lah DYAH-voh-lah

pollo al mattone: chicken grilled with herbs under a brick
POHL-loh ahl maht-TOH-neh

FISH AND SEAFOOD (PESCE E FRUTTI DI MARE)

For more fish and seafood, see p103.

anguilla alla veneziana: eel cooked in tomato sauce, Venetian
   style
ahn-GWEEL-lah AHL-lah veh-neh-TSYAH-nah

aragosta: lobster
ah-rah-GOHS-tah

baccalà: stockfish
bahk-kah-LAH

cacciucco alla livornese: tomato seafood chowder, Leghorn style
kaht-CHOOK-koh AHL-lah lee-vohr-NEH-zeh

cozze ripiene: stuffed mussels
KOHT-seh ree-PYEH-neh

gamberi grigliati: grilled shrimp with garlic
GAHM-beh-ree greel-LYAH-tee

fritto misto: mixed fried fish
FREET-toh MEES-toh

nero di seppie e polenta: baby squid in ink squid sauce served with polenta (corn meal)
NEH-roh dee SEHP-pyeh eh poh-LEHN-tah

pesci al cartoccio: fish baked in parchment paper
PEH-shee ahl kahr-TOHT-choh

SIDE DISHES (CONTORNI)

piselli al prosciutto: peas with ham
pee-ZEHL-lee ahl proh-SHOOT-toh

frittata: omelette
freet-TAH-tah

SWEET BREADS / DESSERTS / SWEETS (DOLCI)

amaretti: almond macaroons
ah-mah-REHT-tee

biscotti: cookies
bees-KOHT-tee

cannoli: crispy pastry rolls filled with sweetened ricotta and candied fruit
kahn-NOH-lee

cassata alla siciliana: traditional Sicilian cake with ricotta, chocolate, and candied fruit
kahs-SAH-tah AHL-lah see-chee-LYAH-nah

gelato: Italian ice cream
jeh-LAH-toh

granita: frozen fruit-juice slush
grah-NEE-tah

panettone: Christmas sweet bread with raisins and candied citrus peel
pah-neht-TOH-neh

panforte: almond, candied citrus, spices, and honey cake
pahn-FOHR-teh

panna cotta: molded chilled cream pudding
PAHN-nah KOHT-ta

semifreddo: soft and airy, partially frozen ice cream
seh-mee-FREHD-doh

tartufo: chocolate ice cream dessert
tahr-TOO-foh

tiramisù: mascarpone, ladyfingers, and coffee dessert
tee-rah-mee-SOO

torta: cake
TOHR-tah

  della nonna: custard shortcrust with pine nuts
  DEHL-lah NOHN-na

  alle mele: with apples
  AHL-leh MEH-le

  al limone: with lemon curd
  ahl lee-MOH-neh

  alle fragole: with fresh strawberries
  AHL-leh FRAH-goh-leh

  ai frutti di bosco: with mixed berries
  eye FROOT-tee dee BOHS-koh

zabaglione: warm custard with Marsala wine
dzah-bahl-LYOH-neh

zuccotto: spongecake filled with fresh cream, chocolate, candied fruit, and liqueur
dzook-KOHT-toh

zuppa inglese: a type of English trifle (spongecake layered with cream and fruit)
DZOOP-pah een-GLEH-zeh

formaggi: cheeses
fohr-MAHD-jee

  asiago: nutty-flavored hard cheese
  ah-ZYAH-goh

  mozzarella di bufala: buffalo mozzarella
  moht-tsah-REHL-lah dee BOO-fah-lah

  formaggio al latte di pecora: ewe's milk cheese
  fohr-MAHD-joh ahl LAHT-teh dee PEH-koh-rah

fontina: semi-soft, melting cheese
fohn-TEE-nah
formaggio al latte di capra: goat's milk cheese
fohr-MAHD-joh ahl LAHT-teh dee KAH-prah
gorgonzola: pungent blue cheese
gohr-gohn-DZOH-lah
mascarpone: rich, dessert cream cheese
mahs-kahr-POH-neh
mozzarella: fresh, soft cow's milk cheese
moht-tsah-REHL-lah
parmigiano: Parmesan
pahr-mee-JAH-noh
provolone: cow's milk cheese, sweet to spicy
proh-voh-LOH-neh
ricotta: fresh, soft and mild cheese
ree-KOHT-tah
taleggio: mild dessert cheese
tah-LEHD-joh
frutta: fruit
FROOT-tah
For a full listing of fruit, see p104.

BUYING GROCERIES

Most Italians shop at **mercati** (open-air markets) or neighborhood
specialty stores. Because fresh ingredients are so essential to their
cuisine, they often purchase just a day or two's worth of groceries.

AT THE SUPERMARKET

Which aisle has _____	**In quale corsia è / sono _____** *een KWAH-leh kohr-SEE-ah EH /* *SOH-noh*
spices?	**le spezie?** *leh SPEH-tsyeh*
toiletries?	**gli articoli di igiene personale?** *lyee ahr-TEE-koh-lee dee ee-JEH-* *neh pehr-soh-NAH-leh*

paper plates and napkins?	**i piatti e tovaglioli di carta?** *ee PYAHT-tee eh toh-vahl-LYOH-lee dee KAHR-tah*
canned goods?	**i cibi in scatola?** *ee CHEE-bee een SKAH-toh-lah*
snack food?	**gli spuntini?** *lyee spoon-TEE-nee*
baby food?	**il cibo per neonati?** *eel CHEE-boh pehr neh-oh-NAH-tee*
water?	**l'acqua?** *LAHK-wah*
juice?	**il succo?** *eel SOOK-koh*
bread?	**il pane?** *eel PAH-neh*
cheese?	**i formaggi?** *ee fohr-MAHD-jee*
fruit?	**la frutta?** *lah FROOT-tah*
cookies?	**i biscotti?** *ee bees-KOHT-tee*

AT THE BUTCHER SHOP

Is the meat fresh?	**È fresca la carne?** *EH FREHS-kah lah KAHR-neh*
Do you sell ____	**Ha ____** *AH*
fresh beef?	**del manzo fresco?** *dehl MAHN-tsoh FREHS-koh*
fresh pork?	**del maiale fresco?** *dehl mah-YA-leh FREHS-koh*
fresh lamb?	**dell'agnello fresco?** *dehl-ahn-NYEHL-loh FREHS-koh*

I would like a cut of ____	**Vorrei un taglio di ____** *vohr-RAY oon TAHL-lyoh dee*
tenderloin.	**filetto.** *fee-LEHT-toh*
T-bone.	**fiorentina.** *fyoh-rehn-TEE-nah*
brisket.	**punta di petto.** *POON-tah dee PEHT-toh*
rump roast.	**scamone.** *skah-MOH-neh*
rump.	**girello.** *jee-REHL-loh*
chops.	**braciole.** *brah-CHOH-leh*
filet.	**filetto.** *fee-LEHT-toh*
Thick / Thin cuts, please.	**Tagli spessi / sottili, per favore.** *TAHL-lyee SPEHS-see pehr fah-VOH-reh*
Please trim the fat.	**Tolga il grasso, per favore.** *TOHL-gah eel GRAHS-soh pehr fah-VOH-reh*
Do you have any sausage?	**Ha della salsiccia?** *AH DEHL-lah sahl-SEET-chah*
Is the ____ fresh?	**È fresco ____?** *EH FREHS-koh*
fish	**È fresco il pesce?** *EH FREHS-koh eel PEH-sheh*
flounder	**È fresca la passera?** *EH FREHS-kah lah PAHS-seh-rah*
sea bass	**È fresco il branzino?** *EH FREHS-koh eel BRAHN-dzee-noh*

shark	**È fresco il palombo?**
	EH FREHS-koh eel pah-LOHM-boh
seafood	**Sono freschi i frutti di mare?**
	SOH-noh FREHS-kee ee FROOT-tee dee MAH-reh
clams	**Sono fresche le vongole?**
	SOH-noh FREHS-kee leh VOHN-goh-leh
octopus	**È fresco il polpo?**
	EH FREHS-koh eel POHL-poh
oysters	**Sono fresche le ostriche?**
	SOH-noh FREHS-kee leh OHS-tree-keh
shrimp	**Sono freschi i gamberi?**
	SOH-noh FREHS-kee ee GAHM-beh-ree
squid	**Sono freschi i calamari?**
	SOH-noh FREHS-kee ee kah-lah-MAH-ree
May I smell it?	**Posso sentire l'odore?**
	POHS-soh sehn-TEE-reh loh-DOH-reh
Would you please ____	**Me lo può ____ per favore?**
	meh loh PWOH ____ pehr fah-VOH-reh
clean it?	**pulire?**
	poo-LEE-reh
filet it?	**sfilettare?**
	sfee-leht-TAH-reh
debone it?	**togliere le lische?**
	TOHL-lyeh-reh leh LEES-keh
remove the head and tail?	**togliere testa e coda?**
	TOHL-lyeh-reh TEHS-tah eh KOH-dah

AT THE PRODUCE STAND / MARKET
Fruits

apple	**mela**
	MEH-lah
banana	**banana**
	bah-NAH-nah
grapes (green, red)	**uva (bianca, nera)**
	OO-vah BYAHN-kah NEH-rah
orange	**arancia (pl. arance)**
	ah-RAHN-chah
lemon	**limone**
	lee-MOH-neh
lime	**limetta**
	lee-MEHT-tah
melon	**melone**
	meh-LOH-neh
mango	**mango**
	MAHN-goh
cantaloupe	**melone**
	meh-LOH-neh
watermelon	**anguria**
	ahn-GOO-ryah
honeydew	**melone verde**
	meh-LOH-neh VERH-deh
cherry	**ciliegia**
	chee-LYEH-jah
peach	**pesca**
	PEHS-kah
apricot	**albicocca**
	ahl-bee-KOHK-kah
strawberry	**fragola**
	FRAH-goh-lah
wild strawberry	**fragolina di bosco**
	frah-goh-LEE-nah dee BOHS-koh
blueberry (European)	**mirtillo**
	meer-TEEL-loh

kiwi	**kiwi** *kiwi*
pineapple	**ananas** *AH-nah-nahs*
blackberries	**more** *MOH-reh*
citron	**cedro** *CHEH-droh*
coconut	**cocco** *KOHK-koh*
fig	**fico** *FEE-koh*
grapefruit	**pompelmo** *pohm-PEHL-moh*
guava	**guava** *GWAH-vah*
gooseberry	**uvaspina** *oo-vah-SPEE-nah*
blood orange	**arancia sanguinella** *ah-RAHN-chah sahn-gwee-NEHL-lah*
papaya	**papaia** *pah-PAH-yah*
pear	**pera** *PEH-rah*
plum	**prugna** *PROON-nyah*
yellow plum	**prugna gialla** *PROON-nyah JAHL-lah*
prune	**prugna secca** *PROON-nyah SEHK-kah*
raspberry	**lampone** *lahm-POH-neh*
tangerine	**mandarino** *mahn-dah-REE-noh*

DINING

Vegetables

artichoke	**carciofo**
	kahr-CHOH-foh
green asparagus	**asparago verde**
	ahs-PAH-rah-goh VERH-deh
white asparagus	**asparago bianco**
	ahs-PAH-rah-goh BYAHN-koh
avocado	**avocado**
	ah-voh-KAH-doh
beans	**fagioli**
	fah-JOH-lee
green beans	**fagiolino verde**
	fah-joh-LEE-noh VERH-deh
bamboo shoots	**germogli di bamboo**
	jehr-MOHL-lyee dee bahm-BOO
bean sprouts	**germoglio di soia**
	jehr-MOHL-lyoh dee SOH-yah
broccoli	**broccoli**
	BROHK-koh-lee
cabbage	**cavolo**
	KAH-voh-loh
carrot	**carota**
	kah-ROH-tah
cauliflower	**cavolfiore**
	kah-vohl-FYOH-reh
celery	**sedano**
	SEH-dah-noh
corn	**mais**
	mice
cucumber	**cetriolo**
	cheh-tree-OH-loh
garlic	**aglio**
	AHL-lyoh
eggplant / aubergine	**melanzana**
	meh-lahn-TSAH-nah

fennel	**finocchio**
	fee-NOHK-kyoh
lettuce	**lattuga**
	laht-TOO-gah
arugula	**rucola**
	ROO-koh-lah
radicchio	**radicchio**
	rah-DEEK-kyoh
mushrooms	**funghi / porcini**
	FOON-gy / pohr-CHEE-nee
white truffles	**tartufi bianchi**
	tahr-TOO-fee BYAHN-kee
black truffles	**tartufi neri**
	tahr-TOO-fee NEH-ree
nettles	**ortiche**
	ohr-TEE-keh
onion	**cipolla**
	chee-POHL-lah
green olives	**olive verdi**
	oh-LEE-veh VERH-dee
black olives	**olive nere**
	oh-LEE-veh NEH-reh
peas	**piselli**
	pee-ZEHL-lee
peppers	**peperoni**
	peh-peh-ROH-nee
red	**rossi**
	ROHS-see
yellow	**gialli**
	JAHL-lee
green	**verdi**
	VERH-dee
hot	**peperoncino**
	peh-peh-rohn-CHEE-noh
potato	**patata**
	pah-TAH-tah

pumpkin	**zucca** *DZOOK-kah*
sorrel	**acetosella** *ah-cheh-toh-ZEHL-lah*
spinach	**spinaci** *spee-NAH-chee*
squash	**zucca** *DZOOK-kah*
tomato	**pomodoro** *poh-moh-DOH-roh*
yam	**patata dolce** *pah-TAH-tah DOHL-cheh*
zucchini	**zucchini** *dzook-KEE-nee*

Fresh herbs and spices

anise	**anice** *AH-nee-cheh*
basil	**basilico** *bah-ZEE-lee-koh*
bay leaf	**alloro** *ahl-LOH-roh*
black pepper	**pepe nero** *PEH-peh NEH-roh*
clove	**chiodo di garofano** *KYOH-doh dee gah-ROH-fah-noh*
dill	**aneto** *ah-NEH-toh*
garlic	**aglio** *AHL-lyoh*
marjoram	**maggiorana** *mahd-joh-RAH-nah*
oregano	**origano** *oh-REE-gah-noh*
paprika	**paprica** *PAH-pree-kah*

parsley	**prezzemolo**
	preht-TSEH-moh-loh
rosemary	**rosmarino**
	rohz-mah-REE-noh
saffron	**zafferano**
	dzahf-feh-RAH-noh
sage	**salvia**
	SAHL-vyah
salt	**sale**
	SAH-leh
sugar	**zucchero**
	DZOOK-keh-roh
thyme	**timo**
	TEE-moh

AT THE DELI

What kind of salad is that?	**Che tipo di insalata è quella?**
	keh TEE-poh dee een-sah-LAH-tah EH KWEHL-lah
What type of cheese is that?	**Che tipo di formaggio è quello?**
	keh TEE-poh dee fohr-MAHD-joh EH KWEHL-loh
What type of bread is that?	**Che tipo di pane è quello?**
	keh TEE-poh dee PAH-neh EH KWEHL-loh
May I have some of that please?	**Posso avere un po' di quello, per favore?**
	POHS-soh ah-VEH-reh oon POH dee KWEHL-loh pehr fah-VOH-reh
Is the salad fresh?	**Questa insalata è fresca?**
	KWEHS-tah een-sah-LAH-tah EH FREHS-kah
I'd like ____, please.	**Vorrei ____, per favore.**
	vohr-RAY ____ pehr fah-VOH-reh
a sandwich	**un panino**
	oon pah-NEE-noh

a salad	**un'insalata** *oon-een-sah-LAH-tah*
tuna salad	**un'insalata di tonno** *oon-een-sah-LAH-tah dee* *TOHN-noh*
chicken salad	**un'insalata di pollo** *oon-een-sah-LAH-tah dee* *POHL-loh*
roast beef	**rosbif** *ROHZ-beef*
shrimp cocktail	**cocktail di gamberetti** *KOHK-tehl dee gahm-beh-* *REHT-tee*
ham	**del prosciutto** *dehl proh-SHOOT-toh*
mustard	**della senape** *DEHL-lah SEH-nah-peh*
mayonnaise	**della maionese** *DEHL-lah mah-yoh-NEH-zeh*
a package of tofu	**un pacchetto di tofu** *oon pahk-KEHT-toh dee TOH-foo*
a pickle	**un cetriolo sott'aceto** *oon cheh-tree-OH-loh soht-tah-* *CHEH-toh*
I'd like that cheese.	**Mi piace quel formaggio.** *mee PYAH-cheh kwehl fohr-* *MAHD-joh*
Is that smoked?	**È affumicato -a?** *EH ahf-FOO-mee-kah-toh -tah*
pound (in kgs)	**mezzo chilo** *MEHD-zoh KEE-loh*
a quarter-pound (in kgs)	**un etto** *oon EHT-toh*
a half-pound (in kgs)	**due etti** *DOO-eh EHT-tee*

CHAPTER FIVE

SOCIALIZING

Italians are a gregarious and curious people. They often initiate conversations with foreigners (some of which can seem quite personal). In this family-oriented country, a solo traveler is often viewed with sympathy; don't assume that every invitation is a scam or flirtation. Here you'll find the language to make new friends.

GREETINGS

Hello.	**Salve.**
	SAHL-veh
Good morning.	**Buon giorno.**
	bwon JOHR-noh
Good afternoon.	**Buon pomeriggio.**
	bwon poh-meh-REED-joh
Good evening.	**Buona sera.**
	BWOH-nah SEH-rah
Good night.	**Buona notte.**
	BWOH-nah NOHT-teh
How are you?	**Come va?**
	KOH-meh vah
Fine, thanks.	**Bene, grazie.**
	BEH-neh GRAH-tsyeh
And you?	**E tu / lei / voi?**
	eh too / lay / voy
I'm exhausted.	**Sono esausto -a.**
	SOH-noh eh-ZOWS-toh -tah
I have a headache.	**Ho il mal di testa.**
	OH eel mahl dee TEHS-tah
I'm terrible.	**Sto male.**
	stoh MAH-leh
I have a cold.	**Ho il raffreddore.**
	OH eel rahf-frehd-DOH-reh

Listen Up: Common Greetings

Ciao.	Hi / Bye.
CHAH-oh	
Salve.	Hello.
SAHL-veh	
È un piacere.	It's a pleasure.
EH oon pyah-CHEH-reh	
Piacere.	How do you do / nice to meet
pyah-CHEH-reh	you.
Molto piacere.	Delighted.
MOHL-toh pyah-CHEH-reh	
Come va?	How's it going?
KOH-meh vah	
Addio.	Goodbye.
ahd-DEE-oh	
Arrivederci.	See you later.
ahr-ree-veh-DEHR-chee	
Ci vediamo.	See you later.
chee veh-DYAH-moh	

THE LANGUAGE BARRIER

I don't understand.	**Non capisco.**
	nohn kah-PEES-koh
Please speak more slowly.	**Parli più lentamente, per favore.**
	PAHR-lee PYOO lehn-tah-MEHN-teh pehr fah-VOH-reh
Please speak louder.	**Parli più a voce alta, per favore.**
	PAHR-lee PYOO ah VOH-cheh AHL-tah pehr fah-VOH-reh
Do you speak English?	**Parla inglese?**
	PAHR-lah een-GLEH-seh
I speak ____ better than Italian.	**Parlo ____ meglio dell'italiano.**
	PAHR-loh ____ MEHL-lyoh DEHL-lee-tah-LYAH-noh

Please spell that.	**Come si scrive, per favore?** *KOH-meh see SKREE-veh pehr fah-VOH-reh*
Please repeat that?	**Me lo ripete, per favore?** *meh loh ree-PEH-teh pehr fah-VOH-reh*
How do you say ____?	**Come si dice ____?** *KOH-meh see DEE-cheh*
Would you show me that in this dictionary?	**Me lo mostra in questo dizionario?** *meh loh MOHS-trah een KWEHS-toh dee-tsyoh-NAH-ryoh*

Curse Words

Here are some common curse words.

merda *MEHR-dah*	shit
figlio di puttana *FEEL-lyoh dee poot-TAH-nah*	son of a bitch (literally "son of a whore")
stronzo *STROHN-tsoh*	jerk (literally "turd", quite common)
Cazzo! *KAHT-soh*	Damn! (literally "dick," stronger than "damn," very frequently used)
Che cazzo vuoi? *keh KAHT-soh VWOH-ee*	What the hell do you want?
culo *KOO-loh*	ass (meaning the behind)
incasinato *een-kah-zee-NAH-toh*	screwed up
Vaffanculo! *vahf-fahn-KOO-loh*	Fuck off!

GETTING PERSONAL

Italians are generally friendly, yet more formal than Americans. Remember to use the formal **lei** (third-person singular) until given permission to employ the more familiar **tu**.

INTRODUCTIONS

What is your name?

Come si chiama?
KOH-meh see KYAH-mah

My name is ____.

Mi chiamo ____.
mee KYAH-moh

I'm pleased to meet you.

Piacere di conoscerla.
pyah-CHEH-reh dee koh-NOSH-ehr-lah

May I introduce my ____

Posso presentarle mio -a ____
POHS-soh preh-zehn-TAHR-leh MEE-oh -ah

  wife?

  moglie?
  MOHL-lyeh

  husband?

  marito?
  mah-REE-toh

  son / daughter?

  figlio -a
  FEEL-lyoh -lyah

  friend?

  il / la mio -a amico-a?
  eel / lah MEE-oh -ah ah-MEE-koh -kah

  boyfriend / girlfriend?

  il / la mio -a ragazzo -a?
  eel / lah MEE-oh -ah rah-GAHT-soh -sah

How is your ____

Come sta -anno il / la suo -a ____
KOH-meh stah -STAHN-noh eel / lah SOO-oh -ah

  family?

  famiglia?
  fah-MEEL-lyah

  mother?

  madre?
  MAH-dreh

father?	**padre?** *PAH-dreh*
brother / sister?	**fratello / sorella?** *frah-TEHL-loh / soh-REHL-lah*
neighbor?	**vicino -a?** *vee-CHEE-noh -nah*
boss?	**capo?** *KAH-poh*
cousin?	**cugino -a?** *koo-JEE-noh -nah*
aunt / uncle?	**zio -a?** *DZEE-oh -ah*
fiancée / fiancé?	**fidanzato -a?** *fee-dahn-TSAH-toh -tah*
partner?	**partner?** *partner*
niece / nephew / grandchild?	**nipote?** *nee-POH-teh*
How are your ___	**Come sta -anno i suoi ___** *KOH-meh stah -STAHN-noh ee soo-OH-ee*
children?	**bambini / figli (if older than teens)** *bahm-BEE-nee / FEEL-lyee*
parents?	**genitori?** *jeh-nee-TOH-ree*
grandparents?	**nonni?** *NOHN-nee*

Dos and Don'ts.

Don't refer to your parents as **i parenti** (*ee pah-REHN-tee*), which means relatives. Do call them **i genitori** (*ee jeh-nee-TOH-ree*).

Are you married?	**È sposato -a?** *EH spoh-ZAH-toh -tah*
I'm married.	**Sono sposato -a.** *SOH-noh spoh-ZAH-toh -tah*
I'm single.	**Non sono sposato -a.** *nohn SOH-noh spoh-ZAH-toh -tah*
I'm divorced.	**Sono divorziato -a.** *SOH-noh dee-vohr-TZYAH-toh -tah*
I'm a widow / widower.	**Sono vedovo -a.** *SOH-noh VEH-doh-voh -vah*
We're separated.	**Siamo separati.** *SYAH-moh seh-pah-RAH-tee*
I live with my boyfriend / girlfriend.	**Vivo con il mio / la mia ragazzo -a.** *VEE-voh kohn eel MEE-oh / lah MEE-ah rah-GAHT-soh -sah*
How old are you?	**Quanti anni ha?** *KWAHN-tee AHN-nee AH*
How old are your children?	**Quanti anni hanno i suoi bambini?** *KWAHN-tee AHN-nee AHN-noh ee soo-OH-ee bahm-BEE-nee*
Wow, that's very young.	**Ah, è molto giovane.** *AH EH MOHL-toh JOH-vah-neh*
No, you're not! You're much younger.	**No, davvero! Lei è molto più giovane.** *noh dahv-VEH-roh lay EH MOHL-toh PYOO JOH-vah-neh*
Your wife / daughter is beautiful.	**Sua moglie / figlia è bellissima.** *SOO-ah MOHL-lyeh / FEEL-lyah EH behl-LEES-see-mah*
Your husband / son is handsome.	**Suo marito / figlio è molto bello.** *SOO-oh mah-REE-toh / FEEL-lyoh EH MOHL-toh BEHL-loh*
What a beautiful baby!	**Che bel -la bambino -a!** *keh behl -lah bahm-BEE-noh -nah*

Are you here on business?	**È qui per affari?** *EH kwee pehr ahf-FAH-ree*
I am vacationing.	**Sono in vacanza.** *SOH-noh een vah-KAHN-tsah*
I'm attending a conference.	**Sto partecipando ad una conferenza.** *stoh pahr-teh-chee-PAHN-doh ah-DOO-nah kohn-feh-REHN-tsah*
How long are you staying?	**Quanto tempo si ferma?** *KWAHN-toh TEHM-poh see FEHR-mah*
I'm a student.	**Sono studente / studentessa.** *SOH-noh stoo-DEHN-teh / stoo-DEHN-tehs-sah*
What are you studying?	**Cosa studia?** *KOH-zah STOO-dyah*
Where are you from?	**Di dov'è?** *Dee dohv-EH*

PERSONAL DESCRIPTIONS

afro	**capigliatura africana** *kah-peel-lyah-TOO-rah ah-free-KAH-nah*
blonde	**biondo -a** *BYOHN-doh -dah*
brunette	**castano -a** *KAHS-tah-noh -nah*
redhead	**rosso -a** *ROHS-soh -sah*
curly hair	**capelli ricci** *kah-PEHL-lee REET-chee*
kinky hair	**capelli crespi** *kah-PEHL-lee KREHS-pee*
long hair	**capelli lunghi** *kah-PEHL-lee LOON-gy*

I capelli
Le sopracciglia
La fronte
Le tempie
Gli occhi
Il naso
Le orecchie
Le guance
I denti
Le labbra
La bocca
Il mento

short hair	**capelli corti**
	kah-PEHL-lee KOHR-tee
straight hair	**capelli dritti**
	kah-PEHL-lee DREET-tee
black	**nero -a**
	NEH-roh -rah
pale	**pallido -a**
	PAHL-lee-doh -dah
mocha-skinned	**dalla pelle color caffè**
	DAHL-lah PEHL-leh koh-LOHR kahf-FEH
olive-skinned	**con la pelle olivastra**
	kohn lah PEHL-leh oh-lee-VAHS-trah
tanned	**abbronzato -a**
	ahb-brohn-DZAH-toh -tah
white	**bianco -a**
	BYAHN-koh -kah
Asian	**asiatico -a**
	ah-ZYAH-tee-koh -kah

biracial	**meticcio -a** *meh-TEET-choh -chah*
African-American	**afroamericano -a** *AH-froh-ah-meh-ree-KAH-noh -nah*
caucasian	**caucasico -a** *kow-KAH-zee-koh -kah*
tall	**alto -a** *AHL-toh -tah*
short	**basso -a** *BAHS-soh -sah*
thin	**magro -a** *MAH-groh -grah*
fat	**grasso -a** *GRAHS-soh -sah*
blue eyes	**occhi azzurri** *OHK-kee ahd-DZOOR-ree*
brown eyes	**occhi castani** *OHK-kee kahs-TAH-nee*
green eyes	**occhi verdi** *OHK-kee VERH-dee*
hazel eyes	**occhi nocciola** *OHK-kee noht-CHOH-lah*
eyebrows	**sopracciglia** *soh-praht-CHEEL-lyah*
eyelashes	**ciglia** *CHEEL-lyah*
freckles	**lentiggini** *lehn-TEED-jee-nee*
moles	**nei** *nay*
face	**viso** *VEE-zoh*

Listen Up: Nationalities

Sono _____	I'm _____
SOH-noh	
brasiliano -a.	Brazilian.
brah-zee-LYAH-noh -nah	
francese.	French.
frahn-CHEH-zeh	
greco -a.	Greek.
GREH-koh -kah	
portoghese.	Portuguese.
pohr-toh-GHEH-zeh	
rumeno -a.	Romanian.
roo-MEH-noh -nah	
russo -a.	Russian.
ROOS-soh -sah	
spagnolo -a.	Spanish.
spahn-NYOH-loh -lah	
svizzero -a.	Swiss.
ZVEET-seh-roh -rah	
tedesco -a.	German.
teh-DEHS-koh -kah	
ungherese.	Hungarian.
oon-gheh-REH-zeh	

For a full list of nationalities, see English / Italian dictionary.

DISPOSITIONS AND MOODS

sad	**triste**
	TREES-teh
happy	**felice**
	feh-LEE-cheh
angry	**arrabbiato -a**
	ahr-rahb-BYAH-toh -tah
tired	**stanco -a**
	STAHN-koh -kah
depressed	**depresso -a**
	deh-PREHS-soh -sah

stressed	**stressato -a**
	strehs-SAH-toh -tah
anxious	**ansioso -a**
	ahn-SYOH-zoh -zah
confused	**confuso -a**
	kohn-FOO-zoh -zah
enthusiastic	**entusiasta**
	ehn-too-ZYAHS-tah

PROFESSIONS

What do you do for a living?	**Che lavoro fa?**
	keh lah-VOH-roh fah
Here is my business card.	**Ecco il mio biglietto da visita.**
	EHK-koh eel MEE-oh beel-LYEHT-toh dah VEE-zee-tah
I am ____	**Sono ____**
	SOH-noh
an accountant.	**contabile.**
	kohn-TAH-bee-leh
an artist.	**artista.**
	ahr-TEES-tah
a craftsperson.	**artigiano -a.**
	ahr-tee-JAH-noh -nah
a designer.	**stilista.**
	stee-LEES-tah
a doctor.	**medico.**
	MEH-dee-koh
an editor.	**redattore / redattrice.**
	reh-daht-TOH-reh / reh-daht-TREE-che
an educator.	**educatore / educatrice.**
	eh-doo-kah-TOH-reh / eh-doo-kah-TREE-cheh
an engineer.	**ingegnere.**
	een-jehn-NYEH-reh

a government employee.	**impiegato -a statale.** *eem-pyeh-GAH-toh -tah stah-TAH-leh*
a homemaker.	**casalinga.** *kah-zah-LEEN-gah*
a lawyer.	**avvocato / avvocassa.** *ahv-voh-KAH-toh / ahv-voh-KAHS-sah*
a military professional.	**un militare.** *oon mee-lee-TAH-reh*
a musician.	**musicista.** *moo-zee-CHEES-tah*
a nurse.	**infermiere -a.** *een-fehr-MYEH-reh -rah*
a salesperson.	**commesso -a.** *kohm-MEHS-soh -sah*
a writer.	**scrittore / scrittrice.** *skreet-TOH-reh / skreet-TREE-cheh*

DOING BUSINESS

I'd like an appointment.	**Vorrei un appuntamento.** *vohr-RAY oon ahp-poon-tah-MEHN-toh*
I'm here to see ____.	**Sono qui per vedere ____.** *SOH-noh kwee pehr veh-DEH-reh*
May I photocopy this?	**Posso fotocopiare questo?** *POHS-soh foh-toh-koh-PYAH-reh KWEHS-toh*
May I use a computer here?	**Posso usare il computer qui?** *POHS-soh oo-ZAH-reh eel computer kwee*
What's the password?	**Qual è la password?** *kwah-LEH lah password*
May I access the Internet?	**Posso accedere a Internet?** *POHS-soh aht-CHEH-deh-reh ah internet*

May I send a fax?	**Posso inviare un fax?** *POHS-soh een-VYAH-reh oon fax*
May I use the phone?	**Posso usare il telefono?** *POHS-soh oo-ZAH-reh eel teh-LEH-foh-noh*

PARTING WAYS

Keep in touch.	**Teniamoci in contatto.** *teh-NYAH-moh-chee een kohn-TAHT-toh*
Please write or email.	**Scriva o invii un e-mail.** *SKREE-vah oh een-VEE-ee oon e-mail*
Here's my phone number. Call me.	**Ecco il mio numero di telefono. Mi chiami.** *EHK-koh eel MEE-oh NOO-meh-roh dee teh-LEH-foh-noh* *mee KYAH-mee.*
May I have your phone number / email, please?	**Posso avere il suo numero di telefono / indirizzo e-mail, per favore?** *POHS-soh ah-VEH-reh eel SOO-oh NOO-meh-roh dee teh-LEH-foh-noh / een-dee-REET-soh e-mail pehr fah-VOH-reh*
May I have your card?	**Posso avere il suo biglietto da visita?** *POHS-soh ah-VEH-reh eel SOO-oh beel-LYEHT-toh dah VEE-zee-tah*
Give me your address and I'll write.	**Mi dia il suo indirizzo e le scriverò.** *mee DEE-ah eel SOO-oh een-dee-REET-soh eh leh skree-veh-ROH*

TOPICS OF CONVERSATION

As in the United States, Europe, or anywhere in the world, the weather and current affairs are common conversation topics.

THE WEATHER

It's _____

È _____
EH

Is it always so _____

È sempre così _____
EH SEHM-preh koh-ZEE

cloudy?

nuvoloso?
noo-voh-LOH-zoh

humid?

umido?
OO-mee-doh

warm?

caldo?
KAHL-doh

cool?

fresco?
FREHS-koh

rainy?

piovoso?
pyoh-VOH-zoh

windy?

C'è sempre così tanto vento?
ch-EH SEHM-preh koh-ZEE TAHN-toh VEHN-toh

sunny?

sole?
SOH-leh

Do you know the weather forecast for tomorrow?

Conosce le previsioni del tempo per domani?
koh-NOH-sheh leh preh-vee-ZYOH-nee dehl TEHM-poh pehr doh-MAH-nee

THE ISSUES

What do you think about ____
Che ne pensa ____
keh neh PEHN-sah

American Republicans?
dei repubblicani americani?
day reh-poob-blee-KAH-nee ah-meh-ree-KAH-nee

American Democrats?
dei democratici americani?
day deh-moh-KRAH-tee-chee ah-meh-ree-KAH-nee

democracy?
della democrazia?
DEHL-lah deh-moh-krah-TSEE-ah

socialism?
del socialismo?
dehl soh-chah-LEEZ-moh

the environment?
dell'ambiente?
DEHL-lahm-BYEHN-teh

women's rights?
dei diritti delle donne?
day dee-REET-tee DEHL-leh DOHN-neh

gay rights?
dei diritti degli omosessuali?
day dee-REET-tee DEHL-lyee oh-moh-sehs-SWAH-lee

the economy?
dell'economia?
dehl-leh-koh-noh-MEE-ah

What political party do you belong to?
A quale partito politico appartiene?
ah KWAH-leh pahr-TEE-toh poh-LEE-tee-koh ahp-pahr-TYEH-neh

What did you think of the election?
Come le sono sembrate le elezioni?
KOH-meh leh SOH-noh sehm-BRAH-teh leh eh-leh-TSYOH-nee

What do you think of the war in ____.
Cosa pensa della guerra in ____.
KOH-zah PEHN-sah DEHL-lah GWEHR-rah een

RELIGION

Do you go to church / temple / mosque?	**Lei frequenta una chiesa / un tempio / una moschea?** *lay freh-KWEHN-tah OO-nah KYEH-zah / oon TEHM-pyoh / OO-nah mohs-KEH-ah*
Are you religious?	**Lei è osservante?** *lay EH ohs-sehr-VAHN-teh*
I'm _____ / I was raised _____	**Sono _____ / Sono cresciuto -a _____** *SOH-noh _____ / SOH-noh kreh-SHOO-toh -tah*

agnostic.
    agnostico -a.
    ahn-NYOHS-tee-koh -kah

atheist.
    ateo -a.
    AH-teh-oh -ah

Buddhist.
    buddista.
    bood-DEES-tah

Catholic.
    cattolico -a.
    kaht-TOH-lee-koh -kah

Greek Orthodox.
    greco ortodosso -a.
    GREH-koh ohr-toh-DOHS-soh -sah

Hindu.
    hindu.
    hindu

Jewish.
    ebreo -a.
    eh-BREH-oh -ah

Muslim.
    mussulmano -a.
    moos-sool-MAH-noh -nah

Protestant.
    protestante.
    proh-tehs-TAHN-teh

I'm spiritual but I don't attend services.	**Sono spirituale ma non osservante.** *SOH-noh spee-ree-TWAH-leh mah nohn ohs-sehr-VAHN-teh*

I don't believe in that.	**Non ci credo.** *nohn chee KREH-doh*
That's against my beliefs.	**È contrario alle mie convinzioni.** *EH kohn-TRAH-ryoh AHL-leh MEE-eh kohn-veen-TSYOH-nee*
I'd rather not talk about it.	**Preferisco non parlarne.** *preh-feh-REES-koh nohn pahr-LAHR-neh*

GETTING TO KNOW SOMEONE

Following are some conversation starters.

MUSICAL TASTES

What kind of music do you like?	**Che tipo di musica le piace?** *keh TEE-poh dee MOO-zee-kah leh PYAH-cheh*
I like _____	**Mi piace _____** *mee PYAH-cheh*
rock 'n' roll.	**il rock 'n' roll.** *eel rock 'n' roll*
hip hop.	**la hip hop.** *lah hip hop*
techno.	**la techno.** *lah techno*
disco.	**La musica de discoteca.** *lah MOO-zee-kah dah dees-koh TEH-kah*
classical.	**la classica.** *lah KLAHS-see-kah*
jazz.	**il jazz.** *eel jazz*
country and western.	**la musica country e western.** *lah MOO-zee-kah country eh western.*

reggae.	**il reggae.** *eel reggae*
calypso.	**la calypso.** *lah calypso*
opera.	**l'opera.** *LOH-peh-rah*
show-tunes / musicals.	**le canzoni da musical.** *leh kahn-TSOH-nee dah musical*
New Age.	**la New Age.** *lah new age*
pop.	**la pop.** *lah pop*

HOBBIES?

What do you like to do in your spare time?	**Cosa le piace fare nel tempo libero?** *KOH-zah leh PYAH-cheh FAH-reh nehl TEHM-poh LEE-beh-roh*
I like _____	**Mi piace _____** *mee PYAH-cheh*
playing guitar.	**suonare la chitarra.** *swoh-NAH-reh lah kee-TAHR-rah*
piano.	**il pianoforte.** *eel pyah-noh-FOHR-teh*

For other instruments, see the English / Italian dictionary.

painting.	**dipingere.** *dee-PEEN-jeh-reh*
drawing.	**disegnare.** *dee-zehn-NYAH-reh*
dancing.	**andare a ballare.** *anh-DAH-reh ah bahl-LAH-reh*
reading.	**leggere.** *LEHD-jeh-reh*

watching TV.	**guardare la TV.**
	ghwar-DAH-reh lah tee-VOO
shopping.	**fare shopping.**
	FAH-reh shopping
going to the movies.	**andare al cinema.**
	anh-DAH-reh ahl CHEE-neh-mah
hiking.	**fare camminate.**
	FAH-reh kahm-mee-NAH-teh
camping.	**andare in campeggio.**
	anh-DAH-reh een kahm-PEHD-joh
hanging out.	**ritrovarmi con gli amici.**
	ree-troh-VAHR-mee kohn lyee
	ah-MEE-chee
traveling.	**viaggiare.**
	vyahd-JAH-reh
eating out.	**mangiare fuori.**
	mahn-JAH-reh FWOH-ree
cooking.	**cucinare.**
	koo-chee-NAH-reh
sewing.	**cucire.**
	koo-CHEE-reh
sports.	**fare sport.**
	FAH-reh sport
Do you like to dance?	**Vuole ballare?**
	VWOH-leh bahl-LAH-reh
Would you like to go out?	**Vuole uscire?**
	VWOH-leh oo-SHEE-reh
May I buy you dinner sometime?	**Posso ti fuori a cena qualche volta?**
	POHS-soh tee FWOH-ree ah CHEH-nah KWAHL-keh VOHL-tah
What kind of food do you like?	**Che tipo di cibo le piace?**
	keh TEE-poh dee CHEE-boh leh PYAH-cheh

For a full list of food types, see Dining in Chapter 4.

Would you like to go _____	**Le piacerebbe andare** _____
	leh pyah-CHEH-rehb-beh ahn-DAH-reh
to a movie?	**al cinema?**
	ahl CHEE-neh-mah
to a concert?	**ad un concerto?**
	ah-DOON kohn-CHEHR-toh
to the zoo?	**allo zoo?**
	AHL-loh DZOH-oh
to the beach?	**alla spiaggia?**
	AHL-lah SPYAHD-jah
to a museum?	**al museo?**
	ahl moo-ZEH-oh
for a walk in the park?	**a passeggiare nel parco?**
	ah pahs-sehd-JAH-reh nehl PAHR-koh
dancing?	**a ballare?**
	ah bahl-LAH-reh
Would you like to get _____	**Andiamo** _____
	ahn-DYAH-moh
lunch?	**a pranzo?**
	ah PRAHN-tsoh
coffee?	**a prendere un caffè?**
	ah PREHN-deh-reh oon kahf-FEH
dinner?	**a cena?**
	ah CHEH-nah
What kind of books do you like to read?	**Che tipo di libri le piace leggere?**
	keh TEE-poh dee LEE-bree leh PYAH-cheh LEHD-jeh-reh
I like _____	**Mi piacciono** _____
	mee PYAHT-choh-noh
mysteries.	**i gialli.**
	ee JAHL-lee

Westerns.	**i romanzi western.**
	ee roh- MAHN-dzee western
dramas.	**le storie drammatiche.**
	leh STOH-ryeh drahm-MAH-tee-keh
novels.	**i romanzi.**
	ee roh- MAHN-dzee
biographies.	**le biografie.**
	leh byoh-grah-FEE-eh
auto-biographies.	**le autobiografie.**
	leh ow-toh-byoh-grah-FEE-eh
romance.	**i romanzi d'amore.**
	ee roh- MAHN-dzee dah-MOH-reh
history.	**gli argomenti storici.**
	lyee ahr-goh-MEHN-tee STOH-ree-chee

For dating terms, see Nightlife in Chapter 10.

CHAPTER SIX

MONEY AND COMMUNICATIONS

This chapter covers money, the mail, phone and Internet service, and other tools you need to connect with the outside world.

MONEY

In 2002, Italy entered the Eurozone, changing its currency from lira to euro. The euro is available in seven different bills (5, 10, 20, 50, 100, 200, and 500) and eight separate coins (1, 2, 5, 10, 20, 50 centesimi, 1 and 2 euro denominations). Bills over 20 euros may be difficult to break.

CURRENCIES

Do you accept _____

Accettate _____
aht-cheht-TAH-teh

Visa / MasterCard / Discover / American Express / Diners' Club? credit cards?

Visa / MasterCard / Discover / American Express / Diners' Club?
carte di credito?
KAHR-teh dee KREH-dee-toh

bills?

banconote?
bahn-koh-NOH-teh

coins?

monete?
moh-NEH-teh

checks?

assegni?
ahs-SEHN-nyee

travelers checks?

traveller's cheques?
traveller's cheques

money transfer?

un bonifico bancario?
oon boh-NEE-fee-koh bahn-KAH-ree-oh

May I wire transfer funds here?	**Posso effettuare un bonifico bancario qui?** *POHS-soh ehf-feht-TWAH-reh oon boh-NEE-fee-koh bahn-KAH-ree-oh kwee*
Would you please tell me where to find ____	**Potrebbe dirmi dove si trova ____** *poh-TREHB-beh DEER-mee DOH-veh see TROH-vah*
a bank?	**una banca?** *OO-nah BAHN-kah*
a credit bureau?	**un banco di credito?** *oon BAHN-koh dee KREH-dee-toh*
an ATM / cashpoint?	**un bancomat?** *oon BAHN-koh-maht*
a currency exchange?	**un cambio?** *oon kahm-byoh*
A receipt, please.	**Una ricevuta, per favore.** *OO-nah ree-cheh-VOO-tah pehr fah-VOH-reh*
Would you tell me ____	**Può dirmi qual è ____** *PWOH DEER-mee kwah-LEH*
today's interest rate?	**il tasso di interesse oggi?** *eel TAHS-soh dee een-teh-REHS-seh OHD-jee*
the exchange rate for dollars to ____?	**il cambio dal dollaro a ____?** *eel KAHM-byoh dahl DOHL-lah-roh ah*
Is there a service charge?	**C'è una tariffa da pagare?** *ch-EH OO-nah tah-REEF-fah dah pah-GAH-reh*

Listen Up: Bank Lingo

Firmi qui, per favore.
*FEER-mee kwee
pehr fah-VOH-reh*

Please sign here.

Ecco la sua ricevuta.
*EHK-koh lah SOO-ah
ree-che-VOO-tah*

Here is your receipt.

Ha un documento d'identità?
*AH oon doh-koo-MEHN-toh
dee-dehn-tee-TAH*

May I see your ID?

Accettiamo traveller's cheques.
aht-cheht-TYAH-moh traveller's cheques

We accept travelers checks.

Solo contanti.
SOH-loh kohn-TAHN-tee

Cash only.

May I have a cash advance on my credit card?

Posso avere un anticipo sulla mia carta di credito?
POHS-soh ah-VEH-reh oon ahn-TEE-chee-poh SOOL-lah MEE-ah KAHR-tah dee KREH-dee-toh kohn-trohl-

Will you accept a credit card?

Accettate la carta di credito?
aht-cheht-TAH-teh lah KAHR-tah dee KREH-dee-toh

May I have smaller bills, please.

Banconote più piccole, per favore.
bahn-koh-NOH-teh PYOO PEEK-koh-leh pehr fah-VOH-reh

Can you make change?

Può cambiare?
PWOH kahm-BYAH-reh

I only have bills.

Ho solo banconote.
OH SOH-loh bahn-koh-NOH-teh

Some coins, please.

Degli spiccioli, per favore.
DEHL-lyee SPEET-choh-lee pehr fah-VOH-reh

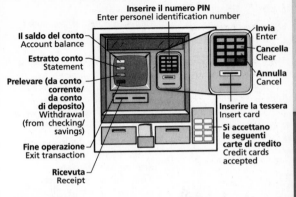

Inserire il numero PIN
Enter personel identification number

Il saldo del conto
Account balance

Estratto conto
Statement

Prelevare (da conto corrente/ da conto di deposito)
Withdrawal (from checking/ savings)

Fine operazione
Exit transaction

Ricevuta
Receipt

Invia
Enter

Cancella
Clear

Annulla
Cancel

Inserire la tessera
Insert card

Si accettano le seguenti carte di credito
Credit cards accepted

COMMUNICATIONS

PHONE SERVICE

Where can I buy or rent a mobile / cell phone?	**Dove posso comprare o noleggiare un cellulare?** *DOH-veh POHS-soh kohm-PRAH-reh oh noh-lehd-JAH-reh oon chehl-loo-LAH-reh*
What rate plans do you have?	**Che piani rateali avete?** *keh PYAH-nee rah-teh-AH-lee ah-VEH-teh*
Is this good throughout the country?	**Questo funziona in tutto il paese?** *KWEHS-toh foon-TSYOH-nah een TOOT-toh eel pah-EH-zeh*
May I have a pre-paid phone?	**Posso avere un telefono pre-pagato?** *POHS-soh ah-VEH-reh oon teh-LEH-foh-noh preh-pah-GAH-toh*

Where can I buy a phone card?	**Dove posso comprare una scheda telefonica?** *DOH-veh POHS-soh kohm-PRAH-reh OO-nah SKEH-dah teh-leh-FOH-nee-kah*
May I add more minutes to my phone card?	**Posso aggiungere altri minuti alla mia scheda telefonica?** *POHS-soh ahd-JOON-jeh-reh AHL-tree mee-NOO-tee AHL-lah MEE-ah SKEH-dah teh-leh-FOH-nee-kah*

MAKING A CALL

May I dial direct?	**Posso chiamare direttamente?** *POHS-soh kyah-MAH-reh dee-reht-tah-MEHN-teh*
Operator, please.	**Il centralista, per favore.** *eel chen-trah-lee-NEES-tah pehr fah-VOH-reh*
I'd like to make an international call.	**Vorrei fare una chiamata internazionale.** *vohr-RAY FAH-reh OO-nah kyah-MAH-tah een-tehr-nah-tsyoh-NAH-leh*

Fuori servizio

Before you stick your coins or bills in a vending machine, watch out for the little sign that says **Fuori Servizio** (Out of Service).

Listen Up: Telephone Lingo

Pronto? / Sì?
PROHN-toh / SEE /

Hello?

Che numero?
keh NOO-meh-roh

What number?

Mi dispiace, la linea è occupata.
mee dee-SPYAH-cheh lah LEE-neh ah EH ohk-koo-PAH-tah

I'm sorry, the line is busy.

Per favore, riagganciare e ricomporre il numero.
pehr fah-VOH-reh ree-ahg-ahg-ghan-CHAH-reh eh ree-kohm-POHR-reh eel NOO-meh-roh

Please, hang up and redial.

Mi dispiace, non risponde nessuno.
mee dee-SPYAH-cheh nohn rees-POHN-deh nehs-SOO-noh

I'm sorry, nobody is answering.

La sua scheda ha ancora dieci minuti a disposizione.
lah SOO-ah SKEH-dah AH ahn-KOH-rah DYEH-chee mee-NOO-tee ah dees-poh-zee-TSYOH-neh

Your card has ten minutes left.

I'd like to make a collect call.	**Vorrei fare una chiamata a carico del ricevente.** *vohr-RAY FAH-reh OO-nah kyah-MAH-tah ah KAH-ree-koh dehl ree-cheh-VEHN-teh*
I'd like to use a calling card.	**Vorrei usare la scheda telefonica.** *vohr-RAY oo-ZAH-reh lah SKEH-dah teh-leh-FOH-nee-kah*
Bill my credit card.	**L'addebiti alla mia carta di credito.** *lahd-DEH-bee-tee AHL-lah MEE-ah KAHR-tah dee KREH-dee-toh*
May I bill the charges to my room?	**Posso addebitare i costi alla mia stanza?** *POHS-soh ahd-deh-bee-TAH-reh ee KOHS-tee AHL-lah MEE-ah STAHN-tsah*
May I bill the charges to my home phone?	**Posso addebitare i costi al mio telefono di casa?** *POHS-soh ahd-deh-bee-TAH-reh ee KOHS-tee ahl MEE-oh teh-LEH-foh-noh dee KAH-zah*
Information, please.	**Informazioni, per favore.** *een-fohr-mah-TSYOH-nee pehr fah-VOH-reh*
I'd like the number for ____.	**Vorrei il numero per ____.** *vohr-RAY eel NOO-meh-roh pehr*
I just got disconnected. / I lost the connection.	**È caduta la linea.** *EH kah-DOO-tah lah LEE-neh-ah*
The line is busy.	**La linea è occupata.** *lah LEE-neh-ah EH ohk-koo-PAH-tah*

INTERNET ACCESS

Where is an Internet café?

Dove si trova un punto di accesso a Internet?
DOH-veh see TROH-vah oon POON-toh di aht-CHESS-soh ah internet

Is there a wireless hub nearby?

C'è un collegamento wireless qui vicino?
ch-EH oon kohl-leh-gah-MEHN-toh wireless kwee vee-CHEE-noh

How much do you charge per minute / hour?

Quanto costa al minuto / all'ora?
KWAHN-toh KOHS-tah ahl mee-NOO-toh / ahl-LOH-rah

Can I print here?

Posso stampare qui?
POHS-soh stahm-PAH-reh kwee

Can I burn a CD?

Posso copiare un CD?
POHS-soh koh-PYAH-reh oon chee-DEE

Would you please help me change the language preference to English?

Può aiutarmi a cambiare l'impostazione della lingua all'inglese?
PWOH ah-yoo-TAHR-mee ah kahm-BYAH-reh leem-pohs-tah-TSYOH-neh DEHL-lah LEEN-gwah ahl-leen-GLEH-seh

May I scan something?	**Posso scannerizzare qualcosa?** *POHS-soh skahn-neh-reed-DZAH-reh kwahl-KOH-zah*
Can I upload photos?	**Posso caricare foto?** *POHS-soh kah-ree-KAH-reh PHOH-toh*
Do you have a USB port so I can download music?	**C'è una presa USB per scaricare musica?** *ch-EH OO-nah PREH-zah oo-ehsseh-bee pehr skah-ree-KAH-reh MOO-zee-kah*
Do you have a machine compatible with iTunes?	**C'è un apparecchio compatibile con iTunes?** *ch-EH oon ahp-pah-REHK-kyoh kohm-pah-TEE-bee-leh kohn iTunes*
Do you have a Mac?	**C'è un Mac?** *ch-EH oon mac*
Do you have a PC?	**C'è un PC?** *ch-EH oon pee-CHEE*
Do you have a newer version of this software?	**C'è una versione più recente di questo software?** *ch-EH OO-nah vehr-SYOH-neh PYOO reh-CHEHN-teh dee KWEHS-toh software*
Do you have broadband?	**C'è il broadband?** *ch-EH eel broadband*
How fast is your connection speed here?	**Che velocità di connessione c'è qui?** *keh veh-loh-chee-TAH dee kohn-nehs-SYOH-neh ch-EH kwee*

GETTING MAIL

Where is the post office?	**Dov'è l'ufficio postale?**
	doh-VEH loof-FEE-choh pohs-TAH-leh
May I send an international package?	**Posso inviare un pacco internazionale?**
	POHS-soh een-VYAH-reh oon PAHK-koh een-tehr-nah-tsyoh-NAH-leh
Do I need a customs form?	**Occorre il modulo doganale?**
	ohk-KOHR-reh eel MOH-doo-loh doh-gah-NAH-leh
Do you sell insurance for packages?	**Offrite l'assicurazione per i pacchi?**
	ohf-FREE-teh lahs-see-koo-raht-SYOH-neh pehr ee PAHK-kee
Please, mark it fragile.	**Lo marchi fragile, per favore.**
	loh MAHR-kee FRAH-jee-leh pehr fah-VOH-reh
Please, handle with care.	**Lo maneggi con cura, per favore.**
	loh mah-NEHD-jee kohn KOO-rah pehr fah-VOH-reh
Do you have twine?	**Ha dello spago?**
	AH DEHL-loh SPAH-goh
Do you have a twine clamp? (sometimes required for packages)	**Ha un sigillo?**
	AH oon see-GEEL-loh
Where is a DHL (express) office?	**Dov'è un ufficio DHL?**
	doh-VEH oon oof-FEE-choh dee-akka-EHLLEH

Listen Up: Postal Lingo

Il prossimo!	Next!
eel PROHS-see-moh	
Lo metta qui.	Set it here.
loh MEHT-tah kwee	
Come lo vuole inviare?	How would you like to send it?
KOH-meh loh VWOH-leh	
een-VYAH-reh	
Che tipo di servizio	What kind of service would
desidera?	you like?
keh TEE-poh dee sehr-	
VEET-syoh deh-ZEE-deh-rah	
Come posso aiutarla?	How can I help you?
KOH-meh POHS-soh	
ah-yoo-TAHR-lah	
Consegne	Dropoff window
kohn-SEHN-nyeh	
Accettazione	Pickup window
aht-cheht-tah-TSYOH-neh	

Do you sell stamps?	**Vende francobolli?**
	VEHN-deh frahn-koh-BOHL-lee
Do you sell postcards?	**Vende cartoline?**
	VEHN-deh kahr-toh-LEE-neh
May I send that first class?	**Posso inviarlo con la posta celere?**
	POHS-soh een-VYAHR-loh kohn
	lah POHS-tah CHEH-leh-reh
How much to send that express / air mail?	**Quanto costa inviarlo espresso / per posta aerea?**
	KWAHN-toh KOHS-tah een-
	VYAHR-loh ehs-PREHS-soh / pehr
	POHS-tah ah-EH-reh-ah

Do you offer overnight delivery?

Offrite la consegna il giorno dopo?
ohf-FREE-teh lah kohn-SEHN-nyah eel JOHR-noh DOH-poh

How long will it take to reach the United States?

Quanto tempo ci vorrà per arrivare negli Stati Uniti?
KWAHN-toh TEHM-poh chee vohr-RAH pehr ahr-ree-VAH-reh NEL-lyee STAH-tee oo-NEE-tee

I'd like to buy an envelope.

Vorrei comprare una busta.
vohr-RAY kohm-PRAH-reh OO-nah BOOS-tah

May I send it airmail?

Posso inviarlo per posta aerea?
POHS-soh een-VYAHR-loh pehr POHS-tah ah-EH-reh-ah

I'd like to send it certified / registered mail.

Vorrei inviarlo per posta raccomandata.
vohr-RAY een-VYAHR-loh pehr POHS-tah rahk-koh-mahn-DAH-tah

CHAPTER SEVEN

CULTURE

CINEMA

Is there a movie theater nearby?	**C'è un cinema qui vicino?** *ch-EH oon CHEE-neh-mah kwee vee-CHEE-noh*
What's playing tonight?	**Cosa danno stasera?** *KOH-zah DAHN-noh stah-SEH-rah*
Is that in English or Italian?	**È in inglese o in italiano?** *EH een een-GLEH-seh oh een ee-tah-LYAH-noh*
Are there English subtitles?	**Ci sono sottotitoli in inglese?** *chee SOH-noh soht-toh-TEE-toh-lee een een-GLEH-seh*
Is the theater air conditioned?	**La sala è climatizzata?** *lah SAH-lah EH klee-mah-teed-ZAH-tah*
How much is a ticket?	**Quanto costa un biglietto?** *KWAHN-toh KOHS-tah oon beel-LYEHT-toh*
Do you have _____	**Ci sono sconti per _____** *chee SOH-noh SKOHN-tee pehr*
senior discounts?	**anziani?** *ahn-TSYAH-nee*
student discounts?	**studenti?** *stoo-DEHN-tee*
children discounts?	**bambini?** *bahm-BEE-nee*

What time is the movie showing?	**A che ora comincia lo spettacolo?** *ah keh OH-rah koh-MEEN-chah loh speht-TAH-koh-loh*
How long is the movie?	**Quanto dura il film?** *KWAHN-toh DOO-rah eel film*
May I buy tickets in advance?	**Posso comprare i biglietti in anticipo?** *POHS-soh kohm-PRAH-reh ee beel-LYEHT-tee een ahn-TEE-chee-poh*
Is it sold out?	**È tutto esaurito?** *EH TOOT-toh eh-zow-REE-toh*
When does it begin?	**Quando inizia?** *KWAHN-doh ee-NEE-tsyah*

PERFORMANCES

Do you have ballroom dancing?	**C'è il ballo da sala?** *ch-EH eel BAHL-loh dah SAH-lah*
Are there any plays showing right now?	**Ci sono spettacoli teatrali al momento?** *chee SOH-noh speht-TAH-koh-lee tehah-TRAH-lee ahl moh-MEHN-toh*
Where can I buy tickets?	**Dove posso comprare i biglietti?** *DOH-veh POHS-soh kohm-PRAH-reh ee beel-LYEHT-tee*
Are there student discounts?	**Ci sono sconti per studenti?** *chee SOH-noh SKOHN-tee pehr stoo-DEHN-tee*
I need ____ seats.	**Mi servono ____ posti.** *mee SEHR-voh-noh ____ POHS-tee*

For a full list of numbers, see p7.

CULTURE

Listen Up: Box Office Lingo

Cosa le piacerebbe vedere?
KOH-zah leh pyah-cheh-REHB-beh veh-DEH-reh

What would you like to see?

Quanti?
KWAHN-tee

How many?

Per due adulti?
pehr DOO-eh ah-DOOL-tee

For two adults?

Vuole del popcorn?
VWOH-leh dehl popcorn

Would you like some popcorn?

Vuole altro?
VWOH-leh AHL-troh

Would you like anything else?

An aisle seat, please.	**Un posto sul corridoio, per favore.** *oon POHS-toh sool kohr-ree-DOH-yoh pehr fah-VOH-reh*
An orchestra seat.	**Un posto in platea.** *oon POHS-toh een plah-TEH-ah*
What time does the play start?	**A che ora inizia lo spettacolo?** *ah keh OH-rah ee-NEE-tsyah loh speht-TAH-koh-loh*
Is there an intermission?	**C'è un intervallo?** *ch-EH oon een-tehr-VAHL-loh*
Do you have an opera house?	**C'è un teatro dell'opera?** *ch-EH oon teh-AH-troh dehl-LOH-peh-rah*

Is there a local symphony? **C'è un'orchestra locale?**
*ch-EH oon-ohr-KEHS-trah
loh-KAH-leh*

May I purchase tickets
over the phone? **Posso comprare i biglietti per
telefono?**
*POHS-soh kohm-PRAH-reh ee beel-
LYEHT-tee pehr teh-LEH-foh-noh*

What time is the box office
open? **A che ora apre il botteghino?**
*ah keh OH-rah AH-preh eel
boht-teh-GHEE-noh*

I need space for a
wheelchair, please. **Ho bisogno di spazio per una
sedia a rotelle, per favore.**
*OH bee-ZOHN-nyoh dee SPAH-
tsyoh pehr OO-nah SEH-dyah
ah roh-TEHL-leh pehr fah-VOH-reh*

Do you have private
boxes available? **Avete palchi privati disponibili?**
*ah-VEH-teh PAHL-kee pree-VAH-tee
dees-poh-NEE-bee-lee*

Is there a church that gives
concerts? **C'è una chiesa che dà concerti?**
*ch-EH OO-nah KYEH-zah keh DAH
kohn-CHEHR-tee*

A program, please. **Un programma, per favore.**
*oon proh-GRAHM-mah
pehr fah-VOH-reh*

Please show us our seats. **Ci mostri i nostri posti, per favore.**
*chee MOHS-tree ee NOHS-tree
POHS-tee pehr fah-VOH-reh*

MUSEUMS, GALLERIES, AND SIGHTS

Do you have a museum guide?	**Ha una guida al museo?** *AH OO-nah GWEE-dah ahl moo-ZEH-oh*
Do you have guided tours?	**Ci sono visite guidate?** *chee SOH-noh VEE-zee-teh gwee-DAH-teh*
What are the museum hours?	**Quali sono gli orari del museo?** *KWAH-lee SOH-noh lyee oh-RAH-ree dehl moo-ZEH-oh*
Do I need an appointment?	**Serve un appuntamento?** *SEHR-veh oon ahp-poon-tah-MEHN-toh*
What is the admission fee?	**Quanto costa l'ingresso?** *KWAHN-toh KOHS-tah leen-GREHS-soh*
Do you have ___	**Ci sono sconti per___** *chee SOH-noh SKOHN-tee pehr*
student discounts?	**studenti?** *stoo-DEHN-tee*
senior discounts?	**anziani?** *ahn-TSYAH-nee*
children discounts?	**bambini?** *bahm-BEE-nee*
Do you have services for the hearing impaired?	**Ci sono servizi per ipoudenti?** *chee SOH-noh sehr-VEET-see pehr ee-poh-oo-DEHN-tee*
Do you have audio tours in English?	**Ci sono guide audiofoniche in inglese?** *chee SOH-noh GWEE-deh ow-dyoh-FOH-nee-keh een een-GLEH-seh*

CHAPTER EIGHT

SHOPPING

This chapter covers the phrases you'll need to shop in a variety of settings: from the mall to the town square artisan market. We also threw in the terminology for a visit to the barber or hairdresser.

For coverage of food and grocery shopping, see Chapter Four, Dining.

GENERAL SHOPPING TERMS

Please tell me _____	**Può dirmi per favore _____** *PWOH DEER-mee pehr* *fah-VOH-reh*
how to get to a mall?	**come si arriva ad un centro** **commerciale?** *KOH-meh see ahr-REE-vah ahd* *oon CHEHN-troh kohm-mehr-* *CHAH-leh*
the best place for shopping?	**il posto migliore per fare** **compere?** *eel POHS-toh meel-LYOH-reh* *pehr FAH-reh KOHM-peh-reh*
how to get downtown?	**come si arriva in centro?** *KOH-meh see ahr-REE-vah een* *CHEHN-troh*

Closed for August

Cities grow hot and steamy in summer, so Italians head for the hills—or the beach. Shops begin closing on August 1st, as well as supermarkets, banks, restaurants, and tourist attractions. The exodus peaks on August 15th, Ferragosto *fehr-rah-GOHS-toh* (Assumption Day), which celebrates the Virgin Mary's ascent to heaven.

Where can I find a _____	Dove trovo _____
	DOH-veh TROH-voh
shoe store?	**un negozio di scarpe?**
	oon neh-GOH-tsyoh dee SKAHR-peh
clothing store for men / women / children?	**un negozio di abbigliamento per uomo / donna / bambini?**
	oon neh-GOH-tsyoh dee ahb-beel-lyah-MEHN-toh pehr WOH-moh / DOHN-nah / bahm-BEE-nee
designer fashion shop?	**una boutique di moda firmata?**
	OO-nah boutique dee MOH-dah feer-MAH-tah
vintage clothing store?	**un negozio di abiti usati?**
	oon neh-GOH-tsyoh dee AH-bee-tee oo-ZAH-tee
jewelry store?	**una gioielleria?**
	OO-nah joh-yehl-leh-REE-ah
bookstore?	**una libreria?**
	OO-nah lee-breh-REE-ah
toy store?	**un negozio di giocattoli?**
	oon neh-GOH-tsyoh dee joh-KAHT-toh-lee
stationery store?	**una cartoleria?**
	OO-nah kahr-toh-leh-REE-ah
antiques shop?	**un negozio di antichità?**
	oon neh-GOH-tsyoh dee ahn-tee-kee-TAH
cigar shop?	**un tabaccaio?**
	oon tah-bahk-KAH-yoh
souvenir shop?	**un negozio di souvenir?**
	oon neh-GOH-tsyoh dee souvenir

Where can I find a flea market?	**Dove trovo un mercatino delle pulci?**
	DOH-veh TROH-voh oon mehr-kah-TEE-noh DEHL-leh POOL-chee

CLOTHES SHOPPING

I'd like to buy ____	**Vorrei comprare ____**
	vohr-RAY kohm-PRAH-reh
men's shirts.	**delle camicie da uomo.**
	DEHL-leh kah-MEE-cheh dah WOH-moh
women's shoes.	**delle scarpe da donna.**
	DEHL-leh SKAHR-peh dah DOHN-nah
children's clothes.	**dei vestiti per bambini.**
	day vehs-TEE-tee pehr bahm-BEE-nee
toys.	**dei giocattoli.**
	day joh-KAHT-toh-lee

For a full listing of numbers, see p7.

I'm looking for a size ____	**Cerco una taglia ____**
	CHEHR-koh OO-nah TAHL-lyah
extra-small.	**molto piccola.**
	MOHL-toh PEEK-koh-lah
small.	**piccola.**
	PEEK-koh-lah
medium.	**media.**
	MEH-dyah
large.	**grande.**
	GRAHN-deh
extra-large.	**molto grande.**
	MOHL-toh GRAHN-deh
I'm looking for ____	**Cerco ____**
	CHEHR-koh
a silk blouse.	**una camicia di seta.**
	OO-nah kah-MEE-chah dee SEH-tah

Gli orecchini
La collana
Il vestito
L'orologio
Itacci alto

La camicia
La cravatta
La giacca
La cintura
I pantaloni
Le scarpe

cotton pants.	**dei pantaloni di cotone.**
	day pahn-tah-LOH-nee dee koh-TOH-neh
a hat.	**un cappello / berretto.**
	oon kahp-PEHL-loh / behr-REHT-toh
sunglasses.	**degli occhiali da sole.**
	DEHL-lyee OHK-kyah-lee dah SOH-leh
underwear.	**della biancheria intima.**
	DEHL-lah byahn-keh-REE-ah EEN-tee-mah
cashmere.	**qualcosa in cashmere.**
	kwahl-KOH-zah een cashmere
socks.	**dei calzini.**
	day kahl-TSEE-nee
sweaters.	**delle maglie.**
	DEHL-leh MAHL-lyeh
a coat.	**una giacca.**
	OO-nah JAHK-kah

gli ochialli

la maglietta

i jeans

le scarpe da tennis

a swimsuit.	**un costume da bagno.**
	oon kohs-TOO-meh dah
	BAHN-nyoh
May I try it on?	**Posso provarlo?**
	POHS-soh proh-VAHR-loh
Where can I try this on?	**Dove posso provarlo?**
	DOH-veh POHS-soh proh-VAHR-loh
This is ____	**Questo è ____**
	KWEHS-toh EH
too tight.	**troppo stretto.**
	TROHP-poh STREHT-toh
too loose.	**troppo largo.**
	TROHP-poh LAHR-goh
too long.	**troppo lungo.**
	TROHP-poh LOON-goh
too short.	**troppo corto.**
	TROHP-poh KOHR-toh
This fits great!	**È perfetto!**
	EH pehr-FEHT-toh

Thanks, I'll take it.	**Grazie, lo prendo.**
	GRAH-tsyeh loh PREHN-doh
Do you have that in ____	**Ce l'ha in ____**
	cheh LAH een
a smaller / larger size?	**una taglia più piccola / grande?**
	OO-nah TAHL-lya PYOO
	PEEK-koh-lah / GRAHN-deh
a different color?	**un altro colore?**
	oon AHL-troh koh-LOH-reh
How much is it?	**Quanto costa?**
	KWAHN-toh KOHS-tah

ARTISAN MARKET SHOPPING

Is there a craft / artisan market?	**C'è un mercato di artigianato?**
	ch-EH oon mehr-KAH-toh dee
	ahr-tee-jah-NAH-toh
That's beautiful. May I look at it?	**Che bello. Posso vederlo?**
	keh BEHL-loh POHS-soh
	veh-DEHR-loh
When is the farmers' market open?	**Quando apre il mercato di frutta e verdura?**
	KWAHN-doh AH-preh eel
	mehr-KAH-toh deeFROOT-tah eh
	vehr-DOO-rah

For full coverage of time, see p12.

Is that open every day of the week?	**È aperto tutti i giorni della settimana?**
	EH ah-PEHR-toh TOOT-tee ee
	JOHR-nee DEHL-lah
	seht-tee-MAH-nah

For full coverage of days of the week, see p14.

How much does that cost?	**Quanto costa?**
	KWAHN-toh KOHS-tah
That's too expensive.	**È troppo caro.**
	EH TROHP-poh KAH-roh

Venditori di falsi (fake designer goods)

Beware unscrupulous vendors who attempt to sell you illegal, contraband, or fake goods. Recent laws penalize buyers as well as sellers.

How much for two?	**Quanto per due?** *KWAHN-toh pehr DOO-eh*
Do I get a discount if I buy two or more?	**Mi fa lo sconto se ne compro due o più?** *mee fah loh SKOHN-toh seh neh KOHM-proh DOO-eh oh PYOO*
Do I get a discount if I pay in cash?	**Mi fa lo sconto se pago in contanti?** *mee fah loh SKOHN-toh seh PAH-goh een kohn-TAHN-tee*
No thanks. Maybe I'll come back.	**No grazie. Magari torno.** *noh GRAH-tsyeh mah-GAH-ree TOHR-noh*
Would you take € ____?	**Vanno bene ___ euro?** *VAHN-noh BEH-neh ___ EH-oo-roh*

For a full list of numbers, see p7.

That's a deal!	**Affare fatto!** *ahf-FAH-reh FAHT-toh*
Do you have a less expensive one?	**Ne ha uno meno caro?** *neh AH OO-noh MEH-no KAH-roh*
Is there tax?	**C'è l'IVA?** *ch-EH LEE-vah*
May I have the VAT forms? (Europe only)	**Posso avere un modulo per il rimborso dell'IVA?** *POHS-soh ah-VEH-reh oon MOH-doo-loh pehr eel reem-BOHR-soh dehl-LEE-vah*

BOOKSTORE / NEWSSTAND SHOPPING

Is there a ____ nearby?	**C'è ____ qui vicino?**
	ch-EH ____ kwee vee-CHEE-noh
bookstore	**una libreria**
	OO-nah lee-breh-REE-ah
newsstand	**un'edicola**
	oon-eh-DEE-koh-lah
Do you have ____ in English?	**Avete ____ in inglese?**
	ah-VEH-teh ____ een een-GLEH-seh
books	**libri**
	LEE-bree
newspapers	**giornali**
	johr-NAH-lee
magazines	**riviste**
	ree-VEES-teh
books about local history	**libri di storia locale**
	LEE-bree dee STOH-ryah loh-KAH-leh
picture books	**libri illustrati**
	LEE-bree eel-loos-TRAH-tee
travel guides	**guide turistiche**
	GWEE-deh too-REES-tee-keh
maps	**cartine**
	kahr-TEE-neh

SHOPPING FOR ELECTRONICS

With some exceptions, shopping for electronic goods in Italy is generally not recommended. The PAL encoding system for DVDs and VHS is different from NTSC and would not work in the United States or Canada.

Can I play this in the U.S.?	**Funziona questo negli Stati Uniti?** *foon-TSYOH-nah KWEHS-toh NEHL-lyee STAH-tee oo-NEE-tee*
Will this game work on my game console in the U.S.?	**Questo gioco funziona su una console americana?** *KWEHS-toh JOH-koh foon-TSYOH-nah soo OO-nah kohn-SOHL ah-meh-ree-KAH-nah*
Do you have this in a U.S. market format?	**C'è questo in formato americano?** *ch-EH KWEHS-toh een fohr-MAH-toh ah-meh-ree-KAH-noh*
Can you convert this to a U.S. market format?	**Si può convertire questo in formato americano?** *see PWOH kohn-vehr-TEE-reh KWEHS-toh een fohr-MAH-toh ah-meh-ree-KAH-noh*
Will this work with a 110V AC adaptor?	**Questo funziona con un adattatore da 110 volts?** *KWEHS-toh foon-TSYOH-nah kohn oon ah-daht-tah-TOH-reh dah CHEHN-toh-DYEH-chee volts*
Do you have an adaptor plug for 110 to 220 volts?	**Avete un adattatore da 110 a 220 volts?** *Ah-VEH-teh oon ah-daht-tah-TOH-reh dah CHEHN-toh-DYEH-chee ah doo-eh-CHEHN-toh-VEHN-tee volts*

Do you sell electronic adaptors here?	**Vendete adattatori per sistemi elettronici?** *vehn-DEH-teh ah-daht-tah-TOH-ree pehr sees-TEH-mee eh-leht-TROH-nee-chee*
Is it safe to use my laptop with this adaptor?	**Posso usare il computer portatile con questo adattatore?** *POHS-soh oo-ZAH-reh eel com puter pohr-TAH-tee-leh kohn KWEHS-toh ah-daht-tah-TOH-reh*
If it doesn't work, may I return it?	**Se non funziona, posso portarlo indietro?** *seh nohn foon-TSYOH-nah POHS-soh pohr-TAHR-loh een-DYEH-troh*
May I try it here in the store?	**Posso provarlo qui in negozio?** *POHS-soh proh-VAHR-loh kwee een neh-GOH-tsyoh*

AT THE BARBER / HAIRDRESSER

Do you have a style guide?	**Ha un catalogo dei vari stili?** *AH oon kah-TAH-loh-goh day VAH-ree STEE-lee*
A trim, please.	**Una spuntatina, per favore.** *OO-nah spoon-tah-TEE-nah pehr fah-VOH-reh*
I'd like it bleached.	**Vorrei ossigenarli.** *vohr-RAY ohs-see-jeh-NAHR-lee*
Would you change the color ____	**Mi fa il colore ____** *mee fah eel koh-LOH-reh*
darker?	**più scuro?** *PYOO SKOO-roh*
lighter?	**più chiaro?** *PYOO KYAH-roh*

For a full list of personal descriptors, see p117.
For a full list of colors, see English / Italian dictionary.

Would you just touch it up a little?	**Me li sistema un po'?**
	meh lee see-STEH-mah oon POH
I'd like it curled.	**Li vorrei arricciati.**
	lee vohr-RAY ahr-reet-CHAH-tee
Do I need an appointment?	**Ci vuole un appuntamento?**
	chee VWOH-leh oon ahp-poon-tah-MEHN-toh
May I make an appointment?	**Posso prendere un appuntamento?**
	POHS-soh PREHN-deh-reh oon ahp-poon-tah-MEHN-toh
Wash, dry, and set.	**Lavaggio, asciugatura, e messa in piega.**
	lah-VAHD-joh ah-shoo-gah-TOO-rah eh MEHS-sah een PYEH-gah
Do you do permanents?	**Fate permanenti?**
	FAH-teh pehr-mah-NEHN-tee
Please use low heat.	**Lo usi tiepido, per favore.**
	loh OO-zee TYEH-pee-doh pehr fah-VOH-reh
Please don't blow dry it.	**Non li asciughi col phon, per favore.**
	nohn lee ah-SHOOG-ee kohl fohn pehr fah-VOH-reh
Please dry it curly / straight	**Li asciughi arricciandoli / stirandoli, per favore.**
	lee ah-SHOO-gy ahr-reet-CHAHN-doh-lee / stee-RAHN-doh-lee pehr fah-VOH-reh
Would you fix my braids?	**Mi fa le trecce?**
	mee fah leh TREHT-cheh
Would you fix my highlights?	**Mi fa i colpi di sole?**
	mee fah ee KOHL-pee dee SOH-leh
Do you wax?	**Fate la ceretta?**
	FAH-teh lah cheh-REHT-tah

Please wax my ___	**Mi faccia la ceretta ___ per favore.** *mee FAHT-chah lah cheh-REHT-tah ___ pehr fah-VOH-reh*
legs.	**alle gambe** *AHL-leh GAHM-beh*
bikini line.	**alla zona bikini** *AHL-lah DZOH-nah bikini*
eyebrows.	**alle sopracciglia** *AHL-leh soh-praht-CHEEL-lyah*
under my nose.	**sotto il naso** *SOHT-toh eel NAH-zoh*
Please trim my beard.	**Mi spunti la barba, per favore.** *mee SPOON-tee lah BAHR-bah pehr fah-VOH-reh*
A shave, please.	**Mi faccia la barba, per favore.** *mee FAHT-chah lah BAHR-bah pehr fah-VOH-reh*
Use a fresh blade, please.	**Usi una lametta nuova, per favore.** *OO-zee OO-nah lah-MEHT-tah NWOH-vah pehr fah-VOH-reh*
Sure, cut it all off.	**Certo, la tagli tutta.** *CHEHR-toh lah TAHL-lyee TOOT-tah*

STAYING FIT

Is there a gym nearby?

C'è una palestra qui vicino?
*ch-EH OO-nah pah-LEHS-trah
kwee vee-CHEE-noh*

Do you have free weights?

Avete pesi liberi?
ah-VEH-teh PEH-zee LEE-beh-ree

I'd like to go for a swim.

Vorrei andare a nuotare.
*vohr-RAY ahn-DAH-reh ah
nwoh-TAH-reh*

Do I have to be a member?

Devo essere socio?
DEH-voh EHS-seh-reh SOH-choh

May I come here for one day?

Posso venire qui per un giorno?
*POHS-soh veh-NEE-reh kwee
pehr oon JOHR-noh*

How much does a membership cost?

Quanto costa associarsi?
*KWAHN-toh KOHS-tah
ahs-soh-CHAHR-see*

I need to get a locker, please.

Mi serve un armadietto, per favore.
*mee SEHR-veh oon ahr-mah-
DYEHT-toh pehr fah-VOH-reh*

161

Do you have locks? **Avete dei lucchetti?**
Ah-VEH-teh day look-KEHT-tee

Do you have _____ **Avete _____**
ah-VEH-teh

a treadmill? **il treadmill?**
eel treadmill

a stationary bike? **la cyclette?**
lah see-KLEHT

handball / squash courts? **campi da pallamano / squash?**
KAHM-pee dah PAHL-lah-MAH-noh / squash

Are they indoors? **Sono campi interni?**
SOH-noh KAHM-pee een-TEHR-nee

I'd like to play tennis. **Vorrei giocare a tennis.**
vohr-RAY joh-KAH-reh ah tennis

Would you like to play? **Vuole giocare?**
VWOH-leh joh-KAH-reh

I'd like to rent a racquet. **Vorrei noleggiare una racchetta.**
vohr-RAY noh-lehd-JAH-reh OO-nah rahk-KEHT-tah

I need to buy some _____ **Devo comprare _____**
DEH-voh kohm-PRAH-reh

new balls. **delle palle nuove.**
DEHL-leh PAHL-leh NWOH-veh

safety glasses. **degli occhiali di sicurezza.**
DEHL-lyee ohk-KYAH-lee dee see-koo-REHT-sah

May I reserve a court for tomorrow? **Posso prenotare un campo per domani?**
POHS-soh preh-noh-TAH-reh oon KAHM-poh pehr doh-MAH-nee

May I have clean towels? **Posso avere asciugamani puliti?**
POHS-soh ah-VEH-reh ah-shoo-gah-MAH-nee poo-LEE-teh

Where are the showers / locker-rooms?	**Dove sono le docce / gli spogliatoi?** *DOH-veh SOH-noh leh DOHT-cheh l lyee spohl-lyah-TOY*
Do you have a workout room for women only?	**Avete un locale per l'allenamento riservato alle donne?** *ah-VEH-teh oon loh-KAH-leh pehr lahl-leh-nah-MEHN-toh ree-sehr-VAH-toh AHL-leh DOHN-neh*
Do you have aerobics classes?	**Avete corsi di aerobica?** *Ah-VEH-teh KOHR-see dee ah-eh-ROH-bee-kah*
Do you have a women's pool?	**Avete una piscina per donne?** *Ah-VEH-teh OO-nah pee-SHEE-nah pehr DOHN-neh*
Let's go for a jog.	**Andiamo a fare jogging.** *anh-DYAH-moh ah FAH-reh jogging*
That was a great workout!	**Che bell'allenamento!** *keh BEHL-lahl-leh-nah-MEHN-toh*

CATCHING A GAME

Where is the stadium?	**Dov'è lo stadio?** *doh-VEH loh STAH-dyoh*
Who is the best goalie?	**Qual è il portiere più bravo?** *kwah-LEH eel pohr-TYEH-reh PYOO BRAH-voh*

Are there any women's teams?	**Ci sono squadre femminili?** *chee SOH-noh SKWAH-dreh fehm-mee-NEE-lee*
Do you have any amateur / professional teams?	**Ci sono squadre dilettanti / professioniste?** *chee SOH-noh SKWAH-dreh dee-leht-TAHN-tee / proh-fehs-syoh-NEES-teh*
Is there a game I could play in?	**C'è una partita in cui posso partecipare?** *ch-EH OO-nah paar-TEE-tah een KOO-ee POHS-soh pahr-teh-chee-PAH-reh*
Which is the best team?	**Qual è la squadra migliore?** *kwah-LEH lah SKWAH-drah meel-LYOH-reh*
Will the game be on television?	**Sarà in TV questa partita?** *sah-RAH een tee-VOO KWEHS-tah paar-TEE-tah*
Where can I buy tickets?	**Dove si comprano i biglietti?** *DOH-veh see KOHM-prah-noh ee beel-LYEHT-tee*
The best seats, please.	**I posti migliori, per favore.** *ee POHS-tee meel-LYOH-ree pehr fah-VOH-reh*
The cheapest seats, please.	**I posti più economici, per favore.** *ee POHS-tee PYOO eh-koh-NOH-mee-chee pehr fah-VOH-reh*
How close are these seats?	**Quanto distano questi posti?** *KWAHN-toh DEES-tah-noh KWEHS-tee POHS-tee*
May I have box seats?	**Posso avere dei posti sul palco?** *POHS-soh ah-VEH-reh day POHS-tee sool PAHL-koh*

Wow! What a game!	**Wow! Che partita!**
	wow keh paar-TEE-tah
Go! Go! Go!	**Vai, vai, vai! / Dai, dai, dai!**
	VAH-ee / DAH-ee
Oh, no!	**Oh, no!**
	oh no
Give it to them!	**Schiacciateli!**
	skyaht-CHAH-teh-lee
Go for it!	**Forza! Vai!**
	FOHR-tsah VAH-ee
Score!	**Gol!**
	gol
What's the score?	**Qual è il punteggio?**
	kwah-LEH eel poon-TEHD-joh
Who's winning?	**Chi sta vincendo?**
	kee stah veen-CHEHN-doh

HIKING

Where can I find a guide to hiking trails?	**Dove trovo una guida ai sentieri per escursioni a piedi?**
	DOH-veh TROH-voh OO-nah GWEE-dah eye sehn-TYEH-ree pehr ehs-koor-SYOH-nee ah PYEH-dee
Do we need to hire a guide?	**Dobbiamo noleggiare una guida?**
	dohb-BYAH-moh noh-lehd-JAH-reh OO-nah GWEE-dah
Where can I rent equipment?	**Dove si possono noleggiare attrezzature?**
	DOH-veh see POHS-soh-noh noh-lehd-JAH-reh aht-treht-tsah-TOO-reh
Do they have rock climbing there?	**Si possono fare arrampicate qui?**
	see POHS-soh-noh FAH-reh ahr-rahm-pee-KAH-teh kwee

We need more ropes and carabiners.	**Ci servono altre corde e moschettoni.** *chee SEHR-voh-noh AHL-treh KOHR-deh eh mohs-keht-TOH-nee*
Where can we go mountain climbing?	**Dove si può andare a fare scalate?** *DOH-veh see PWOH ahn-DAH-reh ah FAH-reh skah-LAH-teh*
Are the routes ____	**I sentieri sono ____** *ee sehn-TYEH-ree SOH-noh*
well marked?	**ben marcati?** *behn mahr-KAH-tee*
in good condition?	**in buone condizioni?** *een BWOH-neh kohn-dee-TSYOH-nee*
What is the altitude there?	**Che l'altitudine c'è là?** *keh ahl-tee-TOO-dee-neh ch-EHLAH*
How long will it take?	**Quanto tempo ci vorrà?** *KWAHN-toh TEHM-poh chee vohr-RAH*
Is it very difficult?	**È molto difficile?** *EH MOHL-toh deef-FEE-chee-leh*
Is there a fixed-protection climbing path?	**C'è una via ferrata?** *CHEH OO-nah VEE-ah fehr-RAH-tah*

I want to hire someone to carry my excess gear.	**Vorrei noleggiare un aiuto che mi porti l'attrezzatura extra.** *VOHR-ray noh-lehd-JAH-reh oon ah-YOO-toh keh mee POHR-tee laht-treht-tsah-TOO-rah extra*
We don't have time for a long route.	**Non c'è tempo per un percorso lungo.** *nohn ch-EH TEHM-poh pehr- oon pehr-KOHR-soh LOON-goh*
I don't think it's safe to proceed.	**Non mi pare sicuro avanzare.** *nohn mee PAH-reh see-KOO-roh ah-vahn-TSAH-reh*
Do we have a backup plan?	**Abbiamo un piano alternativo?** *ahb-BYAH-moh oon PYAH-noh ahl-tehr-nah-TEE-voh*
If we're not back by tomorrow, send a search party.	**Se non torniamo entro domani, mandate una squadra di ricerca.** *seh nohn tohr-NYAH-moh EHN-troh doh-MAH-nee mahn-DAH-teh OO-nah SKWAH-drah dee ree-CHEHR-kah*
Are the campsites marked?	**I siti del campeggio sono marcati?** *ee SEE-tee dehl kahm-PEHD-joh SOH-noh mahr-KAH-tee*
Can we camp off the trail?	**Possiamo campeggiare fuori del sentiero?** *pohs-SYAH-moh kahm-pehd-JAH-reh FWOH-ree dehl sehn-TYEH-roh*
Is it okay to build fires here?	**Si possono fare fuochi qui?** *see POHS-soh-noh FAH-reh FWOH-kee kwee*
Do we need permits?	**Ci servono permessi?** *chee SEHR-voh-noh pehr-MEHS-see*

For more camping terms, see p79.

BOATING OR FISHING

When do we sail?

Quando salpiamo?
KWAHN-doh sahl-PYAH-moh

Where are the life preservers?

Dove sono i salvagenti?
DOH-veh SOH-noh ee sahl-vah-JEHN-tee

Can I purchase bait?

Posso acquistare esche?
POHS-soh ah-kwees-TAH-reh EHS-keh

Can I rent a pole?

Posso noleggiare una canna da pesca?
POHS-soh noh-lehd-JAH-reh OO-nah KAHN-nah dah PEHS-kah

How long is the voyage?

Quanto dura l'escursione?
KWAHN-toh DOO-rah lehs-koor-SYOH-neh

Are we going up river or down?

Andiamo a monte o a valle del fiume?
ahn-DYAH-moh ah MOHN-teh oh ah VAHL-leh dehl FYOO-meh

How far out are we going?

Quanto al largo andiamo?
KWAHN-toh ahl LAHR-goh ahn-DYAH-moh

How deep is the water here?

Quanto è profonda l'acqua qui?
KWAHN-toh EH proh-FOHN-dah LAHK-wah kwee

I got one!

L'ho preso!
LOH PREH-zoh

I can't swim.

Non so nuotare.
nohn soh nwo-TAH-reh

Can we go ashore?	**Possiamo sbarcare?** *pohs-SYAH-moh zbahr-KAH-reh*

DIVING

I'd like to go snorkeling.	**Vorrei fare snorkeling.** *vohr-RAY FAH-reh snorkeling*
I'd like to go scuba diving.	**Vorrei andare in immersione.** *vohr-RAY ahn-DAH-reh een* *eem-mehr-SYOH-neh*
I have a NAUI / PADI certification.	**Ho il certificato NAUI / PADI.** *OH eel chehr-tee-fee-KAH-toh* *NAUI / PADI*
I need to rent gear.	**Devo noleggiare dell'attrezzatura.** *DEH-voh noh-lehd-JAH-reh* *DEHL-laht-treht-tsah-TOO-rah*
We'd like to see some shipwrecks, if we can.	**Vorremmo vedere dei relitti di navi se possibile.** *vohr-REHM-moh veh-DEH-reh day* *reh-LEET-tee dee NAH-vee seh* *pohs-SEE-bee-leh*
Are there any good reef dives?	**Si possono fare belle immersioni lungo la scogliera?** *see POHS-soh-noh FAH-reh BEHL-* *leh eem-mehr-SYOH-nee* *LOON-goh lah skohl-LYEH-rah*
I'd like to see a lot of sea-life.	**Vorrei vedere tanta fauna marina.** *vohr-RAY veh-DEH-reh TAHN-tah* *FOW-nah mah-REE-nah*
Are the currents strong?	**Sono forti le correnti?** *SOH-noh FOHR-tee leh* *kohr-REHN-tee*
How clear is the water?	**È limpida l'acqua?** *EH LEEM-pee-dah LAHK-wah*
I want / don't want to go with a group.	**Voglio / Non voglio andare in gruppo.** *VOHL-lyoh / nohn VOHL-lyoh* *ahn-DAH-reh een GROOP-poh*

Can we charter our own boat?	**Possiamo noleggiare la barca per uso privato?** *pohs-SYAH-moh noh-lehd-JAH-reh lah BAHR-kah pehr OO-zoh pree-VAH-toh*

AT THE BEACH

I'd like to rent a _____ for a day / half a day.

Vorrei noleggiare ___ per un giorno / mezza giornata.
vohr-RAY noh-led-JAH-reh ___ pehr oon JOHR-noh / MED-zah johr-NAH-tah

  a chair

    una sedia a sdraio
    OO-nah SEH-dyah ah ZDRAH-yoh

  an umbrella

    un ombrellone
    oon ohm-brehl-LOH-neh

Is there space _____

C'è posto ___
CHEH POHS-toh

  closer to the water?

    più vicino all'acqua?
    PYOO vee-CHEE-noh ahl-LAHK-wah

  away from the disco music?

    lontano dalla musica?
    lohn-TAH-noh DAHL-lah MOO-zee-kah

Equipped Beaches

Equipped beaches are more common than free ones, and they may charge an admission fee, plus additional fees for chair and umbrella rental.

Do you have ___	**Avete ___** *ah-VEH-teh*
a bar?	**un bar?** *oon bar*
a restaurant?	**un ristorante?** *oon rees-toh-RAHN-teh*
games?	**dei giochi?** *day JOH-kee*
a lifeguard?	**un bagnino?** *oon bahn-NYEE-noh*
a kid's club?	**animazioni per bambini?** *ah-nee-mah-TSYOH-nee pehr bahm-BEE-nee*
pedal boats for rent / hire?	**pedalò a noleggio?** *peh-dah-LOH ah noh-LED-joh*
Is there a free beach nearby?	**C'è una spiaggia libera qui vicino?** *ch-EH OO-nah SPYAD-jah LEE-beh-rah kwee vee-CHEE-noh*
How are the currents?	**Come sono le correnti?** *KOH-meh SOH-noh leh kohr-REHN-tee*
I'd like to go windsurfing.	**Vorrei fare del windsurf.** *vohr-RAY FAH-reh dehl windsurf*
Can I rent equipment?	**Posso noleggiare dell'attrezzatura?** *POHS-soh noh-lehd-JAH-reh DEHL-laht-treht-sah-TOO-rah*

GOLFING

I'd like to reserve a tee-time.

Vorrei prenotare un tee time.
vohr-RAY preh-noh-TAH-reh oon tee time

Do we need to be members to play?

Dobbiamo essere soci per giocare?
dohb-BYAH-moh EHS-seh-reh SOH-chee pehr joh-KAH-reh

How many holes is your course?

Quante buche ha il vostro campo da golf?
KWAHN-teh BOO-keh AH eel VOHS-troh KAHM-poh dah golf

What is par for the course?

Qual è la norma per il campo?
kwah-LEH lah NOHR-mah pehr eel KAHM-poh

I need to rent clubs.

Devo noleggiare delle mazze.
DEH-voh noh-lehd-JAH-reh DEHL-leh MAHT-seh

I need to purchase a sleeve of balls.

Devo acquistare una confezione di palline.
DEH-voh ah-kwees-TAH-reh OO-nah kohn-feh-TSYOH-neh dee pahl-LEE-neh

Do you require soft spikes?

Ci vogliono i soft spikes?
chee VOHL-lyoh-noh ee soft spikes

Do you have carts?

Avete i golf carts?
ah-VEH-teh ee golf carts

I'd like to hire a caddy.	**Vorrei noleggiare un caddy.** *vohr-RAY noh-lehd-JAH-reh oon caddy*
Do you have a driving range?	**Avete un driving range?** *ah-VEH-teh oon driving range*
How much are the greens fees?	**Quanto sono le green fees?** *KWAHN-toh SOH-noh leh green fees*
Can I book a lesson with the pro?	**Posso prenotare una lezione col professionista?** *POHS-soh preh-noh-TAH-reh OO-nah leh-TSYOH-neh kohl proh-fehs-syoh-NEES-tah*
I need to have a club repaired.	**Devo far riparare una mazza.** *DEH-voh fahr ree-pah-RAH-reh OO-nah MAHT-sah*
Is the course dry?	**È asciutto il campo?** *EH ah-SHOOT-toh eel KAHM-poh*
Are there any wildlife hazards?	**Ci sono pericoli da animali selvatici?** *chee SOH-noh peh-REE-koh-lee dah ah-nee-MAH-lee sehl-VAH-tee-chee*
How many meters is the course?	**Quanti metri misura il campo?** *KWAHN-tee MEH-tree mee-ZOO-rah eel KAHM-poh*

CHAPTER TEN

NIGHTLIFE

For coverage of movies and cultural events, see p144, Chapter Seven, "Culture."

NIGHTCLUBBING

Where can I find____	**Dove posso trovare ____**
	DOH-veh POHS-soh troh-VAH-reh
a good nightclub?	**un bel locale notturno / night-club?**
	oon behl loh-KAH-leh noht-TOOR-noh / night club
a club with a live band?	**un locale con musica dal vivo?**
	oon loh-KAH-leh kohn MOO-zee-kah dahl VEE-voh
a reggae club?	**un locale con musica reggae?**
	oon loh-KAH-leh kohn MOO-zee-kah reggae
a hip hop club?	**un locale con musica hip hop?**
	oon loh-KAH-leh kohn MOO-zee-kah hip hop
a techno club?	**un locale con musica techno?**
	oon loh-KAH-leh kohn MOO-zee-kah techno
a gay / lesbian club?	**un locale gay?**
	oon loh-KAH-leh gay
a club where I can dance?	**una discoteca?**
	OO-nah dees-koh-TEH-kah
a club with Italian music?	**un locale con musica italiana?**
	oon loh-KAH-leh kohn MOO-zee-kah ee-tah-LYAH-nah
the most popular club in town?	**il locale più frequentato in città?**
	eel loh-KAH-leh PYOO freh-kwehn-TAH-toh een cheet-TAH

a piano bar?	**un piano bar?**
	oon piano bar.
the most upscale club?	**il locale più di lusso?**
	eel loh-KAH-leh PYOO dee
	LOOS-soh
What's the hottest bar these days?	**Qual è il bar più di moda al momento?**
	kwah-LEH eel bar PYOO dee
	MOH-dah ahl moh-MEHN-toh
What's the cover charge?	**Quant'è il coperto?**
	kwahn-TEH eel koh-PEHR-toh
Do I need a membership?	**Bisogna essere soci?**
	bee-ZOHN-nyah EHS-seh-reh
	SOH-chee
Do they have a dress code?	**Che abbigliamento è richiesto?**
	keh ahb-beel-lyah-MEHN-toh EH
	ree-KYEHS-toh
Is it expensive?	**È caro?**
	EH KAH-roh
What's the best time to go?	**A che ora è meglio andarci?**
	ah keh OH-rah EH MEHL-lyoh
	ahn-DAHR-chee
What kind of music do they play there?	**Che tipo di musica c'è?**
	keh TEE-poh dee MOO-zee-kah
	ch-EH
Is smoking allowed?	**Si può fumare?**
	see PWOH foo-MAH-reh
I'm looking for a tobacconist.	**Cerco un tabaccaio.**
	CHEHR-koh oon tah-bahk-KAH-yoh

I'd like a pack of cigarettes.	**Vorrei un pacchetto di sigarette.**
	vohr-RAY oon pahk-KEHT-toh dee
	see-gah-REHT-teh
I'd like ____, please.	**Vorrei ____, per favore.**
	vohr-RAY pehr fah-VOH-reh
a drink	**qualcosa da bere**
	kwahl-KOH-zah dah BEH-reh
a bottle of beer	**una bottiglia di birra**
	OO-nah boht-TEEL-lyah dee
	BEER-rah
a beer on tap	**una birra alla spina**
	OO-nah BEER-rah AHL-lah
	SPEE-nah
a shot of ____	**un ____**
	oon ____

For a full list of drinks, see p88.

Make it a double, please!	**Doppio, per favore!**
	DOHP-pyoh pehr fah-VOH-reh
With ice, please.	**Con ghiaccio, per favore.**
	kohn GYAT-choh pehr fah-VOH-reh
And one for the lady / the gentleman!	**E uno / a per la signora / il signore!**
	eh OO-noh pehr lah seen-NYOH
	rah / eel seen-NYOH reh
How much for a bottle / glass of beer?	**Quanto costa la birra alla bottiglia / al bicchiere?**
	KWAHN-toh KOHS-tah lah
	BEER-rah AHL-lah boht-TEEL-lyah /
	ahl beek-KYEH-reh

I'd like to buy a drink for that girl / guy over there.

Vorrei offrire da bere a quella ragazza (signora) / quel ragazzo (signore) là.
vohr-RAY ohf-FREE-reh dah BEH-reh ah KWEHL-lah rah-GAHT-sah (seen-NYOH-rah) / kwehl rah-GAHT-soh (seen-NYOH-reh) LAH

May I run a tab?

Posso aggiungere al conto?
POHS-soh ahd-JOON-jeh-reh ahl KOHN-toh

What's the cover?

Quant'è il coperto?
kwahn-TEH eel koh-PEHR-toh

ACROSS A CROWDED ROOM

Excuse me, may I buy you a drink?

Mi scusi, posso offrirle qualcosa da bere?
mee SKOO-zee POHS-soh ohf-FREER-leh kwahl-KOH-zah dah BEH-reh

You look amazing.

Lei è affascinante.
lay EH ahf-fah-shee-NAHN-teh

You look like the most interesting person in the room.

Lei mi sembra la persona più interessante in questo posto.
lay mee SEHM-brah lah pehr-SOH-nah PYOO een-teh-rehs-SAHN-teh een KWEHS-toh POHS-toh

Would you like to dance?

Le va di ballare?
leh vah dee bahl-LAH-reh

Do you like to dance fast or slow?

Le piace il ballo veloce o lento?
leh PYAH-cheh eel BAHL-loh veh-LOH-cheh oh LEHN-toh

Here, give me your hand.

Venga, mi dia la mano.
VEHN-gah mee DEE-ah lah MAH-noh

What would you like to drink?

Cosa le va di bere?
KOH-zah leh vah dee BEH-reh

You're a great dancer.

Come balla bene.
KOH-meh BAHL-lah BEH-neh

I don't know that dance!

Non conosco quella danza!
nohn koh-NOHS-koh KWEHL-lah DAHN-tsah

Do you like this song?

Le piace questa canzone?
leh PYAH-cheh KWEHS-tah kahn-TSOH-neh

You have nice eyes!

Che begli occhi che ha!
kee BEHL-lyee OHK-kee keh AH

For body features, see p118.
May I have your phone number?

Posso avere il suo numero di telefono?
POHS-soh ah-VEH-reh eel SOO-oh NOO-meh-roh dee teh-LEH-foh-noh

GETTING CLOSER

You're very attractive.

Sei molto bello -a.
say MOHL-toh BEHL-loh -ah

I like being with you.

Mi piace stare con te.
mee PYAH-cheh STAH-reh kohn teh

I like you.

Mi piaci.
mee PYAH-chee

I want to hold you.

Voglio tenerti fra le braccia.
VOHL-lyoh teh-NEHR-tee frah leh BRAHT-chah

Kiss me.

Baciami.
BAH-chah-mee

May I give you a hug / a kiss?

Posso abbracciarti / baciarti?
POHS-soh ahb-braht-CHAHR-tee / bah-CHAHR-tee

Would you like a back rub?

Vuoi che ti massaggi la schiena?
VWOH-ee keh tee mahs-SAHD-jee lah SKYEH-nah

Would you like a massage?

Ti piacerebbe un massaggio?
tee pyah-CHEH-rehb-beh oon mahs-SAHD-joh

Don't mix the message	

Ti desidero / Ti voglio. *tee deh-ZEE-deh-roh /* *tee VOHL-lyoh*	I desire you / I want you. These are pretty much physical, erotic expressions, much as in English.
Ti amo. *tee AH-moh*	This means "I love you" and is used seriously.

GETTING INTIMATE

Would you like to come inside?	**Vuoi entrare?** *VWOH-ee ehn-TRAH-reh*
May I come inside?	**Posso entrare?** *POHS-soh ehn-TRAH-reh*
Let me help you out of that.	**Ti aiuto a toglierlo.** *tee ah-YOO-toh ah TOHL-lyehr-loh*
Would you help me out of this?	**Mi aiuti a toglierlo?** *mee ah-YOO-tee ah TOHL-lyehr-loh*
You smell so good.	**Hai un buon profumo.** *eye oon bwon proh-FOO-moh*
You're beautiful / handsome.	**Sei bellissima / bellissimo.** *say behl-LEES-see-mah /* *beh-LEES-see-moh*
May I?	**Posso?** *POHS-soh*
OK?	**Va bene?** *vah BEH-neh*
Like this?	**Così?** *koh-ZEE*
How?	**Come?** *KOH-meh*

HOLD ON A SECOND

Please don't do that.

No, per favore, non farlo.
*noh pehr fah-VOH-reh nohn
FAHR-loh*

Stop, please.

Smetti, per favore.
ZMEHT-tee pehr fah-VOH-reh

Do you want me to stop?

Vuoi che smetta?
VWOH-ee keh ZMEHT-tah

Let's just be friends.

Restiamo solo amici.
*reh-STYAH-moh SOH-loh
ah-MEE-chee*

Do you have a condom?

Hai un preservativo?
eye oon preh-sehr-vah-TEE-voh

Are you on birth control?

Prendi la pillola?
PREHN-dee lah PEEL-loh-lah

I have a condom.

Ho un preservativo.
OH oon preh-sehr-vah-TEE-voh

Do you have anything you
should tell me first?

**Hai qualcosa da dirmi prima di
continuare?**
*eye kwahl-KOH-zah dah
DEER-mee PREE-mah dee
kohn-tee-NWAH-reh*

BACK TO IT

That's it.	**Ecco, sì.**
	EHK-koh SEE
That's not it.	**No, non così.**
	noh nohn koh-ZEE
Here.	**Qui.**
	kwee
There.	**Lì.**
	LEE
More.	**Ancora.**
	ahn-KOH-rah
Harder.	**Più forte.**
	PYOO FOHR-teh
Faster.	**Più veloce.**
	PYOO veh-LOH-cheh
Deeper	**Più profondo.**
	PYOO proh-FOHN-doh
Slower.	**Più lento.**
	PYOO LEHN-toh
Easy / slowly.	**Piano.**
	PYAH-noh
Enough.	**Basta.**
	BAHS-tah

For a full list of features, see p118.
For a full list of body parts, see p190.

COOLDOWN

You're great.	**Sei fantastico -a.**
	say fahn-TAHS-tee-koh -ah
That was great.	**È stato bellissimo.**
	EH STAH-toh behl-LEES-see-moh
Would you like ____	**Vuoi ____**
	VWOH-ee
a drink?	**qualcosa da bere?**
	kwahl-KOH-zah dah BEH-reh
a snack?	**qualcosa da mangiare?**
	kwahl-KOH-zah dah
	mahn-JAH-reh
a shower?	**fare la doccia?**
	FAH-reh lah DOHT-chah
May I stay here?	**Posso stare qui?**
	POHS-soh STAH-reh kwee
Would you like to stay here?	**Vuoi stare qui?**
	VWOH-ee STAH-reh kwee
I'm sorry. I have to go now.	**Mi dispiace. Ora devo andare.**
	mee dee-SPYAH-cheh OH-rah
	DEH-voh ahn-DAH-reh
Where are you going?	**Dove vai?**
	DOH-veh VAH-ee
I have to work early.	**Devo alzarmi presto per andare al lavoro.**
	DEH-voh ahl-TSAHR-mee
	PREHS-toh pehr ahn-DAH-reh ahl
	lah-VOH-roh
I'm flying home in the morning.	**Torno a casa domani mattina.**
	TOHR-noh ah KAH-zah
	doh-MAH-nee maht-TEE-nah
I have an early flight.	**Il mio volo parte presto.**
	eel MEE-oh VOH-loh PAHR-teh
	PREHS-toh

I think this was a mistake.	**Credo che questo sia stato un errore.** *KREH-doh keh KWEHS-toh SEE-ah STAH-toh oon ehr-ROH-reh*
Will you make me breakfast too?	**Puoi preparare la colazione anche per me?** *pwoy preh-pah-RAH-reh lah koh-lah-TSYOH-neh AHN-keh pehr meh*
Stay, I'll make you breakfast.	**Stai qui, ti preparo la colazione.** *STAH-ee kwee tee preh-PAH-roh lah koh-lah-TSYOH-neh*

IN THE CASINO

How much is this table?	**Quanto costa questo tavolo?** *KWAHN-toh KOHS-tah KWEHS-toh TAH-voh-loh*
Deal me in.	**Entro in gioco.** *EHN-troh een JOH-koh*
Put it on red!	**Sul rosso!** *sool ROHS-soh*
Put it on black!	**Sul nero!** *sool NEH-roh*
Let it ride!	**Lascialo girare!** *LAH-shah-loh jee-RAH-reh*
21!	**Ventuno!** *vehn-TOO-noh*
Snake-eyes!	**Due uno!** *DOO-eh OO-noh*
Seven.	**Sette.** *SEHT-teh*

For a full list of numbers, see p7.

Damn, eleven.	**Accidenti, undici.** *at-chee-DEHN-tee OON-dee-chee*
I'll pass.	**Passo.** *PAHS-soh*
Hit me!	**Carte!** *KAHR-te*

Watch that stress!

The meaning of **casinò** (*kah-zee-NOH*) is different from that of **casino** (*kah-ZEE-noh*)! **Casinò** means the gambling house, while **casino** means a mess, a screwed up situation, or . . . "a lot", as in **Mi dispiace un casino** (I'm mad about something or someone).

Split.	**Metà e metà.**
	meh-TAH eh meh-TAH
Are the drinks complimentary?	**Le bevande sono gratis?**
	leh beh-VAHN-deh SOH-noh gratis
May I bill it to my room?	**Posso addebitarlo alla mia stanza?**
	POHS-soh ahd-deh-bee-TAHR-loh AHL-lah MEE-ah STAHN-tsah
I'd like to cash out.	**Vorrei incassare la vincita.**
	vohr-RAY een-kahs-SAH-reh lah VEEN-chee-tah
I'll hold.	**Va bene.**
	vah BEH-neh
I'll see your bet.	**Vedo.**
	VEH-doh
I call.	**Chiamo.**
	KYAH-moh
Full house!	**Full!**
	full
Royal flush.	**Scala reale.**
	SKAH-lah reh-AH-leh
Straight.	**Scala.**
	SKAH-lah

NIGHTLIFE

CHAPTER ELEVEN

HEALTH & SAFETY

This chapter covers the terms you'll need to maintain your health and safety—including the most useful phrases for the pharmacy, the doctor's office, and the police station.

AT THE PHARMACY

Please fill this prescription.	**Mi servono questi farmaci, per favore.** *mee SEHR-voh-noh KWEHS-tee FAHR-mah-chee pehr fah-VOH-reh*
Do you have something for ____	**Ha qualcosa per ____** *AH kwahl-KOH-zah pehr*
a cold?	**il raffreddore?** *eel rahf-frehd-DOH-reh*
a cough?	**la tosse?** *lah TOHS-seh*
I need something for ____	**Mi serve qualcosa per ____** *mee SEHR-veh kwahl-KOH-zah pehr*
corns.	**i calli.** *ee KAHL-lee*
congestion.	**la congestione.** *lah kohn-jehs-TYOH-neh*
constipation.	**la costipazione.** *lah kohs-tee-pah-TSYOH-neh*
diarrhea.	**la diarrea.** *lah dyahr-REH-ah*
indigestion.	**l'indigestione.** *leen-dee-jehs-TYOH-neh*
nausea.	**la nausea.** *lah NOW-zeh-ah*
motion sickness.	**il mal d'auto.** *eel mahl DOW-toh*

seasickness.	**il mal di mare.**
	eel mahl dee MAH-reh
acne.	**l'acne.**
	LAHK-neh
warts.	**le verruche.**
	leh vehr-ROO-keh
to help me sleep.	**aiutarmi a dormire.**
	ah-yoo-TAHR-mee ah dohr-MEE-reh
to help me relax.	**aiutarmi a rilassarmi.**
	ah-yoo-TAHR-mee ah ree-lahs-SAHR-mee
I want to buy ____	**Vorrei ____**
	vohr-RAY
condoms.	**dei preservativi.**
	day preh-sehr-vah-TEE-vee
an antihistamine.	**un antistaminico.**
	oon ahn-tees-tah-MEE-nee-koh
antibiotic cream.	**una crema antibiotica.**
	OO-nah KREH-mah ahn-tee-BYOH-tee-kah
aspirin.	**dell'aspirina.**
	dehl-lahs-pee-REE-nah
non-aspirin pain reliever.	**un analgesico senza aspirina.**
	oon ah-nahl-JEH-zee-koh SEHN-tsah ahs-pee-REE-nah
medicine with codeine.	**un farmaco con codeina.**
	oon FAHR-mah-koh kohn koh-deh-EE-nah
insect repellant.	**un insetto-repellente.**
	oon een-seht-toh reh-pehl-LEHN-teh

AT THE DOCTOR'S OFFICE

I would like to see ____	**Vorrei vedere ____**
	vohr-RAY veh-DEH-reh
a doctor.	**un medico.**
	oon MEH-dee-koh
a chiropractor.	**un chiroterapeuta.**
	oon kee-roh-teh-rah-PEHoo-tah
a gynecologist.	**un ginecologo.**
	oon jee-neh-KOH-loh-goh
an eye / ears / nose / throat specialist.	**un otorinolaringoiatra.**
	oon oh-toh-REE-noh-lah-REEN-goh-YAH-trah
a dentist.	**un dentista.**
	oon dehn-TEES-tah
an optometrist.	**un optometrista.**
	oon ohp-toh-meh-TREES-tah
Do I need an appointment?	**Mi serve un appuntamento?**
	mee SEHR-veh oon ahp-poon-tah-MEHN-toh
I have an emergency.	**È un'emergenza.**
	EH oon-eh-mehr-JEHN-tsah
I need an emergency prescription refill.	**Mi servono questi farmaci urgenti.**
	mee SEHR-voh-noh KWEHS-tee FAHR-mah-chee oor-JEHN-tee
Please call a doctor.	**Chiami un medico, per favore.**
	KYAH-mee oon MEH-dee-koh pehr fah-VOH-reh
I need an ambulance.	**Mi serve un'ambulanza.**
	mee SEHR-veh oon-ahm-boo-LAHN-tsah

SYMPTOMS

For a full list of body parts, see p190.

My ____ hurts.

Mi fa male ____.
mee fah MAH-leh

My ____ is stiff.

____ è rigido -a.
EH REE-jee-doh -ah

I think I'm having a heart attack.

Credo sia un attacco cardiaco.
KREH-doh SEE-ah oon aht-TAHK-koh kahr-DEE-ah-koh

I can't move.

Non riesco a muovermi.
nohn ree-EHS-koh ah MWOH-vehr-mee

I fell.

Sono caduto -a.
SOH-noh kah-DOO-toh -ah

I fainted.

Sono svenuto -a.
SOH-noh zveh-NOO-toh/ah

I have a cut on my ____.

Ho un taglio su ____.
OH oon TAHL-lyoh soo

I have a headache.

Ho mal di testa.
OH mahl dee TEHS-tah

My vision is blurry

La vista è annebbiata.
lah VEES-tah EH ahn-nehb-BYAH-tah

I feel dizzy.

Mi gira la testa.
mee JEE-rah lah TEHS-tah

I think I'm pregnant.

Credo di essere incinta.
KREH-doh dee EHS-seh-reh een-CHEEN-tah

I don't think I'm pregnant.

Non credo di essere incinta.
nohn KREH-doh dee EHS-seh-reh een-CHEEN-tah

I'm having trouble walking.

Faccio fatica a camminare.
FAHT-choh fah-TEE-kah ah kahm-mee-NAH-reh

I can't get up.

Non riesco ad alzarmi.
nohn ree-EHS-koh ahd ahl-TSAHR-mee

Il collo
I seni
L'ombelico
Le anche
La vita
Il sedere
La vagina
Le cosce
Le gambe
Le caviglie

Le spalle
Le mani
Le dita
Le braccia
Il petto
Il torso
Lo stomaco
La vita
Il pene
I polpacci
I piedi
Le dita dei piedi

See p118 for facial features.

I was mugged.	**Sono stato aggredito -a.** *SOH-noh STAH-toh* *ahg-ghreh-DEE-toh -ah*
I was raped.	**Sono stato violentato -a.** *SOH-noh STAH-toh vyo-lehn-* *TAH-toh -tah*
A dog attacked me.	**Un cane mi ha aggredito -a.** *oon KAH-neh mee AH* *ahg-ghreh-DEE-toh -ah*
A snake bit me.	**Mi ha morso un serpente.** *mee AH MOHR-soh oon* *sehr-PEHN-teh*
I can't move my _____ without pain.	**Mi fa male quando muovo _____.** *mee fah MAH-leh KWAHN-doh* *MWOH-voh*
I think I sprained my ankle.	**Credo di essermi slogato la caviglia.** *KREH-doh dee EHS-sehr-mee* *zloh-GAH-toh lah kah-VEEL-lyah*

MEDICATIONS

I need morning-after pills.	**Mi servono delle pillole del giorno dopo.**
	mee SEHR-voh-noh DEHL-leh PEEL-loh-leh dehl JOHR-noh DOH-poh
I need birth control pills.	**Mi servono pillole anticoncezionali.**
	mee SEHR-voh-noh PEEL-loh-leh anti-kohn-CHEH-tsyoh-NAH-lee
I need erectile dysfunction pills.	**Mi servono pillole per la disfunzione erettile.**
	mee SEHR-voh-noh PEEL-loh-leh pehr lah dees-foon-TSYOH-neh eh-REHT-tee-leh
I lost my eyeglasses and need new ones.	**Ho perso gli occhiali da vista e me ne servono di nuovi.**
	OH PEHR-soh lyee ohk-kee-AH-lee dah VEES-tah eh meh neh SEHR-voh-noh dee NWOH-vee
I need new contact lenses.	**Mi servono lenti a contatto nuove.**
	mee SEHR-voh-noh LEHN-tee ah kohn-TAHT-toh NWOH-veh
It's cold in here!	**Fa freddo qui!**
	fah FREHD-doh kwee
I am allergic to ____	**Sono allergico -a ____**
	SOH-noh ahl-LEHR-jee-koh -ah
penicillin.	**alla penicillina.**
	AHL-lah peh-nee-cheel-LEE-nah
antibiotics.	**agli antibiotici.**
	AHL-lyee ahn-tee-BYOH-tee-chee
sulfa drugs.	**ai sulfonamidi.**
	eye sool-foh-NAH-mee-dee
steroids.	**agli steroidi.**
	AHL-lee steh-ROY-dee
I have asthma.	**Soffro d'asma.**
	SOHF-froh DAHZ-mah

HEALTH & SAFETY

DENTAL PROBLEMS

Where can I find a dentist?	**Dove posso trovare un dentista?**
	DOH-veh POHS-soh troh-VAH-reh
	oon dehn-TEES-tah
I have a toothache.	**Mi fa male un dente.**
	mee fah MAH-leh oon DEHN-teh
I chipped a tooth.	**Mi si è rotto un dente.**
	mee see EH ROHT-toh oon
	DEHN-teh
My bridge came loose.	**Mi si è allentato il ponte.**
	mee see EH ahl-lehn-TAH-toh eel
	POHN-teh
I lost a crown.	**Ho perso una capsula.**
	OH PEHR-soh OO-nah
	KAHP-soo-lah
I lost a denture plate.	**Ho perso una piastra della**
	dentiera.
	OH PEHR-soh OO-nah PYAHS-trah
	DEHL-lah dehn-TYEH-rah

AT THE POLICE STATION

I'm sorry, did I do something wrong?	**Scusi, ho fatto qualcosa di male?**
	SKOO-zee OH FAHT-toh kwahl-
	KOH-zah dee MAH-leh
I am ____	**Sono ____**
	SOH-noh
an American.	**americano -a.**
	ah-meh-ree-KAH-noh -ah
a Canadian.	**canadese.**
	kah-nah-DEH-zeh
a European.	**europeo -a.**
	eh-oo-roh-PEH-oh -ah
an Australian.	**australiano -a.**
	ow-strah-LYAH-noh -ah
a New Zealander.	**neozelandese.**
	neh-oh-dzeh-lahn-DEH-zeh

For a full listing of nationalities, see English/Italian dictionary.

Listen Up: Police Lingo

Favorisca la patente, il libretto e l'assicurazione. *fah-voh-REES-kah lah pah-TEHN-teh eel lee-BREHT-toh eh LAHS-see-koo-raht-SYOH-neh-*	Your license, registration and insurance, please.
La multa è di dieci euro. Può pagarla direttamente a me. *lah MOOL-tah EH dee DYEH-chee EH-oo-roh PWOH pah-GAH-reh dee-reht-tah-MEHN-teh ah meh*	The fine is €10. You can pay me directly.
Il suo passaporto, per favore. *eel SOO-oh pahs-sah-POHR-toh pehr fah-VOH-reh*	Your passport, please.
Dov'è diretto? *dohv-EH dee-REHT-toh*	Where are you going?
Perchè tanta fretta? *pehr-KEH TAHN-tah FREHT-tah*	Why are you in such a hurry?

The car is a rental.	**L'auto è a noleggio.** *LOW-toh EH ah noh-LEHD-joh*
Do I pay the fine to you?	**Devo pagare la multa a lei?** *DEH-voh pah-GAH-reh lah MOOL-tah ah lay*
Do I have to go to court?	**Devo andare in tribunale?** *DEH-voh ahn-DAH-reh een tree-boo-NAH-leh*
When?	**Quando?** *KWAHN-doh*

I'm sorry, my Italian isn't very good.	**Scusi, non parlo bene l'italiano.** *SKOO-zee nohn PAHR-loh* *BEH-neh lee-tah-LYAH-noh*
I need an interpreter.	**Mi serve un interprete.** *mee SEHR-veh* *oon-een-TEHR-preh-teh*
I'm sorry, I don't understand the ticket.	**Scusi, non capisco la multa.** *SKOO-zee nohn kah-PEES-koh lah* *MOOL-tah*
May I call my embassy?	**Posso chiamare la mia ambasciata?** *POHS-soh kyah-MAH-reh lah* *MEE-ah ahm-bah-SHAH-tah*
I was robbed.	**Mi hanno derubato.** *mee AHN-noh deh-roo-BAH-toh*
I was mugged.	**Sono stato -a aggredito -a.** *SOH-noh STAH-toh -ah ahg-ghreh-* *DEE-toh -ah*
I was raped.	**Sono stato violentato -a.** *SOH-noh STAH-toh vyo-lehn-* *TAH-toh -tah*
May I make a report?	**Posso sporgere denuncia?** *POHS-soh SPOHR-jeh-reh deh-* *NOON-chah*
Somebody broke into my room.	**Qualcuno è entrato nella mia stanza.** *kwahl-KOO-noh EH ehn-TRAH-toh* *NEHL-lah MEE-ah STAHN-tsah*
Someone stole my purse / wallet.	**Qualcuno mi ha rubato la borsetta / il portafoglio.** *kwahl-KOO-noh mee AH* *roo-BAH-toh lah bohr-SEHT-tah /* *eel pohr-tah-FOHL-lyo*

DICTIONARY KEY

n	noun	m	masculine
v	verb	f	feminine
adj	adjective	s	singular
prep	preposition	pl	plural
adv	adverb	pron	pronoun
interj	interjection		

All verbs are listed in infinitive (to + verb) form, cross-referenced to the appropriate conjugations page. Adjectives are listed first in masculine singular form, followed by the feminine ending.
For food terms, see the Menu Reader (p91) and Grocery Section (p100) in Chaper 4, Dining.

A

able, to be able to (can) *v* potere **p30**

above *prep* sopra p78

accept, to accept *v* accettare **p20**

> **Do you accept credit cards?** Accettate la carta di credito? **p38**

accident *n* l'incidente *m*

> **I've had an accident.** Ho avuto un incidente.

account *n* il conto *m* p135

> **I'd like to transfer to / from my checking account.** Vorrei trasferire dei fondi al / dal mio conto corrente.

> **I'd like to transfer to / from my savings account.** Vorrei trasferire dei fondi al / dal mio conto di risparmio.

acne *n* l'acne *f* p187

across *prep* attraverso, dall'altro lato di **p5**

across the street dall'altro lato della strada

actual *adj* reale

adapter plug *n* lo spinotto adattore *m* p157

address *n* l'indirizzo *m* p124

> **What's the address?** Qual è l'indirizzo?

admission fee *n* il prezzo d'ingresso *m* p148

in advance in anticipo

African-American *adj* afroamericano -a

after *prep* dopo

afternoon *n* il pomeriggio *m*

> **in the afternoon** nel / di pomeriggio

age *n* l'età *f* p116

> **What's your age?** Quanti anni ha?

agency *n* l'agenzia *f* **(travel)** l'agenzia viaggi *m*

agnostic *adj* agnostico -a

air conditioning *n* l'aria condizionata *f* p68

Would you lower / raise the air conditioning? Può abbassare / aumentare l'aria condizionata?

airport *n* l'aeroporto *m*

I need a ride to the airport. Ho bisogno di un passaggio all'aeroporto.

How far is it from the airport? Quanto dista dall'aeroporto?

airsickness bag *n* il sacchetto per il mal d'aria *m* p48

aisle (in store) *n* la corsia *f*

Which aisle is it in? In quale corsia si trova?

alarm clock *n* la sveglia *f*

alcohol *n* l'alcol *m* p88

Do you serve alcohol? Servite bevande alcoliche?

I'd like nonalcoholic beer. Vorrei una birra analcolica.

all *n* il tutto *m* p11

all of the time sempre

That's all, thank you. È tutto, grazie.

all *adj* tutto -a p11

allergic *adj* allergico -a *See common allergens,* p191

I'm allergic to ____. Sono allergico -a a ____.

altitude *n* l'altitudine *f*

aluminum *n* l'alluminio *m*

ambulance *n* l'ambulanza *f*

American *adj* americano -a

amount *n* la quantità *f*

angry *adj* arrabbiato -a

animal *n* l'animale *m*

another *adj* altro -a

answer *n* la risposta *f*

answer, to answer *v* rispondere p20

Answer me, please. Per cortesia, mi risponda.

antibiotic *n* l'antibiotico *m*

I need an antibiotic. Ho bisogno di un antibiotico.

antihistamine *n* l'antistaminico *m* p187

anxious *adj* ansioso -a

any *adj* qualsiasi

anything *n* qualsiasi cosa *f*

anywhere *adv* dovunque

appointment *n* l'appuntamento *m* p148

Do I need an appointment? Ho bisogno di un appuntamento?

April *n* aprile *m* p15

are *See* be, to be, p24

arm *n* il braccio *m*, le braccia *f*

arrival(s) *n* l'arrivo *m* / gli arrivi *m pl* p39

arrive, to arrive *v* arrivare p20

art *n* l'arte *f*

exhibit of art la mostra d'arte

art museum il museo d'arte

fine arts le belle arti

Renaissance art l'arte del Rinascimento

artist *n* l'artista *m f*

Asian *adj* asiatico -a

ask, to ask v chiedere, domandare **p20**

to ask for (to request) chiedere

to ask a question fare una domanda **p23**

aspirin n l'aspirina f **p187**

assist, to assist v assistere **p21**

assistance n l'assistenza f

asthma n l'asma f **p191**

I have asthma. Ho l'asma.

at prep a, in

atheist adj, n ateo -a

ATM / cash machine n il bancomat m **p135**

I'm looking for an ATM / cash machine. Sto cercando un bancomat.

attend, to attend v participare **p20**

audio adj, n l'audio m **p65**

August n agosto m **p15**

aunt n la zia f **p115**

Australia n l'Australia f

Australian adj australiano -a

autumn n l'autunno m

available adj disponibile

B

baby n il / la bambino -a m f

baby adj per bambini **p116**

Do you sell baby food? Vendete cibi per bambini?

babysitter n il / la baby-sitter m f

Do you have babysitters? Avete baby-sitter?

Do you have babysitters who speak English? Avete delle baby-sitter che parlano inglese?

back n la schiena f **p190**

My back hurts. Mi fa male la schiena.

back rub n il massaggio alla schiena m **p179**

backed up (toilet) adj intasato m

The toilet is backed up! Il gabinetto è intasato!

bag n la borsa f, il sacchetto m

airsickness bag il sacchetto per il mal d'aria.

My bag was stolen. La mia borsa è stata rubata.

I lost my bag. Ho perso la mia borsa.

bag, to bag v mettere in borsa **p20**

baggage adj, n il bagaglio m

baggage claim il recupero bagagli

bait n l'esca f **p168**

balance (on bank account) n il saldo m **p135**

balance, to balance v bilanciare **p20**

balcony n il balcone m

ball (sport) n la palla f

ballroom dancing n il ballo da sala m

band (musical ensemble) n il gruppo m

band-aid n il cerotto m

bank *n* la banca *f* p133

Do you know where I can find a bank? Sa dov'è una banca?

bar *n* il bar *m*

barber *n* il barbiere *m*

bass (instrument) *n* il basso *m*

bath *n* il bagno *m*, la toiletta *f*

bathroom (restroom) *n* il bagno *m* p36

Where is the nearest public bathroom? Sa dov'è il bagno pubblico più vicino?

bathtub *n* la vasca da bagno *f*

bathe, to bathe *v* fare il bagno p28

battery (for flashlight) *n* la pila *f*

battery (for car) *n* la batteria *f*

bee *n* l'ape *f*

I was stung by a bee. Mi ha punto un'ape.

be, to be *v* essere p26, stare p25

beach *n* la spiaggia *f* p170

beach, to beach *v* tirare a riva p20

beautiful *adj* bello -a p116

bed *n* il letto *m* p67

beer *n* la birra *f* p88

beer on tap la birra alla spina

begin, to begin *v* cominciare, iniziare p20

behave, to behave *v* comportarsi p20, 35

behind *prep, adv* dietro -a p5

below *prep, adv* sotto -a

belt *n* la cintura *f* p152

conveyor belt il nastro trasportatore

berth *n* la cuccetta *f*

best *adj* il / la migliore

bet *n* la scommessa *f* p184

I'll see your bet. Eguaglio la sua scommessa.

bet, to bet *v* scommettere p20

better *adj* migliore

between *prep* fra, tra

big *adj* grande p11

bilingual *adj* bilingue

bill (currency) *n* la banconota *f*
(check) *n* il conto *m*
(utility bill) *n* la bolletta *f*

bill, to bill *v* mandare il conto p20

biography *n* la biografia *f*

biracial *adj* birazziale

bird *n* l'uccello *m*

birth control *n* la contraccezione *f* p191

birth control (contraceptive) *adj* anticoncezionale p191

I'm out of birth control pills. Non ho più pillole anticoncezionali.

I need more birth control pills. Ho bisogno di più pillole anticoncezionali.

bit (small amount) *n* un poco *m*

black *adj* nero -a

blanket *n* la coperta *f* p47

bleach *n* la candeggina *f*

blind *adj* cieco -a p65

block, to block *v* bloccare p20

blond(e) *adj, n* il / la biondo -a

blouse *n* la camicetta *f* p152

blue *adj* azzurro -a, blu

blurry *adj* annebbiato -a

board *n* l'asse *f*

on board a bordo

board, to board *v* salire a bordo di p21

boarding pass *n* la carta d'imbarco *f* p46

boat *n* l'imbarcazione *f*

bomb *n* la bomba *f*

book *n* il libro *m* p156

bookstore *n* la libreria *f* p156

boss *n* il capo *m*

bottle *n* la bottiglia *f*

May I heat this (baby) bottle someplace? Posso riscaldare questo biberon da qualche parte?

box (seat) *n* il palco *m* p164

box office *n* la biglietteria *f*

boy *n* il ragazzo *m*

boyfriend (friend, date) *n* il ragazzo *m*, boy-friend *m*

braid *n* la treccia *f* p158

braille, American *n* il braille americano *m*

brake *n* il freno *m* p54

emergency brake il freno d'emergenza

brake, to brake *v* frenare p20

brandy *n* il brandy *m* p89

bread *n* il pane *m*

break, to break *v* rompere p20

breakfast *n* la colazione *f*

What time is breakfast? A che ora è la colazione?

bridge (across a river, dental structure) *n* il ponte *m*

I need a new bridge. Ho bisogno di un'altra protesi dentaria.

briefcase *n* la borsa porta-documenti *f* p49

bright *adj* brillante, luminoso -a

broadband *n* la banda larga *f*

bronze *adj* bronzo

brother *n* il fratello *m* p113

brown *adj* marrone

brunette *n* la bruna *f*

Buddhist *adj* il / la buddista

budget *n* il bilancio *m*

buffet *n* il buffet *m* p80

bug *n* l'insetto *m*

burn, to burn *v* bruciare, incendiare p20

Can I burn a CD here? Posso masterizzare un CD qui?

bus *n* l'autobus *m* p60

Where is the bus stop? Dov'è la fermata degli autobus?

Which bus goes to ____? Quale autobus va a ____?

business *n* l'attività *m* p122

business *adj* commerciale

business center il centro affari

busy (restaurant) *adj* affollato -a **(phone)** *adj* occupato -a

butter *n* il burro *m*

buy, to buy *v* acquistare, comprare p20

C

café *n* il caffè *m*, il bar *m*
  Internet café il Internet café
call, to call (shout) *v* gridare
  (telephone) *v* chiamare p20
camp, to camp *v* campeggiare, fare campeggio p20,
28
camper (person) *n* il campeggiatore / la campeggiatrice
  Do we need a camping permit? Abbiamo bisogno d'un
  permesso di campeggio?
campsite *n* l'area di campeggio *f* p79
can *n* la scatola *f*, la lattina *f*
can (to be able to) *v* potere
p30
Canada *n* il Canada *m*
Canadian *adj, n* canadese *m f*
cancel, to cancel *v* cancellare
p20
  My flight was canceled. Il mio
  volo è stato cancellato.
canvas (art) *n* la tela *f*
car *n* l'auto *f*, la macchina *f*
  See car types, p50.
  car rental agency l'autonoleggio
  I need a rental car. Mi serve
  un'auto a noleggio.
card *n* la carta *f* p123
  Do you accept credit cards?
  Accettate le carte di credito?

  **May I have your business
  card?** Posso avere il suo
  biglietto da visita?
  I'd like a greeting card.
  Vorrei un biglietto d'auguri.
car seat (child's safety seat) *n*
  il sedile di sicurezza *m*
  Do you rent car seats for children? Noleggiate sedili di
  sicurezza per bambini?
car sickness *n* il mal d'auto *m*
cash *n* i contanti *m*, i soldi *m*
  cash only solo contanti
cash, to cash *v* incassare p20
  to cash out (gambling)
  incassare la vincita
cash machine / ATM *n* il bancomat *m* p135
cashmere *adj, n* il cashmere *m*
casino *n* il casinò *m* p184
cat *n* il / la gatto -a *m f*
Catholic *adj, n* cattolico -a
cavity (tooth) *n* la carie *f*
  I think I have a cavity.
  Credo di avere una carie.
CD *n* il CD *m* p139
CD player *n* il lettore di CD *m*
celebrate, to celebrate *v* celebrare p20
cell / mobile phone *n* il cellulare *m* p135
centimeter *n* il centimetro *m*
chamber music *n* la musica
  da camera *f*

change (money) n il resto m

I'd like change, please.
Vorrei degli spiccioli, per cortesia.

This isn't the correct change. Questo resto non è esatto.

change (to change money or clothes) v cambiare **p20**

changing room n il camerino m

charge, to charge (money) v addebitare **(a battery)** v caricare **p20**

charmed (greeting) piacere

charred (meat) adj bruciacchiato -a

charter, to charter v noleggiare **p20**

cheap adj economico -a

check / money order n l'assegno m **p132**

Do you accept travelers' checks? Accettate i travellers' checks?

check, to check v verificare **p20**

checked (pattern) adj a quadretti

check-in (airport) n il check-in m **p38**

What time is check-in? A che ora è il check-in?

check-out (hotel) n la partenza f **p78**

check-out time l'orario di partenza

What time is check-out? A che ora è la partenza?

check out, to check out (hotel) v pagare il conto dell'albergo **p20**

cheese n il formaggio m

chicken n il pollo m

child n il / la bambino -a m f

children n i / le bambini -e m f

Are children allowed? Sono ammessi i bambini?

Do you have children's programs? Avete dei programmi per bambini?

Do you have a children's menu? Avete un menu per bambini?

Chinese adj cinese m f

chiropractor n il chiropratico m

chrysanthemum n il crisantemo m

church n la chiesa f **p126**

cigarette n la sigaretta f

a pack of cigarettes un pacchetto di sigarette m

cinema n il cinema m **p144**

city n la città f **p69**

claim n il reclamo m

I'd like to file a claim. Vorrei fare un reclamo.

clarinet n il clarinetto m

class n la classe f **p41**

business class la classe business

economy class la classe economica

first class la prima classe

classical (music, taste) adj classico -a

clean *adj* pulito -a
clean, to clean *v* pulire **p21**
  **Please clean the room
  today.** Per favore, oggi
  pulisca la camera.
clear *adj* chiaro -a
climb, ascent *n* la scalata *f*
climb, to climb *v* scalare,
  salire **p20, 21**
  (a mountain) scalare una
  montagna **p20**
  (stairs) salire le scale
close, to close *v* chiudere **p20**
close (near) *adj* vicino -a
closed *adj* chiuso -a
cloudy *adj* nuvoloso -a
clover *n* il trifoglio *m*
go clubbing, to go clubbing *v*
  andare per locali notturni
  p27
coat *n* il cappotto *m*
coffee *n* il caffè *m* **p88**
  iced coffee il caffè freddo
cognac *n* il cognac *m* **p89**
coin *n* la moneta *f* **p132**
cold *adj* freddo -a **p111**
cold *n* il freddo *m*
  I'm cold. Ho freddo.
  It's cold. Fa freddo.
cold (infection) *n* il raffreddore *m* **p186**
  I have a cold. Ho il raffreddore.
Coliseum *n* il Colosseo *m*
collect *adj* a carico del destinatario

**I'd like to place a collect
  call.** Vorrei fare una telefonata a carico del destinatario.
collect, to collect *v* raccogliere **p20**
college *n* l' università *f*
color *n* il colore *m*
color, to color *v* colorare **p20**
common *adj* comune
computer *n* il computer *m*
concert *n* il concerto *m* **p130**
condition *n* la condizione *f*
  in good / bad condition in
  buone / cattive condizioni
condom *n* il condom *m* **p180**
  Do you have a condom? Hai
  un condom?
  Not without a condom. Non
  senza un condom.
confirm, to confirm *v* confermare **p20**
  I'd like to confirm my reservation. Vorrei confermare
  la mia prenotazione.
confused *adj* confuso -a
congested *adj* congestionato -a
connection speed *n* la velocità di connessione *f*
constipated *adj* stitico -a
  I'm constipated. Sono stitico -a.
contact lenses *n* le lenti a
  contatto *f pl* **p191**
  I lost my contact lenses. Ho
  perso le mie lenti a contatto.

continue, to continue v continuare p20

convertible n la ecappottabile f

cook, to cook v cucinare p20

I'd like a room where I can cook. Vorrei una stanza con uso cucina.

cookie n il biscotto m

copper adj rame

corner n l'angolo m

on the corner all'angolo

correct, to correct v correggere p20

correct adj giusto -a

Am I on the correct train? Mi trovo sul treno giusto?

cost, to cost v costare p20

How much does it cost? Quanto costa?

costume n il costume m

cotton n il cotone m

cough n la tosse f p186

cough, to cough v tossire p21

counter (board) n il banco m

court (legal) n il tribunale m

court (sport) n il campo m

courteous adj cortese p78

cousin n il / la cugino -a m f

cover charge (bar, restaurant) n il coperto m p175

cow n la mucca f

crack (glass) n l'incrinatura f

craftsperson n l'artigiano -a m f p154

cream n la crema f

credit card n la carta di credito f

Do you accept credit cards? Accettate carte di credito?

crib n la culla f p70

crown (dental) n la capsula f

curb n il bordo del marciapiede m

curl n il riccio m

curly adj riccio -a

currency exchange n il cambio di valuta m p133

Where is the nearest currency exchange? Sa dove si trova il cambio di valuta più vicino?

current (water, electricity) n la corrente f

customs n la dogana f p39

cut (wound) n la ferita f

I have a bad cut. Ho una brutta ferita.

cut, to cut v tagliare p20

cybercafé n l'Internet café m

Where can I find a cybercafé? Sa dove posso trovare un Internet café?

D

damaged adj danneggiato -a

Damn! expletive Dannazione!

dance, to dance v ballare p20

danger n il pericolo m

dark adj scuro -a

dark n il buio m

daughter n la figlia f p114

day n il giorno m p161

the day before yesterday
ieri l'altro

these last few days questi
ultimi giorni

dawn n l'alba f

at dawn all'alba

deaf adj sordo -a p65

deal (bargain) n l'affare m

What a great deal! Che
affarone!

deal, to deal (cards) v dare le
carte p28

Deal me in. Dia le carte
anche a me.

December n dicembre m

declined adj rifiutato -a

**Was my credit card
declined?** La mia carta di
credito è stata rifiutata?

declare, to declare v
dichiarare p20

I have nothing to declare.
Non ho niente da
dichiarare.

deep adj profondo -a

delay n il ritardo m p44

How long is the delay?
Quanto dura il ritardo?

delighted adj felicissimo -a

democracy n la democrazia f

dent, to dent v ammaccare
p20

He / She dented the car. Lui
/ Lei ha ammaccato la
macchina.

dentist n il dentista m f p192

denture n la dentiera f

denture plate la piastra
dentale

departure n la partenza f

designer n lo / la stilista m f

dessert n il dolce m p98

dessert menu la lista dei
dolci

destination n la destinazione f

diabetic adj diabetico -a p84

dial, to dial (phone number)
v fare il numero p28

dial direct fare il numero
diretto

diaper n il pannolino m

**Where can I change a dia-
per?** Dove posso cambiare
il pannolino?

diarrhea n la diarrea f p186

dictionary n il dizionario m

different (other) adj diverso -a,
altro -a

difficult adj difficile

dinner n la cena f p80

directory assistance (phone)
n l'assistenza telefonica f

disability n l'invalidità f

disappear, to disappear v
sparire p21

disco n il disco m p174

disconnect, to disconnect v
staccare p20

disconnected adj staccato -a

**Operator, I was discon-
nected.** Centralino, è
caduta la linea.

discount n lo sconto m
Do I qualify for a discount?
Posso ricevere uno sconto?
dish n il piatto m
dive, to dive v tuffarsi p35
scuba dive l'immersione subacquea con le bombole
divorced adj divorziato -a
dizzy adj stordito -a p189
do, to do v fare p28
doctor n il medico m f p121
doctor's office n lo studio del
medico m p188
dog n il cane m
service / guide dog il cane
guida p65
dollar n il dollaro m p132
door n la porta f
double adj doppio -a
double bed il letto a due
piazze
double vision la visione
doppio
down adv giù p5
download, to download v
scaricare p20
downtown n il centro città m
dozen n la dozzina f
drain n lo scarico m
drama n il dramma m
drawing (art) n il disegno m
dress (garment) n il vestito m
dress (general attire) n l'abbigliamento m p152
What's the dress code?
Come ci si deve vestire?

dress, to dress v vestirsi p35
**Should I dress up for that
affair?** Dovrei vestirsi bene
per quella festa?
dressing (salad) n il condimento m
dried adj secco -a
drink n la bevanda f p88
I'd like a drink. Vorrei una
bibita.
drink, to drink v bere p29
drip, to drip v sgocciolare
p20
drive, to drive v guidare p20
driver n l'autista m f
drum n il tamburo m
dry adj secco -a, asciutto -a
This towel isn't dry. Questo
asciugamano non è
asciutto.
dry, to dry v asciugarsi p20
I need to dry my clothes.
Devo asciugarmi i vestiti.
dry cleaner n la lavanderia a
secco f p74
dry cleaning n il lavaggio a
secco m
duck n l'anatra f
duty-free adj esente tasse,
duty-free
duty-free shop n il negozio
duty-free m p37
DVD n il DVD m p157
**Do the rooms have DVD
players?** C'è il lettore di
DVD nelle stanze?

ENGLISH—ITALIAN

Where can I rent DVDs or videos? Sa dove posso noleggiare DVD o video?

E

early *adv* presto
 It's early. E' presto.
eat, to eat *v* mangiare **p20**
 to eat out *v* mangiare fuori
economy *n* l'economia *f*
editor *n* il redattore *m*, la redattrice *f* **p121**
educator *n* l'educatore *m*, l'educatrice *f* **p121**
eight *adj* otto **p7**
eighteen *adj* diciotto **p7**
eighth *adj* ottavo -a **p9**
eighty *adj* ottanta **p7**
election *n* l'elezione *f* **p125**
electrical hookup *n* il collegamento elettrico *m* **p79**
elevator *n* l'ascensore *m*
eleven *adj* undici **p7**
e-mail *n* l'e-mail *f* **p139**
 May I have your e-mail address? Posso avere il suo indirizzo di e-mail?
 e-mail message il messaggio e-mail
e-mail, to send e-mail *v* inviare un'e-mail **p20**
embarrassed *adj* imbarazzato -a
embassy *n* l'ambasciata *f*
emergency *n* l'emergenza *f*
emergency brake *n* il freno d'emergenza *m* **p54**

emergency exit *n* l'uscita d'emergenza *f* **p41**
employee *n* il / la dipendente *m f*
employer *n* il datore di lavoro / la datrice di lavoro *m f*
engine *n* il motore *m* **p54**
engineer *n* l'ingegnere *m f*
England *n* l'Inghilterra *f*
English *n, adj* inglese *m f*
 Do you speak English? Parla inglese? **p1**
enjoy, to enjoy *v* piacere **p33**
enter, to enter *v* entrare **p20**
 Do not enter. Vietato l'ingresso.
enthusiastic *adj* entusiasta
entrance *n* l'entrata *f*
envelope *n* la busta *f*
environment *n* l'ambiente *m*
escalator *n* la scala mobile *f*
espresso *n* il caffè *m*
evening *n* la sera *f*
exchange rate *n* il cambio *m*
 What is the exchange rate for U.S. / Canadian dollars? Qual è il cambio del dollaro USA / canadese?
excuse, to excuse (pardon) *v* scusare **p20**
 Excuse me. Mi scusi.
 (to get through) Permesso.
exhausted *adj* esausto -a
exhibit *n* la mostra *f* **p148**
exit *n* l'uscita *f* **p39**
 not an exit senza uscita
exit, to exit *v* uscire **p32**

ENGLISH–ITALIAN

expensive *adj* caro -a p175
explain, to explain *v* spiegare p20
express *adj* espresso -a
  express check-in il check-in espresso p40
extra (additional) *adj* extra / in più
extra-large *adj* extra-large
eye *n* l'occhio *m* p190
eyebrow *n* il sopracciglio *m*
eyeglasses *n* gli occhiali *m*
eyelashes *n* le ciglia *f pl*

F
fabric *n* il tessuto *m*
face *n* il viso *m* p118
faint, to faint *v* svenire p21
fall (season) *n* l'autunno *m*
fall, to fall *v* cadere p20
family *n* la famiglia *f* p114
fan *n* il ventilatore *m*
far *adj* lontano -a p5
  How far is it to _____?
  Quanto dista _____?
fare *n* la tariffa *f* p57
fast *adj* veloce
fat *adj* grasso -a p11
fat *n* il grasso *m* p11
father *n* il padre *m* p115
faucet *n* il rubinetto *m*
fault *n* il torto *m*
  I'm at fault. E' colpa mia.
  It was his fault. E' colpa sua.
fax *n* il fax *m* p122
February *n* febbraio *m* p15
fee *n* l'onorario *m*, la tassa *f*

female *adj* femminile *f*
female *n* la donna / la femmina *f*
fiancé(e) *n* il / la fidanzato -a *m f* p115
fifteen *adj* quindici p7
fifth *adj* quinto -a p9
fifty *adj* cinquanta p7
find, to find *v* trovare p20
fine (traffic violation) *n* la multa *f*
fine *adj* bello -a p1
  I'm fine (well). Sto bene.
fire *n* il fuoco *m*
  Fire! Al fuoco!
first *adj* primo -a p9
fishing pole *n* la canna da pesca *f* p168
fitness center *n* il centro benessere *m* p66, 161
fit, to fit (size) *v* andare bene p27 (looks) *v* stare bene p25, 35
  This doesn't fit. Questo non mi va bene.
  Does this look like it fits? Sembra che mi stia bene?
fitting room *n* il camerino *m*
five *adj* cinque p7
flight *n* il volo p36
  Where do domestic flights arrive? Dove arrivano i voli nazionali?
  Where do domestic flights depart? Da dove partono i voli nazionali?

Where do international flights arrive? Dove arrivano i voli internazionali?

Where do international flights depart? Da dove partono i voli internazionali?

What time does this flight leave? A che ora parte questo volo?

flight attendant l'assistente di volo *m f*

floor *n* il piano *m* **(ground)** *n* il pavimento *m*

ground floor il pianoterra

first floor il primo piano

flower *n* il fiore *m*

flush (gambling) *n* il flush *m*

flush, to flush *v* tirare l'acqua del water p20

This toilet won't flush. Non si può tirare l'acqua a questo water.

flute *n* il flauto *m*

food *n* il cibo *m* p91

foot (body part) *n* il piede *m*

for *prep* per

forehead *n* la fronte *f* p118

format *n* il formato *m*

formula *n* la formula *f*

Do you sell infants' formula? Vendete il latte in polvere?

forty *adj* quaranta p7

forward *adv* avanti p6

four *adj* quattro p7

fourteen *adj* quattordici p7

fourth *adj* quarto -a p9

one-fourth un quarto *m*

fragile *adj* fragile

freckle *n* la lentiggine *f*

French *adj* francese *m f*

fresh *adj* fresco -a p101

Friday *n* venerdì *m* p15

friend *n* l'amico -a, *m f*

from *prep* da

front *adj* anteriore *adv* davanti p41

front desk la reception

front door la porta principale

fruit *n* il frutto *m* p104 **(collective)** *n* la frutta *f*

fruit juice *n* il succo di frutta *m See fruits,* p104.

full *adj* pieno -a

Full house! *n* Full house! *f*

fuse *n* la valvola fusibile *f* p54

G

garlic *n* l'aglio *m*

gas *n* il gas *m* p53 **(fuel)** *n* la benzina *f*

gas gauge la spia del serbatoio p54

out of gas la benzina è finita

gate (at airport) *n* l'uscita *f*

German *adj, n* tedesco -a *m f*

gift *n* il regalo *m*

girl *n* la ragazza *f*

girlfriend *n* la ragazza *f* p114

give, to give *v* dare p28

glass (drinking) n il bicchiere m

Do you have it by the glass? Lo servite a bicchiere?

I'd like a glass please. Vorrei un bicchiere per favore.

glass (material) n il vetro m

glasses (spectacles) n gli occhiali m, pl p191

I need new glasses. Ho bisogno di nuovi occhiali.

glove n il guanto m

go, to go v andare p27

goal (sport) n il goal m

goalie n il portiere m

gold adj oro

golf n il golf m p172

golf, to go golfing v giocare a golf p20

good adj buono -a

goodbye n arrivederci m See common salutations, p111.

goose n l'oca f

grade (school) n la classe f

gram n il grammo m

grandfather n il nonno m

grandmother n la nonna f

grandparents n i nonni m pl

grape n l'uva f

gray adj grigio -a

Great! adj Eccellente!

Greek adj greco -a

Greek Orthodox adj greco-ortodosso -a

green adj verde

groceries n la spesa f p100

group n il gruppo m

grow, to grow (get larger) v crescere p20

Where did you grow up? Dov'è cresciuto -a?

guard n la guardia f p37

security guard la guardia di sicurezza

guest n l'ospite m f

guide (tour) n la guida f

(publication) n la guida f

guide, to guide v guidare p20

guided tour n la gita guidata f p148

guitar n la chitarra m

gym n la palestra f p161

gynecologist n il / la ginecologo -a m f

H

hair n i capelli m pl p158

haircut n il taglio di capelli m

I need a haircut. Ho bisogno di un taglio ai capelli.

How much is a haircut? Quanto costa il taglio?

hairdresser n il / la parrucchiere -a m f p158

hair dryer n l'asciugacapelli m

half adj mezzo -a

half n la metà f

hallway n il corridoio m

hand n la mano f, le mani f, pl

handbag n la borsetta f

handicapped-accessible adj accessibile ai disabili

handle, to handle v maneggiare p20

ENGLISH–ITALIAN

Handle with care.
Maneggiare con cura.

handsome adj bello -a p116

hangout (hot spot) n il ritrovo m

hang out, to hang out (relax) v rilassarsi p20, 35

hang up, to hang up (end a phone call) v riattaccare p20

hanger n la gruccia f

happy adj felice p120

hard adj duro -a

hat n il cappello m, il berretto m

have, to have v avere p27

hazel adj color nocciola

hazel (nut) n la nocciola f

headache n il mal di testa m

headlight n il faro della macchina m p54

headphones n le cuffie f pl

hear, to hear v udire, sentire p21

hearing-impaired adj ipoudente p65

heart n il cuore m

heart attack n l'infarto m

hectare n l'ettaro m 10

Hello! n Salve! / Ciao! See greetings, p111.

Help! n Aiuto!

help, to help v aiutare p20

hen n la gallina f

her pron lei f p19

her, hers adj, pron suo -a, suoi / sue pl p19

herb n l'erbetta f

here adv qui, qua p5

high adj alto -a

highlights (hair) n i colpi di sole m p158

highway n l'autostrada f

hike, to hike v fare un'escursione a piedi p28

him pron lui p19

Hindu adj indù

hip-hop n l'hip-hop m p174

his adj, pron suo -a, sing, suoi / sue pl p19

historical adj storico -a

history n la storia f

hobby n l'hobby m

hold, to hold v reggere p20

to hold hands tenersi per mano

Would you hold this for me? Può reggermi questo, per favore?

hold, to hold (wait) v aspettare p20

Hold on a minute! Aspetti un attimo!

I'll hold. Sì, attendo.

holiday n la festa f

to go on holiday andare in vacanza

home n la casa f

homemaker n il marito casalingo m / la casalinga f

horn n il corno m

horse n il cavallo m

hostel n l'ostello della gioventù m p66

hot adj caldo -a

hot chocolate *n* la cioccolata calda *f* p88

hotel *n* l'albergo, l'hotel *m*

Do you have a list of local hotels? Ha un elenco di alberghi locali?

hour *n* l'ora *f* p12

hours (schedule) *n* l'orario *m*

how *adv* come p3

humid *adj* umido -a p124

hundred *adj* cento p7

hurry, to hurry *v* aver fretta p27

I'm in a hurry. Ho fretta.
Hurry, please! Si sbrighi per favore!

hurt, to hurt *v* far male p28

Ouch! That hurts! Ahi! Fa male!

husband *n* il marito *m* p114

I

I *pron* io p19

ice *n* il ghiaccio *m*

identification *n* il documento di riconoscimento *m*

in *prep* in

indigestion *n* l'indigestione *f*

inexpensive *adj* economico -a

infant *n* il / la neonato -a *m f*

Are infants allowed? Si possono portare i neonati?

information *n* l'informazione *f*

information booth *n* il banco informazioni *f*

injury *n* la ferita *f* p188

insect repellent *n* l'insetto-repellente *m* p187

inside *adj* interno -a

inside *adv* dentro

insult, to insult *v* insultare p20

insurance *n* l'assicurazione *f*

intercourse (sexual) *n* il rapporto sessuale *m* p180

interest rate *n* il tasso d'interesse *m* p132

intermission *n* l'intervallo *m*

Internet *n* l'Internet *m* p139

High-speed Internet l'Internet ad alta velocità

Do you have Internet access? Avete l'accesso a Internet?

Where can I find an Internet café? Sa dove posso trovare un Internet café?

interpreter *n* l'interprete *m f*

I need an interpreter. Mi serve un interprete.

introduce, to introduce *v* presentare p20

I'd like to introduce you to _____. Ho il piacere di presentarle _____.

Ireland *n* l'Irlanda *f*

Irish *adj* irlandese *m f*

is *See* be, to be, p24.

Italian *adj* italiano -a

J

jacket *n* la giacca *f* p152

January *n* gennaio *m* p14

Japanese *adj* giapponese

jazz *n* il jazz *m*

Jewish *adj* ebreo -a

jog, to run *v* correre p20

juice *n* il succo *m*

July *n* luglio *m* p15

June *n* giugno *m* p15

K

keep, to keep *v* tenere, conservare p20

kid *n* il / la ragazzo -a *m f*

Are kids allowed? Sono ammessi i ragazzi?

Do you have kids' programs? Avete programmi per ragazzi?

Do you have a kids' menu? Avete un menu per i ragazzi?

kilo *n* il chilo *m*

kilometer *n* il chilometro *m*

kind (type) *n* il tipo *m*

(nice) *adj* gentile, simpatico -a

What kind is it? Che tipo è?

kiss *n* il bacio *m* p180

kitchen *n* la cucina *f* p73

know, to know (something) *v* sapere p31

know, to know (someone) *v* conoscere p20

kosher *adj* kasher p85

L

lactose-intolerant *adj* intollerante al lattosio

land, to land *v* atterrare p20

landscape (painting) *n* il paesaggio *m*, **(land)** *n* il panorama *m*

language *n* la lingua *f*

laptop *n* il portatile *m* p139

large *adj* grande p11

last, to last *v* durare p20

last *adj* ultimo -a

late *adv* tardi p13

Please don't be late. Non ritardi per favore.

later *adv* più tardi p4

See you later. A più tardi.

lately *adv* di recente

laundry (shop) *n* la lavanderia *f*, **(clothes)** il bucato *m*

lavender *adj* lavande

law *n* la legge *f*

lawyer *n* l'avvocato *m* / l'avvocassa *f* p121

least *n* il minimo *m*, *adj* minimo -a

leather *n* la pelle *f*

leave, to leave (depart) *v* partire p21

left *adj* sinistro -a p5

on the left a sinistra

(remaining) rimasto -a

leg *n* la gamba *f* p190

lemonade *n* la limonata *f*

less *adv* meno p10

lesson *n* la lezione *f*

license *n* il permesso *m* p50

driver's license la patente *f*

life *n* la vita *f*

the good life la dolce vita *f*

life preserver *n* il salvagente *m*

light (brightness) *adj* luminoso -a

light *n* la luce *f* p47
(for cigarette) l'accendino
May I offer you a light?
Posso offrirle da accendere?
(lamp) la lampada *f*
(weight) leggero -a

like, to like *v* piacere p32
I would like ____. Mi piacerebbe / Vorrei ____.
I like this place. Mi piace questo posto.

limo *n* la limousine *f*
liqueur *n* il liquore *m* p88
liquor *n* il liquore *m* p88
liter *n* il litro *m* p10
little *adj* piccolo -a
live, to live *v* vivere p20
(dwell) *v* abitare p20

Where do you live? Dove abita?
What do you do for a living?
Che mestiere fa?

local *adj* locale
lock *n* la serratura *f* p54
lock, to lock *v* chiudere a chiave p20

I can't lock the door. Non riesco a chiudere la porta a chiave.
I'm locked out. Sono rimasto chiuso fuori.

locker *n* l'armadietto *m* p162
storage locker l'armadietto di deposito
locker room lo spogliatoio

long (length) *adj* lungo -a p10
adv lungo, molto tempo
For how long? Per quanto tempo?
long ago molto tempo fa

look, to look (to observe) *v* guardare, osservare p20
I'm just looking. Sto solo guardando.
Look here! Guarda qui!
look (to appear) *v* sembrare p20
How does this look? Come sembra questo?

look for, to look for (to search) *v* cercare p20
I'm looking for a porter.
Cerco un facchino.

loose *adj* sciolto -a
lose, to lose *v* perdere p20
I lost my passport. Ho perso il mio passaporto.
I lost my wallet. Ho perso il mio portafogli.
I'm lost. Mi sono perso.

lost *adj* perso -a p46
loud *adj* rumoroso -a p77
loudly (voice) *adv* ad alta voce
lounge *n* la sala d'aspetto *f*
lounge, to lounge *v* bighellonare p20
love *n* l'amore *m*
love, to love *v* amare p20
(family) voler bene
(a friend) voler bene
(a lover) amare

to make love fare l'amore **p28**
low *adj* basso -a **p5**
lunch *n* il pranzo *m*
luggage *n* il bagaglio *m* **p48**
  Where do I report lost luggage? Dove posso denunciare la perdita del bagaglio?
  Where is the lost luggage claim? Dov'è l'ufficio bagagli smarriti?

M
machine *m* la macchina *f*
made of *adj* fatto -a di
magazine *n* la rivista *f*
maid (hotel) *n* la cameriera *f*
maiden *adj* nubile *f*
  That's my maiden name. E' il mio nome da nubile.
mail *n* la posta *f* **p141**
  air mail la posta aerea
  registered mail posta assicurata
make, to make *v* fare **p28**
makeup *n* il trucco *m*
make up, to make up (apply cosmetics) *v* truccarsi **p20, 35**
make up, to make up (apologize) *v* fare la pace **p28**
male *adj* maschile *m*
male *n* il maschio *m*
mall *n* il centro commerciale *m*
man *n* l'uomo *m*
manager *n* il manager *m f*, il direttore / il direttrice *m f*
manual *n* il manuale *m*

many *adj* molti -e
map *n* la cartina *f* **p55**
March *n* marzo *m* **p15**
market *n* il mercato *m* **p154**
  flea market il mercatino delle pulci
  open-air market il mercato all'aperto
married *adj* sposato -a **p116**
marry, to marry *v* sposarsi **p20, 35**
massage, to massage *v* massaggiare **p20**
match (sport) *n* la partita *f*
  (stick) il fiammifero
  book of matches una bustina di fiammiferi
match, to match *v* abbinare **p20**
  Does this ____ match my outfit? Questo -a ____ si abbina al mio completo? **p152**
May *n* maggio *m*
may *v* potere **p30**
  May I ____? Posso ____?
meal *n* il pasto *m*
meat *n* la carne *f* **p95**
meatball *n* la polpetta *f*
medication *n* il farmaco *m*
medium (size) *adj* medio -a
medium rare (meat) *adj* quasi al sangue
medium well (meat) *adj* ben cotto -a
member *n* il socio *m*
menu *n* il menu *m* **p91**
  May I see a menu? Posso vedere il menu?

children's menu il menu dei bambini

diabetic menu il menu per i diabetici

kosher menu il menu di piatti kasher

vegetarian menu il menu vegetariano

metal detector n il rivelatore di metalli m

meter n il metro m

middle adj medio -a p10

midnight n la mezzanotte f

mile n il miglio m

military n il militare m

milk n il latte m p88

milk shake n il frappè m

milliliter n il millìlitro m p10

millimeter n il millimetro m

minute n il minuto m p12

in a minute fra un minuto

miss, to miss (a flight) v perdere p20

missing adj perso -a

mistake n l'errore m

moderately priced adj a prezzo modico m p66

mole (facial feature) n il neo m

Monday n lunedì m p14

money n il denaro m, i soldi m pl p132

money transfer il trasferimento di valuta p132

month n il mese m p15

morning n il mattino m p13

in the morning al mattino

mosque n la moschea f p126

mother n la madre f p115

mother, to mother v curare p20

motorcycle n la moto f

mountain n la montagna f

mountain climbing scalata montana

mouse n il topo m

mouth n la bocca f p190

move (change position) v spostare, spostarsi p20, 35

(relocate) v traslocare p20

movie n il film m p144

much adj molto -a

to get mugged essere vittima di un assalto p26

museum n il museo m p148

music n la musica f p128

live music la musica dal vivo

musician n il musicista m f

Muslim adj musulmano -a

my / mine pron mio -a, miei m pl, mie f pl p19

mystery (novel) n il giallo m

N

name n il nome m p111

My name is ____. Mi chiamo ____.

What's your name? Come si chiama?

napkin n il tovagliolo m

narrow adj stretto -a

nationality n la nazionalità f

nausea n la nausea f p186

near adj vicino p5

nearby adv vicino p5

neat (tidy) adj ordinato -a

need, to need v bisognare **p20**

  I need ___. Ho bisogno di ___.

neighbor n il / la vicino -a m f

nephew n il nipote m **p115**

network n la rete f

new adj nuovo -a

newspaper n il giornale m

newsstand n l'edicola f **p37**

New Zealand n la Nuova Zelanda f

New Zealander adj neozelandese m f

next adj prossimo -a

  next to prep accanto a **p5**

  the next station la prossima stazione

nice adj simpatico -a

niece n la nipote f **p113**

night n la notte f **p13**

  at night di notte

  per night a notte

nightclub n il locale notturno m **p174**

nine adj nove **p7**

nineteen adj diciannove **p7**

ninety adj novanta **p7**

ninth adj nono -a **p9**

no adv no **p1**

noisy adj rumoroso -a

none pron nessuno **p10**

no smoking adj vietato fumare

  nonsmoking area la zona non-fumatori

  nonsmoking room la stanza per non-fumatori

noon n il mezzogiorno m

nose n il naso m **p190**

novel n il romanzo m

not adv non

nothing n il niente m

November n novembre m

now adv adesso **p4**

number n il numero m **p7**

  Which room number? Che numero di camera?

  May I have your phone number? Posso avere il suo numero di telefono?

nurse n l'infermiere -a m f

nurse, to nurse (breastfeed) v allattare **p20**

  Do you have a place where I can nurse? C'è un posto dove posso allattare?

nursery n l'asilo infantile m

  Do you have a nursery? Avete un asilo infantile?

nut n la noce f

O

o'clock adv in punto

  two o'clock le due in punto

October n ottobre m

of prep di

offer, to offer v offrire **p21**

officer n il poliziotto m

off-white adj bianco, sporco

oil n l'olio m

okay adv okay, va bene **p2**

old adj vecchio -a

olive n l'oliva f

on prep su, sopra

one adj uno -a **p7**

one way (traffic sign) n il senso unico m

open (business) adj aperto -a
  Are you open? Siete aperti?

opera n l'opera f p146

operator (phone) n il centralino m p135 il / la operatore -trice m f

optometrist n l'optometrista m

orange adj arancio

orange juice n il succo d'arancia m p88

order, to order (demand) v ordinare **(request)** v chiedere **p20**

organic adj organico -a, **(food)** biologico -a

Ouch! interj Ahi!

ours pron nostro -a, nostri -e

out adv fuori

outside adj esterno -a

over prep sopra, su

overcooked adj troppo cotto -a

overheat, to overheat v surriscaldare **p20**
  The car overheated. La macchina si è surriscaldata.

overflowing adj traboccante

oxygen tank n la bombola d'ossigeno f p64

P

package n il pacco m p141

pacifier n il ciuccio m

page, to page (someone) v far chiamare v **p28**

paint, to paint v dipingere **p20**

painting n il quadro m, la pittura f

pale adj pallido -a

paper n la carta f

parade n la parata f

parent n il genitore / la genitrice m f p115

park n il parco m

park, to park v parcheggiare **p20**

parking n il parcheggio m
  no parking sosta vietata
  parking fee la tariffa del parcheggio
  parking garage il garage parcheggio

partner n il / la compagno -a m f

party n il party m, la festa f
  political party il partito politico

pass, to pass v passare **p20**
  I'll pass. Io passo.

passenger n il / la passeggero -a m f

passport n il passaporto m
  I've lost my passport. Ho perso il mio passaporto.

password n la password f

past adj passato

past n il passato m
  (in space) prep dopo, oltre

pay, to pay v pagare **p20**

peanut n l'arachide f

pedestrian n il pedone m

pediatrician n il / la pediatra m f
  Can you recommend a pediatrician? Può consigliarmi un pediatra?

permit n il permesso m
Do we need a permit?
Abbiamo bisogno di un
permesso?
permit, to permit v permettere p20
petrol / gas n la benzina f
phone n il telefono m p135
Do you have a phone directory? Ha una guida telefonica?
May I have your phone number? Può darmi il suo numero di telefono?
Where can I find a public phone? Dove posso trovare un telefono pubblico?
phone operator il operatore m, la operatrice f
Do you sell prepaid phones? Vendete i telefonini prepagati?
phone call n la telefonata f
I need to make a collect phone call. Ho bisogno di fare una telefonata a carico del destinatario.
an international phone call una telefonata internazionale f
photocopy, to photocopy v fotocopiare p20
piano n il pianoforte m
pillow n il cuscino m p47
down pillow il cuscino di piuma m
pink adj rosa

pizza n la pizza f p92
place, to place v mettere p20
plastic n la plastica f
play n il gioco m
play, to play (a game) v giocare, **(an instrument)** v suonare p20
playground n il giardino di ricreazione m
Do you have a playground? Avete un giardino di ricreazione?
plaza n la piazza f
please (polite entreaty) interj per favore p1
please, to be pleasing to v accontentare p20
pleasure n il piacere m
It's a pleasure. E' un piacere.
plug (electrical) n la spina f
plug, to plug v inserire la spina p21
point, to point v indicare p20
Would you point me in the direction of ____? Può indicarmi la direzione per ____?
police n la polizia f p192
police station n la stazione di polizia f
pool n la piscina f **(game)** n il biliardo m
pop music n la musica pop f
popular adj popolare
port (beverage, harbor) n il porto m

ENGLISH–ITALIAN

porter n il facchino m il portiere **(concierge)** m
portion n la porzione f
portrait n il ritratto m
postcard n la cartolina f
post office n l'ufficio postale m
　Where is the post office?
　Dov'è l'ufficio postale?
poultry n il pollame m
prefer, to prefer v preferire p32 (like uscire)
pregnant adj incinta f
prepared adj preparato -a
prescription n la ricetta f
price n il prezzo m p149
print, to print v stampare p20
private berth / cabin n la cabina privata f
problem n il problema m
process, to process v elaborare p20
product n il prodotto m
professional adj professionale
program n il programma m
　May I have a program?
　Posso avere un programma?
Protestant adj protestante
publisher n l'editore m / l'editrice f
pull, to pull v tirare p20
pump n la pompa f
purple adj viola
purse n la borsetta f
push, to push v spingere p20
put, to put v mettere p20

Q
quarter n il quarto m
　one-quarter un quarto m
quick adj veloce
quiet adj tranquillo

R
rabbit n il coniglio m
radio n la radio f p51
　satellite radio la radio satellitare
rain, to rain v piovere p20
　Is it supposed to rain? E' prevista pioggia?
rainy adj piovoso -a p124
　It's rainy. Piove.
ramp n la rampa f p65
rare (meat) adj al sangue
rate (fee) n la tariffa f p52
　What's the rate per day?
　Qual è la tariffa giornaliera?
　What's the rate per week?
　Qual è la tariffa settimanale?
rate plan (cell phone) n il piano rateale m
rather adv preferibilmente
raven n il corvo m
read, to read v leggere p20
really adv davvero
receipt n la ricevuta f p133
receive, to receive v ricevere p20
recommend, to recommend v raccomandare, consigliare p20

red *adj* rosso -a

redhead *n* dai capelli rossi *m f*

reef *n* la scogliera *f* p169

refill, to refill (beverage) *v* riempire p21

refill (of prescription) la ripetizione di una ricetta

reggae *n* la musica reggae *f*

relative *n* il / la parente *m f*

remove, to remove *v* togliere p20

rent, to rent *v* noleggiare p20

I'd like to rent a car. Vorrei noleggiare un'auto.

repeat, to repeat *v* ripetere p20

Would you please repeat that? Può ripeterlo per favore?

reservation *n* la prenotazione *f* p66

I'd like to make a reservation for ___. Vorrei fare una prenotazione per ___. *See numbers,* p7.

restaurant *n* il ristorante *m*

Where can I find a good restaurant? Dove posso trovare un buon ristorante? *See restaurant types,* p80.

restroom *n* il bagno *m* p36

Do you have a public restroom / toilet ? C'è un bagno pubblico?

return, to return (to a place) *v* ritornare p20

return, to return (something to a store) *v* portare indietro p20

ride, to ride *v* viaggiare p20

right *adj* il / la destro -a p5

It is on the right. E' sulla destra.

Turn right at the corner. All'angolo, giri a destra.

rights *n* i diritti *m pl*

civil rights i diritti civili

river *n* il fiume *m*

road *n* la strada *f* p55

road closed sign *n* il segnale della strada bloccata *f*

rob, to rob *v* rubare p20

I've been robbed. Mi hanno derubato.

rock climbing *n* la scalata rocciosa *f*

rocks *n* le roccie *f*

I'd like it on the rocks. Lo gradirei con ghiaccio.

romance (novel) *n* il romanzo *m*

romantic *adj* romantico -a

room (hotel) *n* la camera, la stanza *f* p66

room for one / two la camera singola / doppia

room service il servizio in camera

rope *n* la fune *f*

rose *n* la rosa *f*

royal flush *n* il royal flush *m*

run, to run *v* correre p20

S

sad *adj* triste p120

safe (container) *n* la cassaforte *f* p75

  Do the rooms have safes?
C'è una cassaforte nelle camere?

safe (secure) *adj* sicuro -a

  Is this area safe? Questa zona è sicura?

sail *n* la vela *f* p168

sail, to sail *v* navigare a vela p20

  When do we sail? Quando salpiamo?

salad *n* l'insalata *f* p91

salesperson *n* il / la commesso -a *m f* p121

salt *n* il sale *m* p85

  Is that low-salt? Questo è con poco sale?

satellite *n* il satellite *m* p51

  satellite radio la radio satellitare

  satellite tracking il tracking satellitare

Saturday *n* il sabato *m* p14

sauce *n* il sugo *m* p93

say, to say *v* dire p28

scan, to scan *v* (with a scanner) scannerizzare p20

schedule *n* l'orario *m*

school *n* la scuola *f*

scooter *n* il motorino *m* p50

score *n* il punteggio *m*

Scottish *adj* scozzese

scratch *n* il graffio *m*

scratch, to scratch *v* graffiare p20

scratched *adj* graffiato -a

  scratched surface superficie scalfita

scuba dive, to scuba dive *v* immergersi con le bombole d'ossigeno p20, 35

sculpture *n* la scultura *f*

seafood *n* i frutti di mare *m pl*

search *n* la ricerca *f*

  hand search la perquisizione manuale

search, to search *v* cercare p20

seasick *adj* che soffre il mal di mare p62

  I am seasick. Ho mal di mare.

seasickness pill *n* la pillola antinausea *f*

seat *n* il sedile *m*, il posto *m*

  child seat il sedile per bambini

second *adj* secondo -a p9

security *n* la sicurezza *f*

  security checkpoint il punto di controllo di sicurezza

  security guard la guardia di sicurezza

sedan *n* la berlina *f* p50

see, to see *v* vedere p20

  May I see it? Posso vederlo?

self-serve *n* il self-service *m f*

sell, to sell *v* vendere p20

seltzer *n* la soda *f* p88

send, to send v spedire, mandare, inviare **p20, 21**

separated (marital status) adj separato -a **p116**

September n settembre m

serve, to serve v servire **p21**

service n il servizio m

out of service fuori servizio

services (religious) n le funzioni religiose f

service charge / cover n il coperto m

seven adj sette **p7**

seventy adj settanta **p7**

seventeen adj diciassette **p7**

seventh n adj il / la settimo -a **p9**

sew, to sew v cucire **p21**

sex n il sesso m

sex, to have (intercourse) v avere rapporti sessuali **p27**

shallow adj poco profondo -a

sheet (bed linen) n il lenzuolo m, le lenzuola f

(paper) n il foglio m

shellfish n i crostacei m pl

ship n la nave f **p62**

ship, to ship v spedire **p21**

How much to ship this to
_____? Quanto costa per
spedire questo a _____?

shipwreck n il naufragio m

shirt n la camicia f **p152**

shoe n la scarpa f **p152**

shop n il negozio m

shop, to shop v fare compere **p28**

I'm shopping for mens'
clothes. Sto cercando
abbigliamento da uomo.

I'm shopping for womens'
clothes. Sto cercando
abbigliamento da donna.

I'm shopping for childrens'
clothes. Sto cercando
abbigliamento per bambini.

short adj basso -a **p10**

shorts n i calzoncini corti m

shot (liquor) n il bicchierino m

shout, to shout v gridare **p20**

show (performance) n lo spettacolo m

What time is the show? A
che ora inizia lo spettacolo?

show, to show v mostrare **p20**

Would you show me? Può
mostrarmelo?

shower n la doccia f **p71**

Does it have a shower? C'è
una doccia?

shower, to shower v fare la doccia **p28**

shrimp n il gambero m

shuttle bus n l'autobus navetta m

sick adj malato -a **p48**

I feel sick. Mi sento male.

side n il lato m

on the side (separately) a parte

sidewalk n il marciapiede m

sightseeing n la gita turistica f

sightseeing bus n l'autobus per gite turistiche m

sign, to sign v firmare p20
  Where do I sign? Dove devo firmare?

silk n la seta f

silver n l'argento m

silver adj argento

sing, to sing v cantare p20

single (unmarried) adj single, celibe m, nubile f p116
  Are you single? E' single?

single (one) adj singolo -a

single bed il letto ad una piazza

sink n il lavabo m

sister n la sorella f p115

sit, to sit v sedersi p20, 35

six adj sei p7

sixteen adj sedici p7

sixty adj sessanta p7

size (clothing) n la taglia f
  (shoes) n il numero m

skin n la pelle f

sleeping berth n la cuccetta f

slow adj lento -a

slow, to slow v rallentare p20
  Slow down! Rallenti!

slowly adv lentamente
  Please speak more slowly. Per favore parli più lentamente.

slum n i bassifondi m pl

small adj piccolo -a p11

smell, to smell v puzzare p20

smoke, to smoke v fumare p20

smoking n il fumo m p37

smoking area la zona fumatori
  No Smoking Vietato fumare

snack n lo spuntino m

Snake eyes! n Occhi di serpe!

snorkel, to snorkel v fare snorkeling p28, 169

soap n il sapone m

sock n il calzino m p152

soda n il selz m p88
  diet soda la bibita light

soft adj morbido -a

software n il software m

sold out adj tutto esaurito

some adj qualche p10

someone n qualcuno -a m f

something n il qualcosa f

son n il figlio m p114

song n la canzone f

sorry adj pentito -a
  I'm sorry. Mi dispiace.

soup n la minestra f p93

spa n le terme f pl

Spain n la Spagna f

Spanish adj spagnolo -a

spare tire n la ruota di scorta f

speak, to speak v parlare p20
  Do you speak English? Parla inglese?
  Would you speak louder, please? Può parlare a voce più alta, per favore?
  Would you speak slower, please? Per favore, può parlare più lentamente?

special (featured meal) n la specialità del giorno f

specify, to specify v specificare **p20**

speed limit n il limite di velocità m **p56**

What's the speed limit?
Qual è il limite di velocità?

speedometer n il tachimetro m **p54**

spell, to spell v scrivere correttamente **p20**

How do you spell that?
Come si scrive quello?

spice n la spezia f

spill, to spill v rovesciare **p20**

split (gambling) n la divisione f

sport n lo sport m **p163**

spring (season) n la primavera f **p15**

stadium n lo stadio m **p163**

staff (personnel) n il personale m

stamp (postage) n il francobollo m

stair n la scala f

Where are the stairs? Dove sono le scale?

Are there many stairs? Ci sono molte scale?

stand, to stand v stare in piedi **p24, 25**

start, to start (commence) v iniziare, cominciare **p20**

start, to start (a car) v accendere **p20**

state n lo stato m

station n la stazione f **p58**

Where is the nearest gas station? Dov'è il distributore di benzina più vicino?

Where is the nearest bus station? Dov'è la stazione degli autobus più vicina?

Where is the nearest subway station? Dov'è la stazione della metropolitana più vicina?

Where is the nearest train station? Dov'è la stazione dei treni più vicina?

stay, to stay v restare **p20**

We'll be staying for ___ nights. Pernotteremo per ___ notti. *See numbers,* p7.

steakhouse n il ristorante specializzato in bistecche m

steal, to steal v rubare **p20**

stolen adj rubato -a **p49**

stop n la fermata f

Is this my stop? E' questa la mia fermata?

I missed my stop. Ho passato la mia fermata.

stop, to stop v fermare **p20**

Please stop. Per favore si fermi.

Stop, thief! Fermo, al ladro!

store n il negozio m

straight adj diritto -a **p5**

straight ahead avanti diritto

(drink) liscio **p88**

Go straight (directions). Vada diritto.

straight (gambling) n la scala f

street n la via f, la strada f

across the street dall'altra parte della strada

down the street giù per la strada

Which street? Quale strada?

How many more streets? Ancora quante strade?

stressed adj stressato -a

striped adj a strisce

stroller n il passeggino m

Do you rent baby strollers? Noleggiate passeggini per bambini?

substitution n la sostituzione f

suburb n la periferia f

subway / underground n la metropolitana f, il metrò m p63

subway line la linea della metropolitana

subway station la stazione della metropolitana

Which subway do I take for ____? Che linea del metrò devo prendere per ____?

subtitle n il sottotitolo m

suitcase n la valigia f p48

suite n la suite m p66

summer n l'estate f p15

sun n il sole m

sunburn n la scottatura solare f

I have a bad sunburn. Ho una brutta scottatura.

Sunday n la domenica f p15

sunglasses n gli occhiali da sole m pl

sunny adj soleggiato -a p124

It's sunny out. C'è il sole fuori.

sunroof n il tettuccio apribile m

sunscreen / sunblock n la crema solare protettiva f

Do you have sunscreen / sunblock SPF ____? Avete la crema solare protettiva fattore ____? See numbers, p7.

supermarket n il supermarket m p100

surf, to surf v fare il surf p28

surfboard n la tavola da surf f

suspiciously adv in modo sospetto

swallow, to swallow v inghiottire p21

sweater n la maglia f p152

swim, to swim v nuotare p20

Can one swim here? Si può nuotare qui?

swimsuit il costume da bagno

swim trunks i calzoncini da bagno

symphony n la sinfonia f

T

table n il tavolo m p82

table for two un tavolo per due

tailor n il sarto m

  Can you recommend a good tailor? Può consigliarmi un buon sarto?

take, to take v portare p20

  Take me to the station. Mi porti alla stazione.

  How much to take me to ____? Quanto costa per portarmi a ____?

takeout / takeaway menu n il menu da asporto m

talk, to talk v parlare p20

tall adj alto -a

tan adj marroncino

tanned adj abbronzato -a

taste (flavor) n il sapore m, il gusto m

taste (discernment) n il gusto m

taste, to taste v assaggiare p20

tax n la tassa f p155

  value-added tax (VAT) l'imposta sui valori aggiunti (IVA)

taxi n il taxi / il tassì m p57

  Taxi! Taxi!

  Would you call me a taxi? Mi chiama un taxi per favore?

tea n il tè m p88

team n la squadra f p163

techno n la musica techno f

television n la televisione f

temple n il tempio m p126

ten adj dieci p7

tennis n il tennis m p67

  tennis court il campo da tennis

tent n la tenda f p79

tenth n adj il / la decimo -a p9

terminal (airport) n il terminal m p36

Thank you. interj Grazie. p1

that adj quello -a, quelli -e pl

theater n il teatro m p144

their(s) pron di loro; il / la / i / le loro m f

them pron loro m f p19

there (demonstrative) adv là

  Is / Are there ____? C'è / Ci sono ____?

  It's there. E' là.

these adj questi -e m f p6

thick adj spesso -a

thin adj sottile

third adj terzo -a p9

thirteen adj tredici p7

thirty adj trenta p7

this adj questo -a p6

those adj quelli -e p6

thousand adj mille p7

three adj tre p7

Thursday n il giovedi m p14

ticket n il biglietto m p36

  ticket counter la biglietteria

  one-way ticket un biglietto di sola andata

  round-trip ticket un biglietto di andata e ritorno

tight adj stretto -a

time n il tempo m, l'ora f

  Is it on time? E' in orario?

  At what time? A che ora?

  What time is it? Che ora è?

timetable (train) n l'orario m

tip (gratuity) n la mancia f

tire *n* la gomma *f* p54
I have a flat tire. Ho una gomma a terra.
tired *adj* stanco -a p120
to *prep* a, per
today *adv* oggi p4
toilet *n* il gabinetto *m*, la toiletta *f*
The toilet is overflowing. Il gabinetto trabocca.
The toilet is backed up. Il gabinetto è intasato.
toilet paper *n* la carta igienica *f*
You're out of toilet paper. E' finita la carta igienica.
toiletries *n* articoli da toletta *m pl*
toll *n* il pedaggio *m*
tomorrow *adv* domani p4
ton *n* la tonnellata *f*
too (excessively) *adv* troppo
too (also) *adv* anche
tooth *n* il dente *m* p192
I lost my tooth. Ho perso un dente.
toothache *n* il mal di denti *m*
I have a toothache. Ho il mal di denti.
total *n* il totale *m*
What is the total? Qual è il totale?
tour *n* la gita *f* p148
Are guided tours available? Ci sono gite guidate?
Are audio tours available? Ci sono gite con audio-guida?

towel *n* l'asciugamano *m*
May we have more towels? Possiamo avere altri asciugamani?
toy *n* il giocattolo *m*
toy store il negozio di giocattoli
Do you have any toys for the children? Avete dei giocattoli per i bambini?
traffic *n* il traffico *m*
How's traffic? Com'è il traffico?
Traffic is terrible. Il traffico è orribile.
traffic rules le regole del traffico *f*
trail *n* il sentiero *m* p165
Are there trails? Ci sono dei sentieri?
train *n* il treno *m* p58
express train l'espresso
local train il locale
Does the train go to _____? Questo treno va a _____?
May I have a train schedule? Posso avere un orario del treno?
Where is the train station? Dov'è la stazione dei treni?
train, to train *v* addestrare p20
transfer, to transfer *v* trasferire p32 (like uscire)
I need to transfer funds. Devo trasferire del denaro.

transmission n il cambio m
  automatic transmission il cambio automatico
  standard transmission il cambio manuale
travel, to travel v viaggiare **p20**
traveler's check n il traveller's cheque m **p132**
  Do you cash travelers' checks? Cambiate i traveller's cheque?
trim, to trim (hair) v spuntare **p20**
trip n il viaggio m **p62**
triple adj triplo -a
trumpet n la tromba f
trunk / boot (car) n il bagagliaio m **p54**
try, to try (attempt) v cercare di **(clothing)** v provare **(food)** v assaggiare **p20**
Tuesday n il martedì m **p15**
turkey n il tacchino m
turn, to turn v girare **p20**
  to turn left / right girare a sinistra / destra **p20**
  to turn off / on spegnere / accendere **p20**
twelve adj dodici **p7**
twenty adj venti **p7**
twine n lo spago m
two adj due **p7**

U
umbrella n l'ombrello m
uncle n lo zio m **p115**
under prep sotto **p5**

undercooked adj crudo -a
understand, to understand v capire **p32** (like uscire)
  I don't understand. Non capisco.
  Do you understand? Capisce? / Capite?
underwear n la biancheria intima f
university n l'università f
up adv su, sopra **p5**
update, to update v aggiornare **p20**
upgrade n la categoria superiore f **p52**
upload, to upload v caricare **p20**
upscale adj di lusso
us pron noi **p3**
USB port n la porta USB f
use, to use v usare **p20**

V
vacation n la vacanza f **p44**
  on vacation in vacanza
  to go on vacation andare in ferie **p27**
vacancy n la disponibilità f
van n il furgoncino m **p50**
VCR n il videoregistratore m
  Do the rooms have VCRs? C'è il videoregistratore nelle camere?
vegetable n la verdura f **p106**
vegetarian adj vegetariano -a
vending machine n il distributore automatico m

version n la versione f

very adj molto -a

video n il video m

Where can I rent videos or DVDs? Dove posso noleggiare video o DVD?

view n la vista f p69

beach view la vista della spiaggia

city view la vista della città

vineyard n il vigneto f

vinyl n il vinile m

violin n il violino m

visa n il visto m

Do I need a visa? Ho bisogno del visto?

vision n la visione f

visit, to visit v visitare p20

visually impaired n l'ipovedente m

vodka n la vodka f p88

voucher n il buono m

W

wait, to wait v attendere p20

Please wait. Per favore attenda.

wait n attesa f

How long is the wait? Quanto è lunga l'attesa?

waiter n il / la cameriere -a m f

waiting area n la sala d'aspetto m p36

wake-up call n la chiamata sveglia f p75

wallet n il portafogli m p46

I lost my wallet. Ho perso il mio portafogli.

Someone stole my wallet. Mi hanno rubato il portafogli.

walk, to walk v camminare p20

walker (device) n il girello m

walkway n il passaggio pedonale m

moving walkway la passerella mobile

want, to want v volere p31

war n la guerra f p125

warm adj caldo -a p124

watch, to watch v guardare p20

water n l'acqua f p46

Is the water potable? L'acqua è potabile?

Is there running water? C'è l'acqua corrente?

wave, to wave v salutare con la mano p20

waxing n la depilazione con ceretta f p159

weapon n l'arma f

wear, to wear v indossare p20

weather forecast n le previsioni del tempo f pl

Wednesday n il mercoledì m

week n la settimana f p14

this week questa settimana

last week la settimana scorsa

next week la settimana prossima

ENGLISH—ITALIAN

last week la settimana scorsa

weigh, to weigh *v* pesare p20

I weigh ____ kilos. Peso ____ chili.

It weighs ____. Pesa ____ *See p7 for numbers.*

weights *n* i pesi *m pl*

welcome *adv* benvenuto -a

You're welcome. Prego.

well *adv* bene

well done (meat) ben cotto -a

well done (task) ben fatto -a

I don't feel well. Non mi sento bene.

western *adj* il western

whale *n* la balena *f*

what *adv* che p3

What sort of ____? Che tipo di ____?

What time is ____? Che ora è ____? p7

wheelchair *n* la sedia a rotelle *f* p65

wheelchair access l'accesso alle sedie a rotelle

wheelchair ramp la rampa delle sedie a rotelle

power wheelchair la sedia a rotelle motorizzata

when *adv* quando *See p3 for questions.*

where *adv* dove p3

Where is it? Dov'è? / Dove si trova? *See p3 for questions.*

which *adv* quale p3

Which one? Quale? *See p3 for questions.*

white *adj* bianco -a

who *adv* chi p3

whose *adj* di chi

wide *adj* largo -a

widow, widower *n* la / il vedova -o *m f* p116

wife *n* la moglie *f* p114

wi-fi *n* il wi-fi *m* p139

window *n* la finestra *f*

drop-off window il finestrino di consegna

pick-up window il finestrino di raccolta

windshield / windscreen *n* il parabrezza *m* p54

windshield wiper *n* il tergi-cristallo *m* p54

windsurf, to windsurf *v* fare il windsurf p28

windy *adj* ventoso -a p124

wine *n* il vino *m* p88

winter *n* l'inverno *m* p15

wiper *n* il tergicristallo *m*

with *prep* con

withdraw, to withdraw *v* riti-rare p20

I need to withdraw money. Ho bisogno di prelevare dei soldi.

without *prep* senza

woman *n* la donna *f*

work, to work *v* lavorare p20

This doesn't work. Questo non funziona.

workout *n* l'esercizio fisico *m*
worse *adj* peggiore
worst *adj* il peggiore
write, to write *v* scrivere **p20**
> **Would you write that down for me?** Me lo può scrivere per favore?
writer *n* lo scrittore *m,* la scrittrice *f* **p121**

X
x-ray machine *n* l'apparecchiatura per i raggi X *f*

Y
yellow *adj* giallo -a
yes *interj* sì **p1**
yesterday *adv* ieri **p4**
> **the day before yesterday** ieri l'altro
yield sign *n* il segnale di precedenza *m* **p56**
you (sing. informal) tu **p19**
> **you (sing. formal)** Lei
> **you (pl informal)** voi
> **you (pl formal)** Loro, Voi
your(s) (informal) *pron* tuo -a *m f,* tuoi *m pl,* tue *f pl*
> **your(s) (pl informal)** *pron* vostro -a *m f,* vostri -e *m f pl*
> **yours (formal)** *pron* di lei; suo -a *m f,* suoi *m pl,* sue *f pl*
> **yours (pl formal)** *pron* di loro; il / la loro *m f*
young *adj* giovane

Z
zoo *n* lo zoo *m* **p130**

A

l'abbigliamento m clothes n (general attire) p152

abbinare v to match p20

abbronzato -a tanned adj

abitare v to live p20

Dove abita? Where do you live?

Abito con il / la mio ragazzo -a. I live with my boyfriend / girlfriend.

accendere v to start (a car), to turn on p20

Posso offrirle da accendere? May I offer you a light?

l'accendino m light, lighter n (cigarette)

l'accesso ai disabili m disabled access n

accettare v to accept p20

Si accettano carte di credito. Credit cards are accepted.

accettato -a accepted adj

l'accettazione f check-in n

l'acconciatura afro f afro n

accontentare v to please, to be pleasing to p20

l'acne f acne n p187

l'acqua f water n p142

l'acqua calda hot water
l'acqua fredda cold water

acquistare v to buy p20

addestrare v to train p20

adesso now adv p152

l'aeroporto m airport n p36

l'affare m business, deal, bargain n

Fatti gli affari tuoi. Mind your own business.

affittare v to rent p20

Desidero affittare ____. I'd like to rent ____. See p161 for sporting equipment.

affollato -a crowded, busy adj (restaurant)

l'afroamericano -a African American adj

l'agenzia f agency n

aggiornare v to update p20

l'aglio m garlic n

agnostico -a m f agnostic n

agosto m August n p15

Ahi! Ouch! interj

l'aiuto m help n

Aiuto! m Help! n

aiutare v to help p20

l'alba f dawn n p13

all'alba at dawn

albergo m hotel n p66

l'alcol m alcohol n p88

allattare v to nurse (breast-feed) p20

l'allergia f allergy n

allergico -a allergic adj p191

l'alluminio m aluminum n

l'altitudine f altitude n

alto -a tall, high adj, loudly adv

più alto -a higher, taller
il / la più alto -a the highest, tallest

altro -a (an)other adj

alzare v to lift, raise, turn up (sound) p20

amare *v to love* **p20**
l'ambasciata *f embassy n*
l'ambiente *m environment n*
l'ambulanza *f ambulance n*
l'americano -a *American adj n*
l'amico -a *m f friend n*
ammaccare *v to dent* **p20**
l'ammaccatura *f dent n*
l'amore *m love n*
l'anatra *f duck n*
anche *too, also adv*
andare *v to go* **p27**

> andare fuori al club *to go clubbing* **p174**
> andare bene *to fit*

l'angolo *m corner n*

> all'angolo *on the corner*

l'animale *m animal n*
annebbiato -a *blurry adj*
anni *m pl years n (age)*

> Quanti anni hai? *What's your age?*

l'antibiotico *m antibiotic n*
l'anticipo *m advance n*

> in anticipo *in advance*

anticoncezionale *birth control adj* **p191**

> Non ho più pillole anticoncezionali. *I'm out of birth control pills.*

l'antistaminico *m antihistamine n* **p187**
l'ape *f bee n*
aperto -a *open adj*
l'appartamento in un albergo *m suite n* **p67**

l'appartenenza ad un'associazione *f membership n*
approvare *v approve* **p20**

> La sua carta di credito non è stata approvata. *Your credit card has been declined.*

l'appuntamento *m appointment n* **p148**
aprile *m April n* **p15**
l'arancia *m orange n (fruit)*
arancione *orange adj (color)*
l'area di campeggio *f campsite n* **p79**
l'argento *m silver n*
argento *silver adj (color)*
l'aria *f air n*
l'aria condizionata *f air conditioning n* **p68**
l'arma *f weapon n*
l'armadietto *m locker n* **p162**

> l'armadietto della palestra *gym locker*
> l'armadietto di deposito *storage locker*

arrivare *v to arrive* **p20**
Arrivederci. *See you later. interj*
l'arrivo *m, gli arrivi m pl arrival n, arrivals n pl* **p39**
l'arte *f art n*

> le belle arti *fine arts*
> il museo d'arte *art museum*
> la mostra d'arte *art exhibit*

articoli da toelette *m pl toiletries n*
l'artista *m f artist n*
l'ascensore *m elevator, lift n*

l'asciugacapelli m hair dryer n

l'asciugamano m towel n

asciugare v to dry p20

asciutto -a dry, dried adj

l'asiatico -a Asian adj n

l'asilo infantile m nursery n

l'asino m donkey n

l'asma f asthma n p191

aspettare v to wait, hold p20

l'aspirina f aspirin n p187

assaggiare v to try (food), to taste p20

l'asse f board n

l'assegno m check n p132

l'assicurazione f insurance n

  l'assicurazione sugli scontri collision insurance

  assicurazione sulla responsabilità liability insurance

l'assistenza f assistance n

l'assistenza telefonica f directory assistance n (phone)

assistere v to attend, to assist p20

l'ateo -a atheist adj n

attendere v to wait p20

  Attenda, per favore. Please wait.

atterrare v to land p20

l'attesa f wait n

l'attico m penthouse n

attraverso across prep p5

l'audio m audio adj n p65

  Per favore alza l'audio. Please turn up the audio.

Auguri! Best wishes! interj

l'auricolare m headphones n

l'australiano -a Australian adj n

l'autista m driver n

l'auto f car n p50

  l'autonoleggio car rental agency p50

l'autobus m bus n p60

  la fermata degli autobus bus stop

  l'autobus navetta shuttle bus

  l'autobus per gite turistiche sightseeing bus n

l'automobile f car n p50

l'autunno m autumn n p15

l'autostrada f highway n

avanzato -a forward adj p6

avere v to have p27

  avere rapporti sessuali to have sex

  avere fretta to hurry

l'avvocato -essa m f lawyer n p121

azzurro -a light blue adj

B

il / la baby-sitter m f babysitter n

il bacio m kiss n p180

il bagaglio m, **i bagagli** m pl luggage, baggage n p48

  i bagagli smarriti lost baggage

  il recupero bagagli baggage claim

il bagno m bath, bathroom, restroom n p36

i bagni donne *women's restrooms*

i bagni uomini *men's restrooms*

il balcone *m balcony n*

ballare *v to dance* **p20**

il ballo *m dance n* **p178**

il ballo da sala *m ballroom dancing n*

i bambini *pl children n pl*

cibo per bambini *baby food*

passeggini per bambini *baby strollers*

il / la bambino -a *m f baby, child n* **p116**

la banca *f bank n* **p133**

bancario -a *bank adj*

il conto bancario *bank account*

la tessera bancaria *bank card*

il banco *m counter n* (bar)

il bancomat *m ATM / cash machine n* **p135**

la banconota *f bill n* (currency) **p132**

la banda larga *f broadband n*

il bar *m bar, café n*

il barattolo *m tin can n*

il barbiere *m barber n* **p158**

la barca *f boat n*

basso -a *short, low adj* **p10**

più basso -a *lower*

il / la più basso -a *lowest*

il basso *m bass n* (instrument)

i bassifondi *m pl slum n*

bello -a *beautiful, handsome adj* **p116**

bene *fine, well adv* **p2**

Sto bene. *I'm fine.*

Benvenuto. *Welcome. interj*

Benvenuti in Italia. *Welcome to Italy.*

la benzina *f gasoline, petrol n*

indicatore di benzina *gas gauge* **p54**

La benzina è finita. *It's out of gas.*

Dov'è il distributore di benzina più vicino? *Where is the nearest gas station?*

bere *v to drink* **p29**

la berlina *f sedan n* **p50**

la bevanda *f drink n* **p88**

bevanda offerta dalla casa *complimentary drink*

Desidero una bevanda. *I'd like a drink.*

la bevanda alcolica *f alcoholic drink n* **p88**

la biancheria intima *f underwear n*

bianco -a *white adj*

bianco sporco *off-white adj*

il biberon *m feeding bottle n*

la bibita analcolica *f soda, soft drink n* **p88**

la bibita dietetica *f diet soda*

la biblioteca *f library n*

il bicchiere *m glass n*

Lo servite a bicchiere? *Do you have it by the glass?*

Vorrei un bicchiere per favore. *I'd like a glass please.*

un bicchierino *m shot n*
(liquor)

bighellonare *v to lounge* **p20**

la biglietteria *f ticket
counter, box office n*

il biglietto *m ticket n* **p36**

  un biglietto di sola andata
one-way ticket

  **un biglietto di andata e
ritorno** *round-trip ticket*

  il biglietto da visita *business
card*

bilanciare *v to balance* **p20**

bilanciato -a *balanced adj*

il bilancio *m budget n*

il biliardo *m pool n* (game)

bilingue *bilingual adj*

il / la biondo -a *blond(e) adj n*

la birra *f beer n* **p88**

  birra alla spina *draft beer*

birazziale *biracial adj*

il biscotto *m cookie, biscuit n*

bisognare *v to need* **p20**

  Ho bisogno di ____. *I need
(to) ____.*

bloccare *v to block* **p20**

il blocco *m block n*

la bocca *f mouth n* **p118**

la bomba *f bomb n*

la bomba d'ossigeno *f oxygen tank n* **p64**

il bordo della strada *m curb n*

  a bordo *on board*

la borsa *f bag n*

la borsa portadocumenti *f
briefcase n* **p49**

la borsetta *f purse, handbag
n*

il botteghino *m box office n*

la bottiglia *f bottle n*

il box *m garage n*

il braccio *m arm n* **p190**

il Braille *m Braille n*

brillante *bright adj*

il brillante *m diamond n*

bronzo *bronze adj*

bruciacchiato -a *charred
(food) adj*

bruciare *v to burn* **p20**

bruno -a *brown adj*

  la bruna *f brunette n*

il / la brutto -a *m f ugly n*

il bucato *m laundry n*

il / la buddista *Buddhist adj n*

il buffet *m buffet n* **p80**

buio -a *dark adj*

  il buio *m dark n*

buono -a *good, fine adj*

  buon giorno *good morning*

  buon pomeriggio *good
afternoon*

  buona sera *good evening*

  buona notte *good night*

  il buono *m voucher n*

  il buono per i pasti *meal
voucher*

  il buono per la camera
room voucher

il burro *m butter n*

la busta *f envelope n*

C

la cabina privata f private berth, cabin n

cadere v to fall **p20**

il caffè m café, coffee n **p88**

il caffè freddo iced coffee

caldo -a warm, hot adj **p124**

il calzino m sock n **p152**

i calzoncini corti m pl shorts n

i calzoncini da bagno m swim trunks n

cambiare v to change **p20**

cambiarsi v to change clothes **p35**

il cambio m change n

il cambio della valuta m exchange rate n

il cambio di moneta m money exchange n

il cambio di velocità f transmission n

il cambio di velocità automatico automatic transmission

il cambio di velocità manuale standard transmission

il cambiavalute m currency exchange n **p132**

la camera d'albergo f hotel room n **p66**

il cameriere m waiter n

la cameriera f waitress, maid n

il camerino m changing room n

la camicetta f blouse n **p152**

la camicia f shirt n **p152**

camminare v to walk **p20**

il cammino m walk, path n

campeggiare v to camp, to go camping **p20**

il camper m camper n

il campo m field n (sport)

canadese Canadian adj n

cancellare v to cancel **p20**

la candeggina f bleach n

il cane m dog n

il cane guida service dog **p65**

la canna da pesca f fishing pole n **p168**

il canovaccio m dish towel n

cantare v to sing **p20**

la canzone f song n

i capelli m pl hair n **p158**

dai capelli rossi redhead adj

capire v to understand **p32**

Non capisco. I don't understand.

Capite? Do you understand?

il capo m boss n

il cappello m hat n

il cappotto m coat n

la capra f goat n

il carabiniere m policeman n

caricare v to charge (a battery), to load **p20**

a carico del destinatario collect adj

la carie f tooth cavity n **p192**

la carne f meat n **p95**

caro -a dear, expensive adj

la carta f paper, card n **p123**

la carta igienica f toilet paper

il piatto di carta paper plate

il tovagliolo di carta *paper napkin*

Avete un mazzo di carte? *Do you have a deck of cards?*

la carta di credito *credit card*

Si accettano carte di credito. *Credit cards accepted.*

la carta d'imbarco *f boarding pass* p46

la cartina geografica *f map n*

la carta geografica di bordo *onboard map*

la cartolina *f postcard n*

la casa *f home, house n*

a casa mia *at / in my home*

la casa editrice *publishing house*

la casalinga *f homemaker n*

il casinò *m casino n* p184

la cassaforte *f safe n* (container) p75

il / la cattolico -a *Catholic adj n*

il cavallo *m horse n*

il CD *m CD n* p139

celebrare *v to celebrate* p20

la cena *f dinner, supper n*

il centimetro *m centimeter n*

cento *m hundred n* p7

il centralista *m f operator n* (phone) p135

il centro *m center n*

in centro *m downtown*

il centro benessere *fitness center* p66, 161

il centro commerciale *mall*

il centro affari *m business center*

cercare *v to look for, to attempt* p20

la ceretta *f waxing n* p150

che *what interj* p3

Che tipo di ____? *What sort of ____?*

chi *who pron* p3

di chi *whose* p3

chiamare *v to call, to shout* p20

chiamare all'altoparlante *v to page* (someone) p20

la chiamata sveglia *f waiting call n*

la chiamata a carico del destinatario *collect phone call*

chiarire *v to clear* p21

chiaro -a *clear adj*

la chiave *f key n*

chiedere *v to order* (request), *to ask for* p20

chiedere scusa *v to make up* (apologize) p20

la chiesa *f church n* p126

il chilo *m kilo n*

il chilometro *m kilometer n*

il / la chiropratico *m f chiropractor n*

la chitarra *f guitar n*

chiudere *v to close* p20

chiudere a chiave *v to lock* p20

chiuso -a *closed adj*

il cibo *m* food *n* p91

il cibo in scatola *m* canned goods *n*

cieco -a *blind* adj p65

le ciglia *f* eyelashes *n*

il cigno *m* swan *n*

il cinema *m* cinema *n* p144

il / la cinese *Chinese* adj *n*

cinquanta *fifty* adj p7

cinque *five* adj p7

la cinta *f* belt *n* p152

la cioccolata calda *f* hot chocolate *n* p88

la città *f* city *n* p69

   in città *downtown*

il ciuccio *m* pacifier *n*

il clarinetto *m* clarinet *n*

la classe *f* class *n* p41

   la classe business *business class*

   la classe economica *economy class*

   la prima classe *first class*

il climatizzatore *m* air conditioning *n*

la colazione *f* breakfast *n*

   la prima colazione *f* breakfast *n*

il collegamento elettrico *m* electrical hookup *n* p79

colorare *v* to color p20

il colore *m* color *n*

il Colosseo *m* Coliseum *n*

il colpo di sole ai capelli *m* highlights *n* (hair) p158

come *how* adv p3

cominciare *v* to begin p20

commerciale *business* adj

il / la commesso -a *m f* salesperson *n*

il / la compagno -a *m f* partner *n*

comportarsi *v* to behave p35

comprare *v* to buy p20

compreso -a *included* adj

comune *common* adj

con *with* prep

il concerto *m* concert *n* p130

il condimento *m* salad dressing *n*

la condizione *f* condition *n*

   in buone / cattive condizioni *in good / bad condition*

la conferma *f* confirmation *n*

confermare *v* to confirm p20

confuso -a *confused* adj

il congestionamento *m* congestion *n* (sinus) p186

congestionato -a *congested* adj p186

il coniglio *m* rabbit *n*

conoscere *v* to know (someone) p20

il contachilometri *m* odometer *n* p54

i contanti *m pl* cash *n* p132

   l'acconto in contanti *cash advance*

   solo contanti *cash only*

il contatto d'emergenza *m* emergency contact *n*

contentissimo -a *delighted* adj

continuare *v* to continue p20

il conto *m account* n p135

il contraccettivo *m contraceptive* n p191

la contraccezione *f birth control* n p191

la coperta *f blanket* n p47

il coperto *m service charge, cover charge* n p175

coprire *v to cover* p21

il corno *m horn* n

la corona dentale *f dental crown* n p192

correggere *v to correct* p20

la corrente *f water current* n

correre *v to run, to jog* p20

corretto -a *correct* adj

il corridoio *m hallway* n

la corsia *f aisle* n (in store)

cortese *courteous* adj p78

  per cortesia *please*

cosa *what* n p3

  Cosa c'è? *What's up?*

costare *v to cost* p20

costoso -a *expensive* adj

il costume *m costume* n

  il costume da bagno *swimsuit*

il cotone *m cotton* n

la crema *f cream* n

  la crema solare protettiva *sunscreen*

crescere *v to grow, to get larger* p32

  Dove sei cresciuto -a? *Where did you grow up?*

il crostaceo *m shellfish* n

la cuccetta *f berth* n

la cucina *f kitchen* n p73

cucinare *v to cook* p20

  cotto -a *cooked* adj

  non abbastanza cotto -a *undercooked* adj

il cucinino *m kitchenette* n

cucire *v to sew* p21

il / la cugino -a *m f cousin* n

la culla *f crib* n p70

il cuoio *m leather* n

il cuore *m heart* n

il cuscino *m pillow* n p47

  il cuscino di piume *down pillow*

D

danneggiato -a *damaged* adj

Dannazione! *Damn!* expletive

danno *m damage* n

dare *v to give* p28

  Dia le carte anche a me. *Deal me in.*

il datore di lavoro *m employer* n

davanti *front* adj p4

  la porta d'ingresso *front door*

davvero *really* adv

il dazio *m duty, toll* n

  esente da dazio *duty-free*

decimo -a *tenth* adj p7

del *m /* **della** *f /* **dei** *m pl /* **delle** *f pl any* adj

il delfino *m dolphin* n

la democrazia *f democracy* n

il denaro *m money* n p132

  il denaro liquido *cash*

il dente m tooth n p192

la dentiera f denture n p192

la piastra dentale denture plate

il / la dentista m f dentist n p192

desiderare v to wish **p20**

la destinazione f destination n

la destra f right-hand side n

È sulla destra. It's on the right.

All'angolo, girare a destra. Turn right at the corner.

diabetico -a diabetic adj p84

la diarrea f diarrhea n p186

Al diavolo! Damn! expletive

dicembre m December n p15

dichiarare v to declare **p20**

diciannove nineteen adj p7

diciassette seventeen adj p7

diciotto eighteen adj p7

dieci ten adj p7

dietro -a behind prep adv p5

difficile difficult adj

il / la dipendente m f employee n

dipingere v to paint **p20**

dire v to say **p32**

i diritti m pl rights n

i diritti civili civil rights

diritto -a straight adj adv p5

proprio diritto straight ahead

Andare diritto. Go straight. (giving directions)

il / la disabile m f disabled n

il / la disegnatore -trice m f designer n

il disegno m drawing n (art)

disponibile available adj

la disponibilità f vacancy n

distante distant adj

più distante farther

il / la più distante farthest

il distributore automatico m vending machine n

il divieto m prohibition n

Divieto di balneazione No swimming

divorziato -a divorced adj

la doccia f shower n p71

il documento di riconoscimento m identification n

dodici twelve adj p7

la Dogana f Customs n

il dolce m dessert n p98

la lista dei dolci dessert menu

il dollaro m dollar n p132

la domanda f question n

fare una domanda to ask a question **p28**

domandare v to ask (a question) **p20**

il domani m tomorrow n p4

la domenica f Sunday n p15

la donna f woman n

dopo f after, later adv, prep

dopodomani the day after tomorrow adv

doppio -a double adj

il / la dottore -essa m f doctor n p191

dove where adv p5

Dov'è? / Dove si trova? Where is it?

dovunque anywhere adv

la dozzina f dozen n

il dramma *m drama n*
due *two adj* p7
durare *v to last* p20
duro -a *hard adj*
il DVD *m DVD n* p157

E

è *v is v. See* **essere** p24, 26
ebreo -a *Jewish, Hebrew adj n*
Eccellente! *Great! adj*
l'economia *f economy n*
economico -a *inexpensive adj*
l'educatore *m /* **l'educatrice** *f educator n* p116
elaborare *v to process* (documents) p20
l'elefante *m elephant n*
l'elezione *f election n* p125
l'emergenza *f emergency n*
entrare *v to enter* p20
> **Proibito entrare.** *Do not enter.*
l'entrata *f entrance n*
entusiastico -a *enthusiastic adj*
l'erbetta *f herb n*
l'errore *m mistake n*
esaurito -a *sold out adj*
> **Tutto esaurito** *No vacancy*
l'esca *f bait n* p168
l'esercizio fisico *m workout n*
espresso -a *express adj*
essere *v to be* (permanent quality) p24, 26
> **C'è / Ci sono ____?** *Is / Are there ____?*
l'estate *f summer n* p15

l'esterno *m outside n*
l'età *f age n* p116
l'ettaro *m hectare n* p10
l'etto *m a hundred grams n*
extra / in più *extra* (additional) *adj*

F

il facchino / **il portiere** *m porter / concierge n*
la famiglia *f family n* p114
fare *v to make, to do* p28
> **fare un'escursione a piedi** *to hike* p165
> **Faccio un'escursione a piedi.** *I'm going on a hike.*
> **fare il bagno** *to bathe*
> **fare il numero** *to dial* (phone) p135
> **fare il numero diretto** *dial direct* p135
> **fare il surf** *to surf* p170
> **fare le carte** *to deal* (cards)
> **fare la doccia** *to shower*
> **fare le spese** *to shop*
> **fare l'immersione subacquea** *to snorkel* p169
> **fare bene** *to do good*
> **fare male** *to hurt*
> **Ahi! Questo fa male!** *Ouch! That hurts!*
il farmaco *m medication n*
il faro della macchina *m headlight n* p54
fatto -a di *made of adj*
febbraio *m February n* p15
felice *m f happy adj* p120

femminile *f female adj*

la ferita *f wound, cut n* p188

fermare *v to stop* p20

> **Per favore si fermi.** *Please stop.*

> **Ferma, ladro!** *Stop, thief!*

la fermata *f stop n*

> **la fermata del bus** *bus stop*

la festa *f feast, holiday n*

il fiammifero *m match n* (stick)

il / la fidanzato -a *m f boyfriend / girlfriend n fiancé / fiancée n* p115

il figlio *m son n* 114

la figlia *f daughter n* p114

il filo *m thread, wire n*

la finestra *f window n*

> **il finestrino di consegna** *pickup window*

fino -a *fine adj*

il fiore *m flower n*

firmare *v to sign* p20

> **Firmi qui.** *Sign here.*

il fiume *m river n*

il flauto *m flute n*

il formaggio *m cheese n*

il formato *m format n*

la formula *f formula n*

fotocopiare *v to photocopy* p20

fragile *fragile adj*

il / la francese *French adj n*

il francobollo *m stamp n* (postage)

il fratello *m brother n* p113

la freccia *f turn signal n* (car)

il freddo *m cold n* p186

frenare *v to brake* p20

il freno *m brake n* p54

fresco -a *fresh adj* p190

la fronte *f forehead n* p118

il frullato *m milk shake n*

la frutta *f fruit n* (collective)

i frutti di mare *m pl seafood n*

il frutto *m fruit n* p104

fumare *v to smoke* p20

la fune *f rope n*

funzionare *v to function, to work* p20

le funzioni religiose *f pl religious services n* p126

il fuoco *m fire n*

> **Al fuoco!** *m Fire! interj*

il furgoncino *m van n* p50

G

il gabbiano *m gull n*

il gabinetto *m toilet n*

la gamba *f leg n* p190

il gambero *m shrimp n*

il / la gatto -a *m f cat n*

il / la genitore *m f parent n* p115

gennaio *m January n* p14

il ghiaccio *m ice n*

> **la macchina per il ghiaccio** *ice machine*

la giacca *f jacket n* p152

giallo -a *yellow adj*

> **il giallo** *m mystery novel n*

il / la giapponese *Japanese adj n*

il giardino di ricreazione m
   playground n

il / la ginecologo -a m f gynecologist n p190

giocare v to play (a game)
   p20

giocare a golf to go golfing

il giocattolo m toy n

   il negozio di giocattoli toy
   store

il gioco m play n

il giornalaio m newsstand n

il giornale m newspaper n

il giorno m day n p161

   questi ultimi giorni these
   last few days

giovane young adj

il giovedì m Thursday n p15

girare v to turn p20

   girare a sinistra / destra to
   turn left / right

il girello m walker n (ambula-
   tory device)

il giro turistico m sightseeing n

la gita f tour n p148

   la gita guidata guided tour

giù down, downward adv

giugno m June n p15

giusto -a correct adj

il golf m golf n p172

   il campo da golf golf course

la gomma f rubber n (material), eraser, tire n (wheel)

   Ho una gomma a terra. I
   have a flat tire.

graffiare v to scratch p20

graffiato -a scratched adj

il graffio m scratch n

il grammo m gram n

grande big adj p11

   più grande bigger

   il / la più grande biggest

il grasso m, grasso -a fat adj n

Grazie. Thank you. interj p1

il / la greco -a Greek adj n

gridare v to shout p20

grigio -a gray adj

la gruccia f clothes hanger n

il gruppo m band n (musical
   ensemble), group n

il guanto m glove n

guardare v to look, watch
   p20

   Guarda qui! Look here!

la guardia f guard n p37

   la guardia di sicurezza security guard

la guerra f war n p125

la guida f guide (publication), tour guide n

guidare v to drive, guide p20

il gusto m taste n (discernment)

H

la hostess f flight attendant n

I

ieri m yesterday n adv

   ieri l'altro the day before
   yesterday

imbarazzato -a *embarrassed adj*

l'imbarcazione *f boat n* p62

immergersi con l'apparecchiatura subacquea *v to scuba dive* **p35**

importante *important adj*

> **Non è importante.** *It's no big deal.*

l'imposta *f tax n*

> **l'imposta sui valori aggiunti (IVA)** *value-added tax (VAT)*

incassare *v to cash, to collect (money)* **p20**

> **incassare la vincita** *to cash out (gambling)*

incendiare *v to burn* **p20**

l'incidente *m accident n*

incinta *pregnant adj*

incominciare *v to start, to begin* **p20**

l'incrinatura *f crack n* (glass)

indicare *v to point* **p20**

l'indigestione *m indigestion n*

l'indirizzo *m address n* p124

> **Qual'è l'indirizzo?** *What's the address?*

indossare *v to wear* **p20**

l'indù *Hindu adj n*

l'infarto *m heart attack n*

l'infermiere -a *m f nurse n*

l'informazione *f information n*

> **il chiosco delle informazioni** *information booth*

l'ingegnere *m engineer n*

inghiottire *v to swallow* **p21**

l'inglese *m f English adj n*

l'Inghilterra *f England n*

l'ingorgo stradale *m congestion n* (traffic)

l'insalata *f salad n* p91

inserire la spina *v to plug in* **p21**

l'insetto *m bug, insect n*

insultare *v to insult* **p20**

intasato -a *backed up* (toilet) *adj*

interno -a *inside adj*

l'interprete *m f interpreter n*

l'intervallo *m intermission n*

intollerante al lattosio *lactose-intolerant adj*

l'invalidità *f disability n*

l'inverno *m winter n*

io *I pron* p19

l'ipovedente *m f visually-impaired n* p65

l'irlandese *m f Irish adj n*

l'italiano -a *m f Italian adj n*

J

il jogging *m jogging n*

K

kasher *kosher adj* p85

L

là *there adv* (demonstrative)

> **di là** *over there*

la lampada *f light n* (lamp)

largo -a *wide adj*

il lato *m side n*

dall'altro lato di *across prep*
dall'altro lato della strada *across the street*
il latte *m milk n*
 il latte in polvere *formula*
il lavabo *m sink n*
il lavaggio a secco *m dry cleaning n*
lavanda *f lavender n*
la lavanderia a secco *f dry cleaner n* p74
lavorare *v to work* **p20**
 Io lavoro per _____. *I work for _____.*
la legge *f law n*
leggere *v to read* **p20**
leggero -a *light adj*
lei *f she, her pron* p19
lentamente *slowly adv*
le lenti a contatto *f contact lens n* p191
la lentiggine *f freckle n*
lento -a *slow adj*
le lenzuola *f sheets n* (linens)
il letto *m bed n* p67
il lettore di DVD *m DVD player n*
levare *v to take off* **p20**
la lezione *f lesson n*
libero -a *free adj*
la libreria *f bookstore n* p156
il libro *m book n* p156
il limite di velocità *m speed limit n* p56
la limousine *f limo n*
la lingua *f language n*

il liquore *m liqueur n* p88
liscio -a *smooth adj, straight adj* (drinks)
il litro *m liter n* p10
locale *local adj*
lontano -a *far adj* p5
 più lontano -a *farther*
 il / la più lontano -a *farthest*
loro *they, them pron* p19
la luce *f light n* p47
luglio *m July n* p15
lui *m he, him pron* p19
luminoso -a *bright adj*
luna *f moon n*
lunedì *m Monday n* p15
lungo -a *long adj* p10
 più lungo -a *longer*
 il / la più lungo -a *longest*
di lusso *upscale adj*

M

la macchina *f machine, car n*
 la macchina decappottabile *convertible car*
la madre *f mother n* p115
maggio *m May n* (month)
la maglia *f sweater n* p152
il maiale *m pig n*
malato -a *sick adj* p48
male *badly adv*
 il mal d'auto *carsickness*
 il mal di denti *toothache*
 il mal di mare *seasickness*
 il mal di testa *headache*
il / la manager *m f manager n*

la mancia *f tip n* (gratuity)
  Mancia compresa. *Tip included.*
mandare *v to send* p20
  mandare la posta elettronica / e-mail *to send e-mail*
  mandare il conto *to bill*
maneggiare *v to handle* p20
  Maneggiare con cura. *Handle with care.*
mangiare *v to eat* p20
  mangiare fuori *to eat out*
la mano *f sing / le mani f pl hand n* p190
mantenere *v to hold, to keep* p20
il manuale d'istruzioni *m manual n* (book)
il marciapiede *m sidewalk n*
il marito *m husband n* p114
marroncino -a *tan adj*
marrone *brown adj*
il martedì *m Tuesday n* p14
marzo *m March n* (month)
maschile *male adj*
il maschio *m male n*
massaggiare *v to massage* p20
il massaggio alla schiena *m back rub n* p179
il mattino *m morning n*
  al mattino *in the morning*
medio -a *middle, medium adj* (size) p10
meno *adv less* p10
meno *adv lesser*
il meno *n least*

il menù *m*, la lista *f menu n*
  il menù dei bambini *children's menu*
  il menù per i diabetici *diabetic menu*
  il menù da asporto *takeout menu*
il mercato *m market n* p154
  il mercatino delle pulci *flea market*
  il mercato all'aperto *open-air market*
il mercoledì *m Wednesday n*
il mese *m month n*
il mestiere *m occupation, trade n*
  Che mestiere fa? *What do you do for a living?*
la metà *f half n*
il metro *m meter n*
il metrò *m*, la metropolitana *f the subway, tube n* p63
  la linea della metropolitana *subway line*
  la stazione della metropolitana *subway station*
  Che linea di metropolitana devo prendere per____? *Which subway do I take for ____?*
mettere *v to place, to put* p20
  mettere in borsa *to bag*
la mezzanotte *f midnight*
il mezzogiorno *m noon n*
migliore *better, best adj*
il militare *m military n*

mille *thousand adj n* p7

il millilitro *m milliliter n* p10

il millimetro *m millimeter n*

la minestra *f soup n* p93

il minimo *m least n*

il minuto *m minute n* p12

in un attimo *in a minute*

la misura *f size n* (clothing)

in modo sospetto *suspiciously adv*

la moglie *f wife n* p115

molti -e *many adj*

molto -a *much, very adj adv*

la moneta *f coin n* p132

la montagna *f mountain n*

scalare la montagna *mountain climbing*

morbido -a *soft adj*

la moschea *f mosque n* p126

la mostra *f exhibit n* p148

mostrare *v to show* p20

Può mostrarmelo? *Would you show it to me?*

la moto *f motorcycle n*

il motore *m engine n* p54

il motorino *m scooter n* p50

la mucca *f cow n*

la multa *f fine n* (penalty)

il museo *m museum n*

la musica *f music n* p128

il / la musicista *m f musician n*

il / la musulmano -a *Muslim adj n*

N

il naso *m nose n* p118

il nastro trasportatore *m conveyor belt n*

il naufragio *m shipwreck n*

la nausea *f nausea n* p186

la nave *f ship n* p62

la navetta *f shuttle n* (transportation)

navigare a vela *v to sail* p20

la nazionalità *f nationality n*

il negozio *m store, shop n*

il negozio duty-free *duty-free shop* p37

il neo *m mole n* (facial feature)

il / la neonato -a *f baby, infant n* p116

nero -a *black adj*

nessuno -a *m f nobody n*

il niente *m nothing n*

il night *m nightclub n*

il / la nipote *m f nephew, niece, grandchild n* p115

no *no adv* p1

la nocciolina americana *f peanut n*

la noce *f nut n*

noi *us pron* p19

noleggiare *v to charter* (transportation), *to rent* p20

a noleggio *chartered, rented*

il nome *m name n* p111

nome e cognome *first and last name*

non-fumatori *nonsmoking adj*

la zona non-fumatori *nonsmoking area*

la carrozza non-fumatori *nonsmoking car*

la **sala non-fumatori** *non-smoking room*

la **nonna** *f grandmother n*

il **nonno** *m grandfather n, grandparent n* p115

nono -a *ninth adj 9*

la **notte** *f night n* p13

a **notte** *per night*

novanta *ninety adj* p7

nove *nine adj n* p7

novembre *m November n* p15

nubile *f maiden adj n*

lo conservato il mio **nome da nubile**. *I kept my maiden name.*

il **numero** *m number, size n* (shoes) p7

nuotare *v to swim* p20

la **Nuova Zelanda** *f New Zealand n*

il / la **neozelandese** *New Zealander adj n*

nuovo -a *new adj*

nuvoloso -a *cloudy adj* p124

O

l'**oca** *f goose n*

gli **occhiali** *m pl glasses n pl* (spectacles) p191

gli **occhiali da sole** *sun-glasses*

l'**occhio** *m eye n* p190

occupato -a *busy adj* (phone line), *taken adj* (seat)

Questo posto è **occupato**? *Is this seat taken?*

offrire *v to offer* p21

l'**oggi** *m today n* p4

l'**olio** *m oil n*

l'**oliva** *f olive n*

l'**ombrello** *m umbrella n*

l'**onorario** *m fee n*

l'**opera** *f opera, work n* p148

il / la **operatore -trice** *m f phone operator n* p135

l'**optometrista** *m f optometrist n*

l'**ora** *f hour, time n* p12

A che **ora**? *At what time?*

Che **ora** è? *What time is it?*

l'**orario** *m hours* (at museum), *schedule, timetable n* (train)

È in **orario**? *Is it on time?*

ordinare *v to order* p20

ordinato -a *neat adj* (tidy)

organico -a *organic adj*

l'**organo** *m organ n*

l'**oro** *m gold adj n*

l'**orso** *m bear n*

l'**ospite** *m guest n*

l'**ostello** *m hostel n* p66

l'**otorino** *m ear / nose / throat specialist n* p188

ottanta *eighty adj* p7

l'**ottavo** *a eighth adj* p9

tre **ottavi** *three eighths n*

otto -a *eight adj* p7

ottobre *October n* p15

P

il **pacco** *m package n* p141

il **padre** *m father n* p115

il **paesaggio** *m landscape n* (painting)

pagare *v to pay* **p20**

  pagare il conto dell'albergo *check out (of hotel)* **p78**

la palestra *f gym n* **p161**

la palla *f ball n*

  il pallone *ball, soccer* (sport)

pallido -a *pale adj*

il pane *m bread n*

il pannolino *m diaper n*

  il pannolino di stoffa *cloth diaper*

il parabrezza *m windshield n*

la parata *f parade n*

parcheggiare *v to park* **p20**

il parcheggio *m parking n*

il parco *m park n*

il parente *m relative n*

parlare *v to talk, to speak* **p20**

  Si parla inglese. *English spoken here.*

la parola di accesso *f password n*

il parrucchiere *m hairdresser n*

la partenza *f departure n*

la partita *f match m* (sport)

il partito politico *m political party n*

il passaggio pedonale *m walkway n*

passare *v to pass* **p20**

il passaporto *m passport n*

il passeggero *m passenger n*

il passeggino *m stroller n*

la passerella *f walkway, cat-walk n*

la passerella mobile *moving walkway*

il passero *m sparrow n*

il pasto *m meal n*

  il pasto per diabetici *diabetic meal*

  il pasto kasher *kosher meal*

  il pasto vegetariano *vegetarian meal*

la patente *f driver's license n*

il pavimento *m floor n* (ground)

pazzo -a *m crazy n*

il pedaggio *m toll n*

il pediatra *m pediatrician n*

pedonale *pedestrian adj*

  la zona pedonale *pedestrian area*

il pedone *m pedestrian n*

la pelle *f skin, leather n*

pentito -a *sorry adj*

perdere *v to lose, to miss* (a flight) **p20**

  Mi sono perso. *I'm lost.*

per favore *please* (polite entreaty) *interj* **p1**

il pericolo *m danger n*

la permanente *f permanent* (hair) *n* **p158**

il permesso *m license, permit n* **50**

  Permesso. *Excuse me, pardon me.*

permettere *v to permit* **p20**

il personale *m staff n*

pesare *v to weigh* **p20**

  Pesa ____. *It weighs ____.*

i pesi *m pl* weights *n*

il pettine *m* comb *n*

il pettirosso *m* robin *n*

il pezzo *m* / il pezzetto *m* bit (small amount) *n*

piacere *v* to like (take pleasure in) p33

Mi piacerebbe _____. / would like ____.

il piacere *m* pleasure *n*

per piacere please (polite entreaty)

È un piacere. It's a pleasure.

il piano *m* floor *n*

il piano terra ground floor

il secondo piano first floor

poco profondo -a shallow *adj*

il piano rateale *m* rate plan *n* (for purchases)

il piatto *m* dish *n* p85

il piatto del giorno special (featured meal)

il piccione *m* pigeon *n*

piccolo -a little, small *adj*

più piccolo -a littler, smaller

il più piccolo, la più piccola littlest, smallest

il piede *m* foot (body part) *n*

pieno -a full *adj*

il pieno full tank (fuel)

la pila *f* battery (electric) *n*

la pillola *f* pill *n*

la pillola contro il mal di mare seasickness pill

piovere *v* to rain p20

piovoso -a rainy *adj* p124

la piscina *f* swimming pool *n*

la pista *f* runway *n*

più tardi later *adv*

A più tardi. See you later.

piuttosto rather *adv*

la pizza *f* pizza *n* p92

la plastica *f* plastic *n*

lo pneumatico *m* tire *n* (wheel) p54

Ho lo pneumatico sgonfio. / have a flat tire.

poco -a (a) little *adj* (quantity)

poco costoso -a cheap *adj*

meno costoso -a cheaper

il / la meno costoso -a cheapest

poco profondo -a shallow *adj*

poi then, later *adv*

la polizia *f* police *n* p192

il poliziotto *m* officer *n*

il pollame *m* poultry *n*

il pollice *m* thumb *n* p190

il pollo *m* chicken *n*

la polpetta *f* meatball *n*

le poltroncine nella sezione orchestra *f pl* orchestra seats *n pl*

il pomeriggio *m* afternoon *n*

nel pomeriggio / di pomeriggio in the afternoon

la pompa *f* pump *n*

il ponte *m* bridge (across a river, dental prosthesis) *n*

popolare popular *adj*

la porta *f* door *n*

il portabagagli *m* trunk *n* (car) p54

il portafogli *m* wallet *n*

portare *v* to take, to bring p20

portare indietro v to return (something to a store) **p20**

il portiere m goalie (sport), concierge n

il porto m port (beverage, ship mooring) n

la porzione f portion n

la posta f mail n **p141**

  la posta aerea air mail

  la posta raccomandata certified mail

  la posta celere express mail

  la posta prioritaria first class mail

  spedire per assicurata to send by registered mail

posta elettronica f e-mail n

  messaggio di posta elettronica, messaggio e-mail e-mail message

  Posso avere il suo indirizzo di posta elettronica / e-mail per favore? May I have your e-mail address?

il posto m seat, place n

  il posto sul corridoio aisle seat

  Sei a posto? Are you okay?

potere v can (be able to), may v aux **p30**

  Posso ____? May I ____?

la pozza f pool n

il pozzo m pit, well n

il pranzo m lunch, dinner, meal n

preferire v to prefer **p32**

prelevare v to withdraw **p20**

il prelievo m withdrawal n

la prenotazione m reservation n **p66**

preoccupato -a anxious adj

preparato -a prepared adj

presentare v to introduce **p20**

  Ho il piacere di presentarti ____. I'd like to introduce you to ____.

il preservativo m condom n

  Hai un preservativo? Do you have a condom?

  non senza un preservativo not without a condom

preventivare v to budget **p20**

le previsioni del tempo f weather forecast n **p125**

il prezzo m price n **p148**

  il prezzo del biglietto fare / ticket price

  il prezzo d'ingresso admission fee

  a prezzo modico moderately priced

presto -a early, quick adj

  È presto. It's early.

  Fai presto! Be quick!.

la primavera f spring (season) n **p15**

primo -a first adj **p9**

il problema m problem n

il prodotto m product n

professionale professional adj

profondo -a deep adj

il programma m program n

prossimo -a next adj

  la prossima stazione the next station

il / la **protestante** Protestant
adj n

provare v to try, to try on
(clothing) **p20**

provare gioia to enjoy **p20**

pulire v to clean **p21**

la **pulizia** f cleanliness n

puntare v to bet, to put
(gambling) **p20**

Punti sul rosso / nero! Put it
on red / black!

il **punteggio** m score n

in **punto** o'clock adv

puzzare v to smell **p20**

Q

a **quadretti** checked (pattern)
adj

il **quadro** m painting n

qualche some adj **p10**

qualcosa f something n

qualcuno -a someone adj n

quale which adv **p6**

qualsiasi cosa f anything n

quando when adv **p4**

la **quantità** f amount n

quanto sing / **quanti** pl how
much adj pron **p3**

Quanti? How many? **p3**

Quanto? How much? **p3**

quaranta forty adj **p7**

quarto -a fourth adj

il **quarto** m quarter n

quasi al sangue medium rare
(steak) adj

quattordici m fourteen adj **p7**

quattro m four adj **p7**

quello -a that adj **p19**

quelli -e those adj

questo -a this adj **p19**

questi -e these adj

qui here n **p5**

quindici m fifteen adj **p7**

quinto -a fifth adj **p9**

R

raccomandare v to recommend **p20**

Ti raccomando! I beg you!

la **radio** f radio n **p51**

la **radio satellitare** satellite
radio

il **raffreddore** m cold n (sickness)

il **ragazzo** m boy, boyfriend n

la **ragazza** f girl, girlfriend n

i **ragazzi** m f pl kids n

rallentare v to slow down
p20

Rallenta! Slow down!

il **rame** m copper n

la **rampa** f ramp n **p65**

il **rapporto sessuale** m sexual
intercourse n **p180**

il **recapito domiciliare** m
home address n

il **reclamo** m complaint n

il / la **redattore -trice** m f editor n **p121**

il **regalo** m gift n

reggere v to hold **p20**

il **repellente insetticida** m
insect repellent n **p187**

restare v to stay **p20**

resto m change n (money)

la rete *f* network *n*

riappacificarsi *v* to make up, to make peace **p35**

riccio -a curly *adj*

il ricciolo *m* curl *n*

la ricerca *f* search *n*

la ricetta medica *f* prescription *n* **p188**

ricevere *v* to receive **p20**

la ricevuta *f* receipt *n* **p133**

richiesta *f* order, request *n*

riempire *v* to fill **p21**

rifiutare *v* to refuse, to decline **p20**

il rifornimento *m* stock *n*

rilassarsi *v* to relax, to hang out **p35**

ripetere *v* to repeat **p20**

Può ripetere per favore?
Would you please repeat that?

riscuotere *v* to collect (pay) **p20**

rispondere *v* to answer, to reply **p20**

Per cortesia, rispondimi.
Answer me, please.

risposta *f* answer *n*

Ho bisogno di una risposta.
I need an answer.

il ristorante *m* restaurant *n*

il ritardo *m* delay *n* **p44**

Per favore non fare ritardo.
Please don't be late.

in ritardo late *adv*

ritirare *v* to withdraw **p20**

ritornare *v* to return (go back to) **p20**

il ritratto *m* portrait *n*

il ritrovo *m* hangout (hot spot) *n*

il rivelatore di metalli *m* metal detector *n*

la rivista *f* magazine *n* (periodical)

la roccia *f* rock *n*

scalare le roccie rock climbing

romantico -a romantic *adj*

il romanzo *m* novel *n*

rompere *v* to break **p20**

rosa pink *adj*

la rosa *f* rose *n*

rosso -a red *adj*

a rotelle wheeled *adj* (luggage)

la rottura *f* break *n*

rovesciare *v* to spill **p20**

rubare *v* to steal, to rob **p20**

Qualcuno ha rubato il mio portafogli. *Someone stole my wallet.*

rubato -a stolen *adj* **p49**

il rubinetto *m* faucet *n*

rumoroso -a loud, noisy *adj*

la ruota di scorta *f* spare tire *n*

S

il sabato *m* Saturday *n* **p14**

il sacchetto *m* bag *n*

il sacchetto per il mal d'aria airsickness bag **p48**

la sala d'aspetto *f* lounge *n*

la sala non-fumatori *f non-smoking room n*

il saldo *m balance (bank account) n* p135

il sale *m salt n*

Con poco sale *low-salt*

salire *v to climb* p21

salire le scale *to climb the stairs*

salire a bordo di *to board*

Lei salirà a bordo della nave. *She will board the ship.*

salpare *v to set sail, to sail away* p20

Quando salpiamo? *When do we sail?*

il saluto *m greeting n*

il salvagente *m life preserver n*

al sangue *rare (meat) adj*

sapere *v to know (something)* p20

il sapone *m soap n*

il sapore *m taste (flavor) n*

il sapore di cioccolato *chocolate flavor*

il sarto *m tailor n*

il satellite *m satellite n* p51

la radio satellitare *satellite radio*

il tracking satellitare *satellite tracking*

sazio -a *full adj (after a meal)*

sbagliare *v to make a mistake* p20

lo sbaglio *m mistake n*

la scala *m staircase, straight (gambling) n*

la scala mobile *f escalator n*

scalare *v to climb* p20

scalare una montagna *to climb a mountain*

scalare delle rocce *rock climbing*

la scalata *f climbing n*

l'attrezzatura per scalate *climbing gear*

le scale *f pl stairs n*

scalfito -a *scratched adj*

la scalinata *f steps n*

scaricare *v to download, to unload* p20

lo scarico *m drain n*

la scarpa *f shoe n* p151

la scheda *f phone card n*

la schiena *f back n* p190

sciolto -a *loose adj*

la scogliera *f reef n* p169

la scommessa *f bet n* p184

Eguaglio la tua scommessa *I'll see your bet.*

scommettere *v to bet* p20

scomparire *v to disappear* p21

lo sconto *m discount n*

lo sconto per i bambini *children's discount*

lo sconto per gli anziani *senior discount*

lo sconto per gli studenti *student discount*

lo scontrino *m receipt n*

la **scottatura solare** f sunburn n

il / la **scozzese** Scottish adj

lo / la **scrittore -trice** m f writer n p122

scrivere v to write **p20**

Come si scrive? How do you spell that?

Per favore potreste scrivermelo? Would you write that down for me?

la **scultura** f sculpture n

la **scuola** f school n

la **scuola media** junior high / middle school

la **scuola superiore** high school

la **facoltà di giurisprudenza** law school

la **facoltà di medicina** medical school

la **scuola elementare** primary school

scusare v to excuse (pardon) **p20**

Mi scusi. Excuse me.

secco -a dry adj

secondo -a second adj p9

sedersi v to sit **p35**

la **sedia a rotelle** f wheelchair n p65

l'**accesso alle sedie a rotelle** wheelchair access

la **rampa delle sedie a rotelle** wheelchair ramp

la **sedia a rotelle motorizzata** power wheelchair

sedici sixteen adj p7

il **sedile** m seat n

il **sedile di sicurezza** m car seat, child's safety seat n

il **segnale di strada bloccata** m road-closed sign n

il **segnale di precedenza** m yield sign n

sei six adj p7

self-serve self-serve adj

sembrare v to look, to appear **p20**

sempre always adv

senso unico one way (traffic sign) adj p56

il **sentiero** m trail n p165

sentire v to hear, to feel **p21**

senza without prep

separato -a separated (marital status) adj p116

la **sera** f evening n

di sera at night

la **serratura** f lock n p54

servire v to serve **p21**

servizio m service n

Fuori servizio Out of service

sessanta sixty adj p7

il **sesso** m sex (gender, activity) n

la **seta** f silk n

settanta seventy adj p7

sette seven adj p7

settembre m September n

la **settimana** f week n p14

questa settimana this week

la **settimana scorsa** last week

tra una settimana / la settimana prossima *a week from now / next week*

il settimo -a *seventh adj* p9

sgocciolare *v to drip* **p20**

si *yes adv* p1

la sicurezza *f security, safety n*

il sedile di sicurezza *child's safety seat*

il punto di controllo di sicurezza *security checkpoint*

la guardia di sicurezza *security guard*

sicuro -a *safe (secure) adj*

il sigaro *m cigar n*

la sigaretta *f cigarette n*

un pacchetto di sigarette *a pack of cigarettes*

silenzioso -a *quiet adj*

simpatico -a *nice adj*

la sinfonia *f symphony n*

single *single (unmarried) adj*

E' single? *Are you single?*

singolo -a *single (one) adj*

sinistro -a *left adj* p5

a sinistra *on the left*

smarrirsi *v to get lost, to go astray* **p35**

Ho smarrito il mio passaporto. *I lost my passport.*

smarrito -a *missing adj*

il socialismo *m socialism n*

il socio *m member n*

la soda *f seltzer n* p88

soffrire *v to suffer* **p21**

che soffre il mal di mare *seasick* p62

il sole *m sun n*

soleggiato -a *sunny adj* p124

solo -a *alone adj adv*

solo scotch *straight scotch*

sopra *above prep adv* p78

il sopracciglio *m eyebrow n*

sordo -a *deaf adj* p65

la sorella *f sister n* p115

la sostituzione *f substitution n*

sottile *thin adj*

sotto *below prep, adv*

il sottotitolo *m subtitle n*

spaccare *v to break* **p20**

la Spagna *f Spain n*

il / la spagnolo -a *Spanish adj n*

lo spago *m twine n*

le spalle *f back n* p190

la spazzola *f brush n*

le spazzole del tergicristallo *f wiper blades n* p54

specificare *v to specify* **p20**

spedire *v to send, to ship* **p21**

le spesa *f groceries n* p100

lo spettacolo *m show n (performance)*

la spezia *f spice n*

la spia *f spy, lamp n (dashboard)* p54

la spia dell'olio *oil light*

la spiaggia *f beach n* p170

gli spiccioli *m change (money) n* p132

spiegare *v to explain* **p20**

la spina *f plug n*

spingere *v to push* **p20**

lo spinotto adattore *m* adapter plug *n* p157

sporco -a *dirty adj*

gli sport *m* sports *n* p163

sposarsi *v* to marry **p35**

sposato -a *married adj*

spuntare *v* to trim (hair) **p20**

lo spuntino *m* snack *n*

la squadra *f* team *n* p163

staccato -a *disconnected, detached adj*

lo stadio *m* stadium *n* p163

stampare *v* to print **p20**

stanco -a *tired, exhausted adj*

stare *v* to be *v* (temporary state, condition, mood) **p24**

stare in piedi *to stand*

lo stato *m* state *n*

gli Stati Uniti *the United States*

la stazione *f* station *n*

la stazione di polizia *police station* p192

la stazione termale *spa*

la stella di Natale *f* poinsettia *n*

stitico -a *constipated adj*

lo STOP *m* STOP (traffic sign)

stordito -a *dizzy adj* p189

la storia *f* history *n*

storico -a *historical adj*

la strada *f* road, street *n*

dall'altra parte della strada *across the street*

giù per la strada *down the street*

stressato -a *stressed adj*

stretto -a *tight, narrow adj*

a strisce *striped adj*

lo studio del medico *m* doctor's office *n* p188

su *up adv prep*

subire un furto *v* to get mugged, to get robbed **p21**

Ho subito un furto. *I've been robbed.*

il succo *m* juice *n*

il succo d'arancia *orange juice*

il succo di frutta *fruit juice*

il sugo *m* sauce *n* p93

suo -a *his adj* p19

suonare *v* to play (an instrument) **p20**

surriscaldare *v* to overheat **p20**

la sveglia *f* alarm clock *n*

svenire *v* to faint **p21**

T

il tachimetro *m* speedometer *n* p54

il tacchino *m* turkey *n*

la taglia *f* size *n* (clothes)

tagliare *v* to cut **p20**

il taglio *m* cut *n*

il tamburo *m* drum *n*

la targa *f* license plate *n*

la tariffa *f* fare, rate *n* (car rental, hotel) p57

la tassa *f* tax, fee *n*

il tasso d'interesse *m* interest rate *n* p132

la tavola di surf *f* surfboard *n*

il tavolo *m* table *n* p82

il taxi *m* taxi *n* p57

la stazione dei taxi *taxi stand*

il tè *m* tea *n* p88

il tè con latte e zucchero *tea with milk and sugar*

il tè con il limone *tea with lemon*

la tisana *herbal tea*

il teatro *m* theater *n* p144

il teatro dell'opera *m* opera house *n* p145

la tecno-musica *f* techno *n*

il / la tedesco -a *m f* German *adj n*

telefonare a *v* to call (phone) p20

la telefonata *f* phone call *n*

una telefonata internazionale *an international phone call*

una telefonata interurbana *a long-distance phone call*

telefonico -a *telephone adj*

elenco telefonico *phone directory*

il telefonino *m* cell / mobile phone *n*

Vendete i telefonini prepagati? *Do you sell prepaid phones?*

il telefono *m* phone *n* p135

Può darmi il suo numero di telefono? *May I have your phone number?*

la televisione *f* television *n*

la televisione via cavo *cable television*

la televisione satellitare *satellite television*

il televisore *m* television set *n*

il tempio *m* temple *n* p126

il tempo *m* time *n* p12

Per quanto tempo? *For how long?*

la tenda *f* curtain, tent *n*

tenere *v* to keep, to hold p20

tenersi per mano *to hold hands*

il tennis *m* tennis *n* p79

il campo da tennis *tennis court*

il tergicristallo *m* windshield wiper, wiper *n* p54

il terminale *m* terminal *n* (airport) p37

terzo -a *third adj* p9

la tessera *f* permit *n*

Abbiamo bisogno di una tessera? *Do we need a permit?*

il tessuto *m* fabric *n*

il tettuccio apribile *m* sunroof *n* p54

il tipo *m* kind *n* (type)

Che tipo è? *What kind is it?*

tirare *v* to pull p20

Tira vento. *It's windy out.*

tirare a riva *to beach*

tirare l'acqua del gabinetto *to flush*

togliere *v* to remove p20

la tonnellata *f* ton *n*

il topo *m* mouse *n*

il torto *m* fault *n*

Ho torto. *I'm at fault.*

Lui ha torto. *He's at fault.*

la tosse *f* cough *n* p86

tossire *v* to cough **p21**

il totale *m* total *n*

  Qual'è il totale? *What is the total?*

il tovagliolo *m* napkin *n*

traboccante *overflowing adj*

il traffico *m* traffic *n*

  Com'è il traffico? *How's the traffic?*

  Il traffico è orribile. *The traffic is terrible.*

  il regolamento del traffico *traffic rules*

la transazione *f* transaction *n*

il trasferimento *m* transfer *n*

  trasferimento di valuta / di fondi *money transfer*

  Ho bisogno di fare un trasferimento dei fondi. *I need to transfer funds.*

trasferire dei dati *v* to upload **p21**

traslocare *v* to move **p20**

trasmettere *v* to transfer **p20**

tre *three adj* p7

la treccia *f* braid *n* p158

tredici *thirteen adj* p7

il treno *m* train *n* p58

trenta *thirty adj* p7

  Sono le due e trenta. *It's two-thirty.*

il tribunale *m* court (legal) *n*

triplo -a *triple adj*

triste *sad adj* p120

troppo *too* (excessively) *adv*

  troppo caldo -a *too hot*

  troppo cotto -a *overcooked*

trovare *v* to find **p20**

truccarsi *v* to make up (apply cosmetics) **p35**

il trucco *m* makeup *n*

tu *you pron* (singular, informal) **p19**

tuffarsi *v* to dive **p35**

tuo *m sing /* **tua** *f sing /* **tuoi** *m pl /* **tue** *f pl* your *adj* p19

il tuo *m /* **la tua** *f /* **i tuoi** *m pl /* **le tue** *f pl* yours *n* p19

tutto- a *all adj* p11

  È tutto, grazie. *That's all, thank you.*

  tutto esaurito -a *sold out adj*

U

l'uccello *m* bird *n*

udire *v* to hear **p21**

l'ufficio postale *m* post office *n*

  Dov'è l'ufficio postale? *Where is the post office?*

ultimo -a *last adj*

umido -a *humid adj* p124

undici *eleven adj* p7

l'università *f* university, college *n*

uno -a *one adj* p7

l'uomo *m* man *n*

usare *v* to use **p20**

uscire *v* to exit **p32**

l'uscita f gate (at airport), exit n p39

senza sbocco not an exit

l'uscita d'emergenza emergency exit n p41

l'uscita USB f USB port n

l'uva f grapes n

V

la vacanza f vacation, holiday n

il vagone letto m sleeping car n p59

la valigia f suitcase n p48

la valvola fusibile f fuse n

la vasca da bagno f bathtub n

vecchio -a old adj

vedere v to see p22

Posso vederlo? May I see it?

il / la vedovo -a m f widower, widow n

il vegetale m vegetable n

vegetariano -a vegetarian adj

la vela f sail n p168

veloce fast adj

la velocità di connessione f connection speed n p139

vendere v to sell p20

il venditore all'aperto m street vendor n

venerdì m Friday n p15

il ventaglio m fan n

venti twenty adj p7

verde green adj

la verdura m vegetables n (food) p106

verificare v to check p20

la verruca f wart n

la versione f version n

il vestito m dress (garment) n

vestirsi v to dress p35

viaggiare v to travel, to ride p20

il viaggio m trip, tour n p62

vicino -a close, near adj, nearby adj, adv p5

più vicino -a closer, nearer

il / la più vicino -a closest, nearest

il / la vicino -a neighbor

il video (registratore) m VCR, video n

Vietato Fumare No Smoking (sign)

Vietato l'ingresso Do not enter (sign)

il vigneto m vineyard n

il vinile m vinyl n

il vino m wine n p88

il vino bianco white wine

il vino rosso red wine

il vino frizzante sparkling wine

il vino dolce sweet wine

viola purple adj

la viola del pensiero f pansy n

il violino m violin n

la visione f vision n

visitare v to visit p20

il viso m face n p118

la vista f view n p69

la vista della spiaggia beach view

ITALIAN—ENGLISH

la vista della città *city view*

il **visto** *m visa n*

la **vita** *f life n*

il **vivere** *m living n*

il **vocabolario** *m dictionary n*

voi *you* (pl informal) *pron* p19

volere *v to want* p31

il **volo** *m flight n* p36

la **volpe** *f fox n*

votare *v to vote* p20

il **voto** *m grade, mark n*
  (school)

W

il **water** (*VAH-tehr*) *m toilet
  bowl n*

X

Y

Z

la **zia** *f aunt n* p115

lo **zio** *m uncle n* p115

zitto -a *quiet adj*

la **zona periferica** *f suburb n*

la **zona non-fumatori** *f nonsmoking area n*

lo **zoo** (*ZOH-oh*) *m zoo n* p130